Fifth Edition

Legal Forms
for
Everyone

HALT

Founded in 1978, HALT– *An Organization of Americans for Legal Reform* is a non-partisan, non-profit public interest organization.

HALT pursues an ambitious education and advocacy program that challenges the legal establishment to improve access and reduce costs in the civil justice system. To join HALT, or for more information, visit *www.halt.org*.

Legal Forms

for

Everyone

Carl W. Battle

Fifth Edition

Allworth Press, New York

Previously published as *Legal-Wise®:Self-Help Legal Guide for Everyone.*

10 09 08 07 06   6 5 4 3 2

Published by Allworth Press
An imprint of Allworth Communications
10 East 23rd Street, New York, NY 10010

Cover design, page composition, and typography by Douglas Design Associates, New York, NY

Library of Congress Cataloging-in-Publication Data
Battle, Carl W.
    Legal forms for everyone / Carl W. Battle.—5th ed.
        p.   cm.
    Includes index.
    ISBN 1-58115-451-8 (pbk.)
    1. Forms (Law)—United States.   2. Law—United States—Popular works.
  I. Title.

    KF170.B37   2006
    347.73'55—dc22

                         2006016399

Legal-Wise® is a registered trademark of Legal Information Services, Philadelphia, Pennsylvania.

Printed in Canada

Table of Contents

Preface

We live in an extremely complex society, and our interactions with other people and with countless institutions are becoming even more complex. If there is any doubt about the validity of this observation, you need only consider that ours is the most litigious society in the world. With this in mind, it has become clear that the protection and enforcement of individual rights, the need to solve disputes, and the management of legal affairs are rapidly becoming the routine concerns of each and every one of us.

It is a deeply rooted principle in American law that "ignorance of the law is no excuse." Therefore, it is imperative that you have a basic understanding of law to protect your legal rights and interests and to conduct your legal affairs properly.

Renting an apartment? Buying your first home? Thinking about a will? Starting your own business? This book was designed for your use with these questions and many others in mind. While not designed to replace in any way the advice and services of a lawyer, this book is a self-help guide dedicated to the proposition that the information revolution has finally reached the courthouse and the lawyer's office.

Included here are detailed and easy-to-follow forms, instructions, and advice for individual representation in areas such as wills, leases, patents, copyrights, trademarks, small claims court, name changes, divorce, bankruptcy, and IRS audits—each accompanied by a concise and lucid presentation of the relevant laws and rules. Other forms and discussions explain how to close on your house, make an assignment, prepare a power of attorney, contract for repairs and services, and several other very useful and potentially expense-saving procedures.

The idea here is to put together in a simple, non-threatening form the kinds of things you might need in your daily life. This book should provide you with a basic familiarity with the laws, legal forms, and procedures such that you can manage your simple legal affairs, or make an informed decision to seek appropriate legal counsel. This book also provides in many cases an estimated cost for typical legal services if you decide you need a lawyer.

This edition of *Legal Forms for Everyone* reflects important changes in the law since publication of the prior edition in 2001. As the laws are constantly changing, you are advised to check with the court clerk or an attorney in your jurisdiction for new developments. The sample forms and instructions in this book are appropriate for most, if not all, states and jurisdictions. You can typically call or write your court clerk for specific court rules and requirements.

1 *Managing Your Legal Affairs*

Your Participation in the American Legal System

Do you have faith in the American legal system? A large number of people would probably answer this question with a resounding "No." But despite a lack of public confidence, the American legal system is one of the best in the world.

Although it may appear to suffer from many problems and inequities, our legal system is remarkable. Our Constitution, the bedrock of our legal system, is a brilliantly crafted document designed to safeguard individual interests and freedoms while concurrently promoting public, societal needs. Our judicial and legislative processes assure that the intent of the Constitution is carried out. Our country has a well-trained and active judiciary. Our legal profession has an abundance of talent and resources. But to work most effectively, our legal system requires public awareness and participation.

Our legal system needs a public desirous of being knowledgeable of the law. It needs a public willing to monitor, evaluate, and formulate legal policies. Further, it needs public confidence and support. American democracy cannot flourish without the will of the people. The American legal system cannot, and will not, function effectively without you.

The American legal system affects virtually every aspect of our daily lives. Laws regulate our family relationships, commercial activities and social conduct. Regula-

tions govern the food we eat, the garbage we throw away, and the places we park our cars. While our individual liberties, such as freedom of speech, press, and assembly, are protected by the Constitution, our legal system regulates countless aspects of our daily lives.

The laws regulating American society do not necessarily represent a destruction of individual rights. Many of the laws were enacted for the very purpose of protecting such rights. The protection of the law may be lost, however, because of lack of public awareness and mismanagement of legal affairs. Because an unwanted lawsuit or loss of important legal rights can destroy families, fortunes, and lives, you need to manage your legal affairs as routinely and carefully as you balance your checkbook. The magic formula is simply knowing your legal rights and knowing how to enforce them. For example, always read the fine print in an agreement before you sign it. Also, make sure important legal transactions are reduced to writing. A written document, such as a contract, a deed, or a will, can be extremely important as evidence of your legal rights and obligations. Never rely on oral promises or handshakes to protect your rights.

The importance of an informed public cannot be overemphasized. The growing popularity of televised trials and increasing news coverage of these events has resulted in many people now seeing our legal system at work. But despite this greater exposure through our mass media, many people still do not have a clear understanding of how the legal system operates and how cases are won or lost in court. You may want to personally attend court proceedings to see first-hand how the court system functions. Serving as a juror on a civil or criminal trial is another excellent way to see how the legal system works.

Your Right to Represent Yourself

More and more people are starting to take the law into their own hands. People are becoming hungry for information about law and self-help legal material. The 1980s and 90s will be remembered as the era of self-help. Many people are taking the do-it-yourself route in auto repairs, carpentry, home improvements, and many other areas. You also need to take the self-help approach in handling your simple legal affairs. Hiring a lawyer simply is not necessary for many of your routine legal matters.

The right to represent yourself is a basic concept of federal constitutional law. Although this right is nowhere spelled out in the Constitution, its existence is recognized by the courts as fundamental to our system of individual liberties. However, the right to represent yourself is not advantageous unless you have knowledge of the law. This includes knowing how to prepare legal forms and other documents, as well as how to safeguard and enforce legal rights.

Moreover, knowledge of the law encourages more public participation in the legal system. It eliminates the dependence that people have on lawyers in handling legal matters. Also, if you are familiar with the law, you will be better able to monitor a lawyer's work if you need to hire one.

Some areas of law can be very complex and may require the services of a good lawyer. But, to the extent that you can, try to represent yourself in your simple legal matters. You may consider consulting with an attorney only for guidance as you prepare to handle the matter yourself.

Using This Book as a Legal Resource

The material in this book will enable you to manage many of your legal affairs by yourself. Each chapter covers a legal issue you are likely to encounter in your personal or professional life, such as how to prepare a will, how to hire a contractor, how to deal with a suit in small claims court, or other important legal topics. Following most chapters are sample forms and checklists to help you organize the steps you should take and the papers you need to prepare. At the back of the book are sources of additional information which can provide you with further help and information. Finally, your local law library and court clerks can be very helpful. You are encouraged to use all these resources. This book is not intended to replace the advice of legal counsel.

Even with all the help available from this book and other sources, at times you may find that handling a legal problem by yourself is too difficult. Some issues are just too complex, or perhaps you do not have enough time. There may be instances when you find it best to hire an attorney. The next chapter discusses the steps you should take when engaging the services of an attorney.

2

Finding the Best Lawyer for You

Which Lawyer Is Right for You?
With the complexities of life and the laws governing us, the need for competent and effective legal advice arises on many occasions. Finding a good lawyer who is right for you and your particular situation can sometimes be difficult. There are, however, several sources you can use in helping you locate good legal counsel.

In searching for a good lawyer, you should use your personal contacts, local bar associations, telephone directories, legal publications, and community organizations. Each of these may be a good source of information and assistance in obtaining the right lawyer. Your final selection of a lawyer should involve an analysis of your specific facts, the complexity of your case, and the character and experience of the individual lawyer.

Unquestionably, the best approach for you in choosing a suitable lawyer is through personal contacts with relatives, friends, and business associates. Relatives and friends who have had similar legal matters satisfactorily handled can recommend their own personal lawyers. Such recommendations are the truest measure of a lawyer's reputation and zeal. Moreover, relatives and friends will generally have your best interests at heart and are less likely to do a disservice in referring you to a lawyer.

Local bar associations usually maintain a lawyer referral service which can be employed in directing you to appropriate legal counsel. Specific information on these services can be obtained by calling or writing to the bar association in your area. They are usually listed in the telephone directory under "Association" or "Professional Organization." The referral services typically involve a brief telephone discussion with a lawyer who reviews the general facts and refers you to one or more lawyers handling such cases.

Although this service does help in narrowing your search for the proper lawyer, it gives little aid in measuring a lawyer's eagerness, character, and integrity. All lawyers are required to meet the standards of the Code of Professional Responsibility, such as zealously representing you, safeguarding your confidential discussions, and providing competent legal services. You need to find a lawyer who measures up to these standards.

As a supplement to their referral services, the bar associations in many cities provide taped lectures over the telephone. This is a good program for providing some basic legal information to the public. The taped lectures usually run from five to fifteen minutes and cover a variety of subjects such as criminal law, divorce, landlord/tenant relationships, and much more. The law tapes can be a valuable resource for helping you understand your legal problems and make informed decisions to seek legal advice. You can usually find these services in the telephone directory under such names as "Lawline," "TeleLaw," or the like. Also, you can generally contact your bar association for information on these law tapes.

As you can see, your local telephone directory is a very good source to use in locating a lawyer. The Yellow Pages, in particular, gives an extensive listing of lawyers and law firms. These can typically be found under the heading of "Attorneys" or "Lawyers." Many Yellow Pages listings present basic information such as telephone numbers, office hours, fee schedules, and areas of concentration.

Legal directories, publications, and community organizations are additional sources for help in finding a lawyer. Many large urban areas have directories of lawyers, which often give information on both educational background and training. Legal magazines and newspapers frequently carry articles and advertisements by and about lawyers which may be useful to you. Community organizations such as neighborhood centers, local chapters of the American Civil Liberties Union, legal aid societies, law school clinical programs, consumer agencies, and tenants associations can also be excellent references.

In many areas, legal services plans can provide relatively inexpensive legal services for monthly membership fees of about $10–20. Many employers, unions, and associations offer legal services plans as part of their benefits packages. Legal services plans typically provide a list of plan lawyers who are available to you for handling some simple, routine legal matters at no additional cost. Examples of some normal services are the following:

- legal consultation and advice in person, by phone, or mail during normal business hours;

- legal letters and phone calls on your behalf;

- preparation of a simple will;

- review of documents, such as leases, real estate papers, contracts, etc., up to a specified number of pages;

- advice in representing yourself in small claims court;

- advice on your rights under government programs, such as Social Security and veterans' programs; and

- emergency bail service.

Check the telephone directory or your employee benefit manual for legal services plans that may be available in your area. Directories of legal services may also be available on the on-line computer services such as CompuServe, Prodigy, and America Online.

Legal clinics can also be a source for relatively inexpensive routine legal services. These clinics usually handle high volumes of simple cases such as bankruptcies, wills, uncontested divorces, personal injuries, and many others.

Your search for legal counsel should always focus on finding the right lawyer for you. This necessarily will involve an evaluation of many factors, such as the lawyer's reputation, experience, loyalty, personality, and fees. You should always choose a lawyer that you can afford and trust.

You should try to find a lawyer who is experienced in handling cases such as yours. This is especially true in cases involving complex areas such as taxes, patents, malpractice, immigration, commercial activities, and other specialized areas.

It is important that you find out as much as possible about a lawyer before retaining him or her. Explore the lawyer's reputation in the community and with former clients. Is the lawyer honest and loyal to clients? Is the lawyer responsible and conscientious about his or her work? To assist you in answering these questions, ask the lawyer for references and then contact them to investigate the lawyer's reputation.

It is important that you review and understand fully all financial aspects of your case with your lawyer. You should get information on the lawyer's fees, witness fees, court costs, and other charges in writing from the lawyer in advance. Avoid lawyers who are unwilling to discuss fees and charges up front. Try to get the lawyer to handle your case on a contingency basis, if possible. On this basis, you only pay your lawyer a percentage (typically one third) of your actual recovery. Lawyers typically handle accidents, personal injury, property damage, collections, and some estate cases on a contingency-fee basis.

You should review the merits of your case with the lawyer in detail. He or she should be willing to explain the legal issues and procedures to you. Watch out for lawyers who guarantee to win your case for you. Although a lawyer may be able to give you an estimated probability of success, he or she cannot ensure the outcome in any case.

If you have done your homework by becoming generally familiar with the law, you will be better able to monitor the lawyer's work. All too often, however, people retain lawyers in complete ignorance of their legal rights and remedies, and with no understanding of what the lawyer is to do. There is no substitute for an informed client in ensuring proper integrity and performance by a lawyer.

Using the Sample Attorney's Retainer Agreement

When hiring a lawyer, be sure to enter into a written retainer agreement. A sample Attorney's Retainer Agreement is provided at the end of this chapter. Item 1 of the sample Attorney's Retainer Agreement should be filled in by giving the date, the client's name and address, and the lawyer's name and office address. Item 1 should also describe as completely as possible the transaction or matter for which legal representation is sought.

Item 2 should include a complete listing of the duties and services the lawyer is to perform. This can become a handy checklist for gauging the lawyer's performance.

Item 3 should set forth the manner in which you will pay the lawyer for legal services. This should include amounts, payment dates, and all other terms and conditions regarding payment of legal fees. The agreement may provide for a retainer or flat fee to be paid to the lawyer for handling the entire matter. Many times, the retainer is only a first payment or advance against an hourly or contingency fee. Alternately, provisions can be made to pay the lawyer an hourly rate, with the lawyer providing an accounting for his or her time. Also, the lawyer may accept payment on a contingency arrangement based on a certain percentage of any funds received.

Payment for costs and expenses such as court fees, filing fees, witness fees, long distance telephone calls, travel, copying of documents, and investigative services should be provided for in item 4. Generally, the client pays for these costs, but agreement may be made otherwise. In any event, try to obtain a good faith estimate of these costs from your lawyer and list them in item 4. You should require that the lawyer obtain your approval before incurring any costs and expenses greater than some specified amount.

Item 5 provides that you can terminate your attorney retainer agreement at any time and for any reason. Your lawyer can terminate the agreement for valid cause, such as your noncooperation or nonpayment, or with your consent. In any event, termination of the agreement should not be allowed when it would harm or prejudice your case.

Item 6 provides for the immediate refund of the money paid to your lawyer if the agreement is terminated, except that you and your lawyer may agree to deduct payment for time, costs, and expenses from your refund or credit.

Item 7 obligates your lawyer to give you or any new attorney a copy of all documents in your file at your request. Any additional terms that you or your lawyer may have can be added to item 8.

The agreement should be signed by both you and your lawyer. It is also recommended that the Attorney's Retainer Agreement, as well as any other agrements or documents used from this book, be initialed and dated on each page to prevent fraud and substitution of pages. You should keep a copy for your records.

Form 1: Attorney's Retainer Agreement

1. This is an Agreement made as of the _____ day of _____, 20____, between

(Client's name)_____,

(Client's address)_____,

(hereinafter referred to as the "Client") and

(Attorney's name)_____,

(Attorney's address)_____,

(hereinafter referred to as the "Lawyer"), which defines the terms and conditions under which Client has retained Lawyer to provide legal counsel and services relating to the following matter:

_____

_____

_____

_____

_____(hereinafter referred to as "Client's Case").

2. Lawyer agrees to provide competent legal counsel and services to Client in connection with Client's Case and to perform the services provided below:

_____

_____

_____

_____

3. In consideration for the legal counsel and services performed by Lawyer, Client agrees to make payment to Lawyer as follows:

_____

_____

_____

_____

4. a) Client agrees to pay all reasonable costs and expenses incurred by Lawyer in connection with Client's Case. Lawyer estimates in good faith that these costs are as follows:

_____

_____

_____

b) Lawyer agrees to obtain Client's prior approval before incurring any costs and any other expenses on behalf of Client in an amount greater than $_____.

5. Client has the right to terminate this Agreement at any time at Client's discretion. Lawyer may terminate this agreement for valid cause upon Client's consent, provided that Client's Case is not prejudiced or harmed thereby.

6. Upon termination of this Agreement, Client shall be entitled to the immediate refund or credit of all amounts paid or due, except as provided below:

_____

_____

_____

_____

7. After termination of this Agreement, Lawyer agrees to provide to any new attorney or to Client, upon Client's request, a copy of all documents which Lawyer has possession of relating to Client's Case.

8. Additional terms and conditions:

Client and Lawyer, intending to be legally bound, have signed this Agreement on the date first indicated above.

_____   _____
Client's signature   Lawyer's signature

3

Preparing Your Will

What Is a Will?

A will is a legal document which is prepared with certain formalities and under which you direct what will happen to your property after your death. Your will is effective only upon your death and it can be modified or revoked by you at any time during your life. If you should die without leaving a will, your property will be distributed according to state law and will generally go to your spouse and children or other next of kin.

There are several good reasons why you should prepare a will. Your will expresses your specific wishes as to how you want your property distributed and it eliminates speculation and confusion about how your estate will be given away. Also, it states who you want to handle your estate and can identify who you would want as guardian of any minor children. Equally important, your will provides a good inventory of your property and assets. Without this, it may be difficult for someone to identify and locate any real estate, bank accounts, safe deposit boxes, securities, or other personal property you may have in various places. Preparing your will is also good because it causes you to seriously consider the extent of your property, family, and friends and to plan your estate accordingly.

Before making your will, you should prepare a list of all of your real and personal property. This list should be complete with all your real estate, bank accounts, safe deposit boxes, stocks and bonds, automobiles, furniture, jewelry, artwork, and all other assets. It is also good to list any insurance policies you may have, even though insurance proceeds will generally be paid directly to the beneficiary named in the policy without going through probate of the will. You should also prepare a list of your children, spouse, other family members, friends, charities and others who you would like to make beneficiaries in your will.

Next, you should prepare a distribution plan which shows how you want your property distributed among your family, friends, and others. Identify someone that you would like to name as Executor (male) or Executrix (female) to carry out your wishes and the distribution of your estate. You should also identify an alternate person in the event that the first Executor or Executrix is unable to serve. With all the information you have just gathered, you can now prepare your will.

Requirements of a Valid Will

The formal requirements for making a valid will depend on state law. However, most, if not all, of the states recognize four general requirements in the formation of a valid will. First, there must be the necessary intent to make a will. This means that you must intend for the document and the words contained therein to operate as your will upon your death. Secondly, you must be of legal age and have the legal capacity to make a will. This means that you must have actual knowledge of the act that you are performing. You must also have an understanding of your property and your relationship to others at the time of making your will. Third, your will must be made free of fraud, duress, undue influence, and mistake. Fourth, your will must be executed in accordance with the formal requirements of your state law. This generally requires that your will be signed by you and by two disinterested witnesses in the presence of each other. Some states, however, may require that the will be witnessed by three people. Therefore, it is recommended that you have at least three people sign your will as witnesses. An extra witnesses may provide validity if another witness is disqualified.

Intent to Make a Will

A valid will generally requires that you, as the maker, have the intent to make a will. This is a question of fact which is determined from the circumstances surrounding the making of your will. Where your will is a sham or was executed as a joke, the required testamentary intent is lacking and your will is invalid. If you prepare a document or agreement which shows an intent to make a will in the future, this document or agreement is not a valid will. For your will to be valid, it must show your present intent to make a will.

Capacity to Make a Will

For the required testamentary capacity to make a will, you must be of legal age and sound mental capacity. The legal age in most states is 18 years. The sound mental capacity requires that you be able to (1) understand the relationship between you and the natural objects of your generosity, such as your spouse, children, and other family members; (2) understand the nature and extent of your property; and (3) understand that you are executing your will. The required mental capacity must exist at the time that you make your will. If you should later lose the required mental capacity, this does not affect the validity of an earlier will

executed when you did have the required mental capacity.

Your capacity to make a will can be influenced by alcohol, drugs, medications, illness, and mental disease. To help avoid questions about your capacity to make a will, your will should contain an introductory clause declaring that you are of sound mind and body, have full testamentary intent and capacity, and voluntarily execute that document as your last will and testament. Your will should also include a witness attestation clause in which the witnesses declare that you are of sound mind and body and signed of your free will.

Signing Your Will

The valid execution of your will requires that it be signed by you. Your signature generally must appear at the end of the will. However, it is recommended that you sign at the end of each page to prevent fraud and substitution of pages. You should use your regular and complete signature, although any name or mark used by you and intended as your signature is generally acceptable. You should sign your will in the presence of the witnesses who will be attesting to it. If you are unable to sign your will, generally you can have another person sign for you. This must be done in your presence and in the presence of the witnesses and be at your specific direction.

The Witnesses to Your Will

It is required that your will be witnessed by two or three people, depending on state law. This usually requires that the witnesses observe your signing and also sign the will themselves in your presence and the presence of each other.

Who may be a proper witness to your will is also governed by your state law. Generally, any competent person who is of legal age can be a witness. Some states require that the witnesses not be beneficiaries under the will or lose their gift under the will if they act as witnesses. Therefore, it is recommended that your will be witnessed by disinterested witnesses who will not be beneficiaries under your will.

Your will should contain a witness attestation clause which declares that the will was signed and published in their presence and that you were of sound mind and body and acting from your free will at that time. This witness attestation clause may be useful in preventing challenges to your will that might be based on arguments that you lacked testamentary intent and capacity.

Your witnesses should include their addresses along with their signatures so they will be easier to find. In some states, your will can be "self-proving" if your signature and that of your witnesses are notarized. If your will is "self-proving," your signature and your witnesses' signatures are presumed to be valid.

Using the Sample Will Form

A sample will form is provided at the end of this chapter for your use in preparing a simple will. It is useful for most cases involving simple bequests and provisions and is adaptable for most states.

Clause 1 is a declaration that you are of sound mind and body and free will, that you have full testamentary intent and capacity, and that you voluntarily make your will.

In Clause 2 you include your current domicile.

Clause 3 is an express revocation of all wills and codicils previously executed by you. A codicil is an amendment to a will which does not revoke it, but merely modifies it. A sample codicil form is also provided at the end of this chapter. Note that a valid codicil must be prepared with the same requirements for making a valid will.

Clause 4 provides for the appointment of an Executor or Executrix for your estate. Your will should provide that no bond be required for the Executor or Executrix to carry out his or her duties in your will.

Clause 5 directs your Executor or Executrix to pay all of your just debts and other expenses of the administration of your estate. These debts and expenses are usually paid directly from the assets of your estate before any distribution is made to your beneficiaries.

In Clause 6 you provide for your gifts to the beneficiaries. In the simplest form these can be gifts of specific property to named individuals. You may also make gifts to members of a class, such as your children, brothers or sisters and the like. Care must be taken to make certain that any gift will vest within 21 years after the life of some specific person. For complicated will and trust provisions you should consult an attorney. Typical legal fees for preparing a simple will range from about $200 to about $1,000, depending on complexity and location.

In many states, your surviving spouse may be entitled to a certain minimum portion (usually from ¼ to ½) of your estate regardless of what your will provides. Thus, you may need to indicate in your will whether any bequest or devise to your spouse is in lieu of, or in addition to, any minimum portion mandated by state law.

Likewise, some states provide that a child who is not mentioned or provided for in your will may be entitled to a share of your estate. Similar provisions may apply to children born after execution of your will. For these reasons, your state laws should be checked for specific provisions to testamentary gifts to children. It is recommended that all your children be acknowledged and mentioned in your will, even if you do not leave them anything or only leave a small token gift.

Clause 7 is a residuary clause wherein you can give the remainder of your estate. This provision is important in case you have omitted to give any of your property under Clause 6, or if any of your other gifts should fail for any reason.

You should date and sign your will with your legal signature in the presence of your witnesses.

Other Clauses for Your Will

Depending on your particular circumstances you may want to include additional provisions in your will, such as a guardianship clause and trust clause for your minor children, a simultaneous death clause, or predeceased clause in case a beneficiary should predecease you. These sample clauses are given at the end of this chapter and can be included in Clause 8 of the sample will. Remember to consult an attorney if your will involves non-routine or complicated situations or if you should have any questions about preparing your will.

The guardianship clause nominates someone whom you would like to act as guardian of your minor children. The trust clause provides the terms and conditions as to how a gift to your minor children will be held and distributed. In the trust clause, you should appoint a trustee and give instructions as to how the trustee should distribute the gifts. The simultaneous death clause provides that, if you and a beneficiary should die together, the gift to that beneficiary will pass through your estate rather than the estate of the beneficiary. The predeceased clause provides that, if beneficiaries should die before you, their gifts will pass to their lawful descendents who survive you. Otherwise, the gifts become part of your residuary estate. You may also want to include a pledge of your body or organs in your will. A discussion on how to make such a pledge is provided in chapter 7.

Revoking Your Will

You can revoke your will at any time before your death. You can revoke your will by tearing, cancelling, burning, or otherwise destroying it with the intent of revoking it. Your will can also be revoked by making a new will. Your new will can revoke the old one by explicit language of revocation or by conflicting provisions. The best ways of revoking a will are to execute a new will which expressly revokes the old one, or to cancel or otherwise revoke the will in the presence of witnesses.

Reviewing Your Will

It is important that you review your will on a periodic basis and whenever there is a change in your personal circumstances, such as marriage, children, death of a beneficiary, disposition or acquisition of property, and the like. For example, in many states, getting married will automatically invalidate any wills made by you prior to marriage. Other states may give your spouse and children a statuary share of your estate regardless of the provisions in your will. Likewise, the death of a beneficiary or a change in property ownership could dramatically affect the provisions in your will. Be sure that your will is always consistent with your current wishes.

Checklist for Preparing Your Will

❏ Prepare a list of all real estate and personal property.

❏ Prepare a list of children, family members, and other beneficiaries.

❏ Prepare a plan of distribution of your property.

❏ Identify an Executor or Executrix for your estate.

❏ Prepare your will according to your wishes using the sample will form.

❏ Obtain three witnesses who will not be beneficiaries under your will.

❏ Sign and date your will in the presence of the witnesses.

❏ Have the witnesses sign your will in your presence and in the presence of each other.

❏ For a "self-proving" will, have the signatures notarized.

❏ Consult an attorney if your will involves complex or difficult provisions.

❏ Review your will periodically to make sure that it is up-to-date and appropriate for your current situation.

Form 2: Last Will and Testament

1. I, _____, being of sound mind and body and free will, and having full testamentary intent and capacity, do hereby voluntarily make, publish, and execute this document as my Last Will and Testament.

2. My current domicile is as follows:

3. I hereby revoke all wills and codicils previously executed by me.

4. I hereby appoint _____ as Executor/Executrix of my estate. I direct that no bond be required in any jurisdiction for the faithful exercise of his/her duties.

5. I hereby direct my Executor/Executrix to pay all of my just debts and other expenses of the administration of my estate.

6. I hereby devise and give the following items:

7. All the rest, residue, and remainder of my estate, whether real or personal, I devise and give as follows:

8. Other provisions:

In Witness Whereof, I have signed this document as my Last Will and Testament on this _____ day of _____ 20__.

_____

Maker's Legal Signature

The foregoing Will of _____, dated _____, was signed and published in our presence as his/her Last Will and Testament. We declare that the maker was of sound mind and body and free will at that time, and we have hereto signed our names as witnesses in the presence of the maker and of each other.

_____

Name

_____   _____

Witness' Signature   Address

_____

Name

_____   _____

Witness' Signature   Address

_____

Name

_____   _____

Witness' Signature   Address

Subscribed and sworn to before me on this ____ day of _____, 20__.

_____

Notary

Sample Clauses for Wills

Guardianship Clause

I hereby nominate and appoint _____ as the Guardian of any of my children during their respective minority ages and upon my death.

Simultaneous Death Clause

If any beneficiary named in this Will and I shall die together, or under any circumstances where it is impracticable to determine the order of death, I hereby direct that the terms of this Will shall be construed as if said beneficiary had predeceased me and that my estate shall be administered accordingly.

Predeceased Clause

If any beneficiary named in this will shall predecease me, then I hereby direct that his/her bequest, devise, or gift shall be given by per stirpes right of representation to his/her lawful descendents who are living at the time of my death. If said beneficiary leaves no lawful descendents who are living at the time of my death, then his/her gift shall lapse and become part of my residuary estate.

Trust Clause for Minor Children

If any of my children named as a beneficiary under this Will is a minor at the time of my death, then I direct that his/her bequest, devise, or gift under this Will shall be held in trust by my Executor/Executor as Trustee, and distributed according to the following terms and conditions for the support, maintenance and education of said children:

Form 3: Codicil

1. I, _____, being of sound mind and body and free will, and having full testamentary intent and capacity, do hereby voluntarily make, publish and execute this document as a codicil to my Last Will and Testament which was made on the _____ day of _____, 20__.

2. I hereby amend and modify the provisions of my Last Will and Testament identified above as follows:

3. Except as expressly modified by this codicil, all remaining terms and provisions of my Last Will and Testament identified above shall remain in full force and effect.

In Witness Whereof, I have signed this document as a codicil to my Last Will and Testament identified above on this _____ day of _____, 20__.

_____
Maker's Signature

The foregoing codicil of _____, dated this _____ day of_____, 20__, was signed and published in our presence as a codicil to his/her Last Will and Testament. We declare that the maker was of sound mind and body and free will at that time, and we have hereto signed our names as witnesses in the presence of the maker and of each other.

_____
Name

_____   _____
Witness' Signature   Address

_____
Name

_____   _____
Witness' Signature   Address

_____
Name

_____   _____
Witness' Signature   Address

Subscribed and sworn to before me on this _____ day of _____, 20__.

_____
Notary

4 *Easy Steps to Probate a Will*

Definition of Probate

Probate is the legal process by which an estate is settled and the property of the estate is distributed. Technically, probate refers to applying to the court to admit a will for settlement of an estate. More generally, probate refers to the entire process involved with administering a will. This involves opening the estate for probate; taking inventory and appraising the estate; closing the estate, including settling all accounts and debts, and paying any applicable estate and inheritance taxes; and distributing the property to the beneficiaries or heirs. The person probating a will is generally called the personal representative. All of these steps will be described in this chapter.

A will has no real effect until it has been probated. Probate proceedings are generally held in the probate court in the county and state where the decedent resided on the date of his or her death. The procedures for probating an estate are governed by the law of the state where the decedent was domiciled. Many states follow the rules of the Uniform Probate Code, which simplify many probate procedures and give the personal representative freedom to conduct probate independently, thus reducing delays and costs. If real estate is located in other states, supplementary probate proceedings may also be required in those states to settle title to any real estate.

If a will has not been left, the decedent is said to have died "intestate," and the estate will be administered and distributed according to the "laws of intestacy" in the state where the decedent resided. If a will has been prepared it will be offered for probate and administered according to the stipulations in the will.

Obviously, you will not be handling the probate of your own estate after your death. However, the information in this chapter will be useful to others who will be probating your estate, and to you if you should ever have to probate the estate of a family member or friend.

You should be able to do most of the work involved with settling an estate without hiring an attorney. However, if you decide to hire an attorney in a complex case, be certain to find one who is experienced in handling estate and probate matters. Typical attorney's fees in probate cases range from about three percent to about seven percent of the value of the decedent's estate. The personal representative is also generally paid a fee for administering the estate in the range of three to five percent of the value of the estate. These legal and administrative fees are usually paid out of the proceeds of the decedent's estate. The time and expense of probate can be avoided by setting up a living trust. Information and forms for setting up a living trust are presented in chapter 5.

Opening the Estate

Generally, opening the estate begins by submitting the will to the probate court in the county where the decedent was last domiciled to be proved valid. This may be done by the designated Executor or Executrix of the will, a beneficiary, an heir, a creditor, or anyone with a claim against or interest in the estate. Proving the will may require a brief hearing attended by witnesses to the will who can vouch for its authenticity. If there is no will, an intestacy form must be submitted to the probate court instead of a will. These forms are usually available from the probate registrar.

In addition to submitting the will to prove its validity, opening the estate also usually includes providing the following information to probate court: the date and place of death of the decedent; the decedent's domicile at the time of death; a copy of the decedent's death certificate; a list of all known interested persons, including the decedent's surviving spouse and next of kin; and an estimate of the estate's total value.

Opening the estate also involves the formal appointment by the court of a personal representative. The personal representative may be the executor or executrix named in the will, an heir, a beneficiary, or someone appointed by the court. The personal representative is responsible for performing and administering the steps outlined in this chapter.

All interested persons must be notified of the decedent's death and the opening of the estate. This notice is usually done by the personal representative. The validity of all or part of a will may be contested by any interested party within a specified number of days following notice. This may initiate a will contest that can either be settled by agreement of all interested persons or by a formal will contest proceeding in the courts. Generally, an attorney will have to be engaged if there is a will contest.

Estate Inventory and Appraisal

After the estate has been opened, it must be inventoried and appraised by the personal representative. This must usually be done within the time specified by state law. During this process the personal representative will account for all assets owned by the decedent at the time of death, as well as all debts and other claims against the estate. In addition, as the estate's representative, you are empowered by the court to become the legal custodian of the assets, and you should make certain that the assets are released to you for distribution under the terms of the decedent's will.

One of the first things you should do when you inventory the estate is open a bank account in the name of the estate, with you as the signator of the account. The cash assets of the estate will be deposited into this account and debts and administrative fees will be paid from this account. An interest-bearing checking account is most advisable.

Before taking a detailed inventory, try to get a preliminary estimate of the value of the estate by talking to those who you believe would be most knowledgeable of the decedent's affairs. Also, locate and try to value the major assets of the estate (e.g., bank accounts, deed to house). This preliminary estimate will help you focus on the details of the inventory, as well as help you determine if the estate qualifies for small-estate administration. Small-estate administration is an expedited probate procedure for estate below a certain amount, as determined by state law.

Taking inventory of the estate requires searching for and valuing all of the estate's assets. To do this, you should contact all those who might know about the decedent's affairs—surviving spouse, other close relatives, close friends, business partners. They will help you locate personal papers that will direct you to bank accounts, insurance policies, brokerage accounts, real estate interests, etc. You should be as thorough as possible in this search. Valuing some of the assets, such as jewelry and real estate, may require the services of a professional appraiser.

As you inventory the estate, list each asset by value and type of asset. In addition, categorize the assets as probate or non-probate assets. Not all assets are subject to probate. Non-probate assets can pass directly to the heir, beneficiary or co-owner without going through probate, and include property legally designated as jointly owned in the title of ownership; and benefits such as death benefits from insurance policies, or benefits from private retirement plans, Social Security, the Veteran's Administration, and other sources. The probate court may require documentation to prove the assets are not subject to probate, but this documentation is usually easy to obtain. It may include a notarized affidavit stating that the co-owners have a right to the jointly owned property or a statement from the decedent's employer in the case of retirement benefits.

In addition to locating, valuing, and categorizing the assets, you must also identify and value all outstanding liabilities of the estate. These include reasonable funeral expenses; costs and expenses of estate administration, including legal fees and your expenses as personal representative; outstanding medical expenses; unpaid bills for rent, utilities, telephone, etc.; and taxes. Check for claims against the estate as you did for the estate's assets. Valid claims are to be paid from the estate's assets. Depending on the size of the claim, the probate court may need to approve their payment.

Finally, during this process you must arrange to pay state and federal taxes. These taxes include: a) income taxes earned by the decedent during the tax year in which he or she died; b) state and federal taxes earned by the *estate* after the death of the decedent until the estate has been distributed; c) state taxes assessed either as an inheritance tax on each heir's share of the estate or as an estate tax on the total value of the estate, and; d) federal estate tax that must be filed for the estate of every decedent where the gross estate exceeds the sum of $600,000. These taxes should be calculated before the estate is closed in order that enough money

is set aside prior to the distribution of the estate to the heirs or beneficiaries. For information about federal inheritance or estate taxes, you can call your regional IRS office.

Closing the Estate and Distributing the Assets

Once the estate has been inventoried and appraised the next step is to pay all valid claims and expenses, and to complete all tax returns. The estate can then be formally closed, and the remaining assets can be distributed to the heirs and beneficiaries. Make sure you have set aside enough money to pay taxes and estate administration fees. Closing the estate merely involves preparing a final accounting and either filing it with the court or giving it to the heirs. This final accounting lists the total assets and expenses, including taxes due. There are different procedures for formally closing an estate. In some states the estate can be closed by a sworn statement, in other states the probate court may require a brief hearing. After the estate has been formally closed by notification from the court, the assets can be distributed.

So far, all of the estate's assets have been in your custody. The distribution of the assets means that they will now be handed over in accordance with the terms in the decedent's will. In some instances, most of the decedent's assets are in real estate or personal property. Distribution of the assets according to the will may require a probate sale in order to convert this property into cash. Because a probate sale may be time consuming and not cost effective, many states allow the distribution of the physical assets of the estate in place of their cash value. If the heirs demand cash, then the property will have to be sold. Any assets remaining after all grants in the will have been distributed are to be distributed according to the commonly found residuary clause in the will.

Each person receiving assets should give you a receipt acknowledging that he or she received their full share of the estate.

To help resolve any disputes (should they arise), keep copies of all receipts for distribution, payment of claims, expenses, etc. for a few years after the estate is closed.

Using the Sample Petition/ Application to Probate a Will

A sample petition/application to probate a will is provided at the end of this chapter. This petition/application can be completed and filed without the assistance of an attorney if the probate proceeding is a simple one. However, if you decide to hire an attorney in a complex probate, be certain to find an attorney who is experienced in handling estate and probate matters. Typical attorney's fees in probate cases range from about three percent to about seven percent of the value of your decedent's estate. The Executor, Executrix, or other administrator is generally paid a fee for administering the estate in the range of three percent to five percent of the value of the estate. These legal and administrative fees are usually paid out of the proceeds of the decedent's estate. The time and expense of probate can be avoided by setting up a living trust. Information and forms for setting up a living trust are presented in chapter 5.

The caption of the sample petition/application should include the full name of the decedent and the name of the court. The docket number is obtained from the court clerk at the time the petition/application is filed. Be sure to check with the court clerk to find out if multiple copies of the petition/application must be filed and what filing fees may be involved. You should keep one copy of the petition/application for your records.

Item 1 of the sample petition/application should include the complete address of the petitioner/applicant.

Item 2 should include the date and place of death of the decedent.

The decedent's domicile at the time of his or her death should be included in item 3. Remember that the decedent's domicile is important in determining the place of probate. A person's domicile is his or her fixed or permanent place of residence.

Item 4 makes reference to a list of decedent's surviving spouse, heirs at law, and next of kin which are known to you, the petitioner/applicant. This list should be attached to the petition/application as an exhibit.

Item 5 makes reference to the decedent's Last Will and Testament. A copy of the decedent's will should be attached to the petition/application as an exhibit.

Reference is made to the decedent's Death Certificate in item 6. A copy of the decedent's Death Certificate should be attached to the petition/application as an exhibit.

Item 7 is a certification that all information in the petition/application is true.

You should sign the petition/application and include your address and telephone number for easy reference by the probate court. Because some courts may require that your signature be verified, (particularly if someone else will be filing the petition/application on your behalf) it should be notarized.

The sample petition/application is adaptable for use in most states for probating an estate where a valid will is involved. You should check the rules and requirements for your particular state. If no will is involved, the petition/application should be one for administration of the decedent's estate. In such a case, item 4 of the sample petition/application is deleted and replaced with a declaration that the decedent has not left a will. The application should also contain a clause, such as the following: Petitioner/Applicant requests that_____ be appointed as administrator of the decedent's estate.

Checklist for Probating a Will

The following checklist will help you organize the tasks you must perform in order to serve as a personal representative.

- ❏ Obtain a copy of decedent's Last Will and Testament

- ❏ Obtain a copy of decedent's Death Certificate

- ❏ Submit the will to the court for it to be proved

- ❏ Submit an intestacy form to the court if there is no will

- ❏ Submit a list of all known interested persons

- ❏ Apply for appointment by the court as personal representative

- ❏ Notify all interested persons of the decedent's death and the opening of the estate

- ❏ Open estate bank account

- ❏ Prepare an inventory of the decedent's assets and an estimate of the estate's worth

- ❏ Collect all property of the estate

- ❏ Engage an appraiser, if necessary

- ❏ Determine whether the assets are probate or non-probate assets

- ❏ Determine all claims against the estate

- ❏ Close the estate by preparing a final accounting for filing with the court or heirs

- ❏ Prepare a plan of distribution according to the will

- ❏ Pay off the claims against the estate

- ❏ Distribute all assets

- ❏ Obtain receipts for all claims paid and all assets distributed

- ❏ Retain all receipts and other records for several years

- ❏ Consult an attorney if the probate of decedent's estate will involve complex or difficult issues

Form 4: Petition/Application to Probate Will

Court: _____

Estate of _____, Deceased.   Docket No.: _____

Petitioner/Applicant, _____ (Name of petitioner/applicant), declares the following:

1. Petitioner/Applicant resides at _____

_____.

2. Decedent died on _____(Date) at_____(Place of Death).

3. Decedent's domicile at the time of his/her death was_____

_____.

4. Attached is a list of decedent's surviving spouse, heirs at law, and next of kin known to the petitioner/applicant.

5. Attached is decedent's Last Will and Testament executed on _____(Date).

6. Attached is a copy of the Death Certificate of _____(Name of Decedent).

7. Petitioner/Applicant certifies that all information contained herein is true to the best of his/her knowledge and belief.

_____   _____
Signature   Date

_____
Address

_____
Phone

Subscribed and sworn to before me this _____ day of_____, 20____.

_____
Notary

5 Using a Living Trust to Avoid Probate

Making Use of a Living Trust

A living or "inter vivos" trust can be used to avoid the expenses, time, and procedures of probating your estate. Basically, a living trust is the establishment of a separate legal entity during your lifetime to hold, manage, and distribute property according to the terms of a trust agreement.

A living trust can serve important functions in planning your estate for both probate and tax purposes. If you retain the right to revoke the trust, your estate must pay federal estate taxes on the trust assets. Also, income that the revocable trust earns will be taxable to you even if this income is paid to someone else. Federal estate taxes can be avoided by making the trust irrevocable or revocable only upon the occurrence of an event outside of your control.

A trust is established when you transfer real estate or personal property to someone to act as trustee pursuant to a trust agreement. A valid trust requires that title to the trust property actually be transferred to the trust. This is generally done by transferring the property to the trustee with a designation such as "to Carl Battle, trustee." The requirements as to who can serve as a trustee are governed by the laws of your specific state. Generally, any person or entity who is capable of contracting can serve as trustee. The trustee usually is a bank, an insurance company, a certified public accountant, an attorney, or any other person competent in business affairs. In

many states, you can be the maker (or "settlor") of the trust and also serve as trustee, provided that you are not the only beneficiary under the trust.

Assets that you transfer to a living trust are generally not included in your estate for probate purposes. Instead, the assets of your living trust are distributed by your trustee according to the terms of your trust agreement. Therefore, it is important that your trust agreement provide for the disposition of trust property and income after your death, particularly if you are the trustee or the initial life beneficiary. If you are the trustee, it is also important that you have appointed an alternate trustee in case of your death so that the trust provisions can be carried out.

Any property can be transferred to your living trust, whether it is real or personal property. The trust agreement can also provide for additional property to be added to the trust in the future. Your living trust can also be coordinated with your will to avoid probate by providing that any property that would be probated shall be transferred to your living trust upon your death. The trust property should be handled separately from and not commingled with your individual property or the trust may be invalidated as merely a sham.

There are many tax and estate issues that may arise in setting up a trust. Complicated and difficult trust arrangement may require the assistance of an attorney or tax specialist. Typical legal fees for establishing a simple trust range from about $500 to $1,000.

Understanding the Trust Agreement

A sample trust agreement is provided at the end of this chapter. The sample trust agreement is designed to be simple and adaptable for use in most situations. Each trust is a unique arrangement which should be tailored to your desires. Therefore, it is important that you complete the provisions of the trust agreement with clear terms and conditions that reflect your particular wishes.

The trust agreement is made between you (the maker or "settlor") and the trustee. Remember, you can serve as settlor and trustee in many states.

In Item 1(a) of the sample trust agreement you identify the property that you are transferring to the trust. You may make future transfers of property, but these should be clearly identified as transfers of property to the trust pursuant to your trust agreement.

Item 2 provides that you may revoke or amend the trust agreement except as provided by any terms and conditions that you may specify.

Item 3 provides for the payment of the trust income during your lifetime to any beneficiary and according to any terms you indicate.

In Item 4 you can specify the beneficiaries and terms for the distribution of trust income and trust property upon your death.

Item 5 is a spendthrift provision which may protect the trust income and property from the legal claims of creditors of the beneficiaries. The spendthrift provision may not be effective if the settlor is the sole beneficiary. Item 6 gives the trustee broad powers to manage the trust in the trustee's best judgment and discretion. Item 7 appoints an alternate trustee in the event of the death, resignation, or incapacity of the initial trustee.

Item 8 provides for the trustee to receive reasonable compensation or be paid as otherwise agreed. The trustee is also reimbursed for trust expenses and not required to post a bond. Item 9 provides that any pertinent taxes on trust property shall be paid from the trust.

To avoid the "rule against perpetuities," item 10 provides that the trust shall not continue for more than 21 years after the later of your death or the death of the last surviving beneficiary. Any trust property remaining thereafter will be distributed according to the terms that you specify.

In item 11 you identify the state where the trust agreement is made and will be interpreted and administered.

The trust agreement should be signed by both the settlor and trustee. If you will be serving as the trustee of your trust, then you should sign the trust agreement both as the settlor and trustee.

Checklist for Establishing a Living Trust

❏ Prepare a list of property which you will transfer to the trust.

❏ Prepare a list of beneficiaries and your plan for the distribution of trust income and trust property.

❏ Identify a trustee and an alternate.

❏ Prepare the trust agreement according to your plan of distribution and wishes.

❏ Settlor and Trustee sign the trust agreement.

❏ Transfer any identified property to the trust.

❏ If your trust involves difficult tax or estate issues, consult an attorney.

❏ Review your trust arrangement periodically to assure that it is up-to-date.

Form 5: Trust Agreement

It is declared that this Trust Agreement has been made and executed on this _____ day of _____, 20____, between _____(the "Settlor")

_____(Settlor's address)

and _____(the "Trustee")

_____(Trustee's address)

according to the following terms and conditions:

1. **(a)** The property listed below is transferred by the Settlor to the Trustee, and the Trustee's successor in trust, subject to the terms, conditions, and purposes set forth herein:

    (b) The property listed above and any other property that the Trustee may acquire pursuant to this Agreement (hereinafter "Trust Property"), shall be held, administered and distributed by the Trustee in accordance with the provisions of this Trust Agreement.

2. The Settlor may revoke or amend this Trust Agreement in writing at any time during his/her lifetime; except as provided by the following terms and conditions:

3. The Trustee shall pay and distribute the net income from this trust during the lifetime of the Settlor to the following beneficiary or beneficiaries and pursuant to the following terms:

4. Upon the death of the Settlor, the Trustee shall pay and distribute the net income from this trust and the Trust Property to the following beneficiary or beneficiaries and pursuant to the following terms:

5. The interests of the beneficiaries in the Trust Property and trust income shall not be subject to the claims of their creditors or any other party by way of garnishment, attachment, or any other legal process, and shall not be transferred or encumbered. Any such transfer or encumbrance shall be null and void.

6. The Trustee shall have the power pursuant to this Trust Agreement to hold, manage, operate, lease, sell, exchange, convey, repair, insure, protect, and invest the Trust Property and to collect the trust income and to employ other's assistance, all in the Trustee's best judgment and discretion.

7. In the event of death, resignation or other incapacity of the Trustee first named herein, the following person, persons or entity shall serve as the Trustee pursuant to this Trust Agreement:

8. The Trustee shall be entitled to receive reasonable and just compensation, or be paid as otherwise provided by agreement, for the Trustee's services, and shall be reimbursed for all reasonable expenses incurred in managing the Trust Property. The Trustee shall not be required to post a bond in any state for the exercise of the Trustee's duties pursuant to this Trust Agreement.

9. If any estate, inheritance, or transfer taxes are assessed against the Trust Property, the Trustee shall pay such taxes from the Trust Property.

10. No trust established herein shall continue for more than 21 years after the death of the last survivor of the Settlor or any beneficiary named herein. At the expiration of such period any Trust property remaining shall be immediately distributed as follows:

11. This Trust Agreement has been made in and shall be interpreted and administered in accordance with the laws of the State of _____.

Settlor and Trustee, intending to be legally bound, have signed this Agreement on the date first indicated above.

_____
Settlor's Signature

_____
Trustee's Signature

Subscribed and sworn to before me on this _____ day of _____, 20___.

_____
Notary

6

Making a Living Will

The Functions of a Living Will

A "living will" is not a will at all, but instructions and a power of attorney to family members or doctors regarding the continuation or termination of medical life-support systems. Living wills can be useful to avoid life-support measures which only prolong the dying process.

Beginning with California in 1976, most other states and the District of Columbia adopted "living will," "death-with-dignity," or "right-to-die" laws which recognize the rights of terminally ill patients to stop life support. The purpose of these laws is to protect doctors, hospitals, and others from civil and criminal liability and to honor the wishes of patients who are dying from a terminal condition.

The requirements for making a living will vary for each state. Generally, the laws require that the living will be signed and dated by the maker. It generally must be witnessed by two or more people who are not the maker's relatives, doctor (or doctor's employees), beneficiaries, or creditors. The maker and witnesses generally must be of legal age (i.e., 18 years old in most states). If you make a living will, give copies to your doctor and family so that they will know your wishes.

A typical "death with dignity" law provides that a terminally ill patient can request by a conscious directive or by a living will that life-support systems be withheld or withdrawn. The hospital, staff, and family will be free from liability if such a request is honored. The laws also protect any insurance that the terminal patient may have, by declaring that honoring a living will does not constitute suicide.

The living will document itself basically provides: If the situation should arise in which there is no reasonable expectation of recovery from terminal physical or mental disability, you request that you be allowed to die naturally, and not be kept alive by artificial means or extraordinary measures.

Before your living will is honored, usually a determination of terminal illness must be made by your attending physician and at least one other doctor. However, the living will must normally be made by you when you are in a stable mental and physical condition. You can revoke or modify your living will at any time.

Some doctors or hospitals may be reluctant to honor a living will and terminate life-support systems. For this reason, many states allow you to make a durable power of attorney or medical proxy whereby you appoint someone to make medical decisions for you when you are unable to do so. The medical proxies and durable power of attorney are more likely to be honored by doctors and hospitals because someone has been appointed by you who can make decisions regarding specific circumstances as they arise. Most jurisdictions now recognize medical proxies or durable powers of attorney whereby you can appoint someone to make medical decisions, including withdrawal or withholding of life support.

It is recommended that a medical proxy or durable power of attorney be included in your living will. A sample living will form is provided at the end of this chapter and is adaptable for use in most jurisdictions. It incorporates a durable power of attorney.

Checklist for Making a Living Will

❑ Check to see if your state recognizes living wills and what the requirements are.

❑ Identify two or more people as witnesses who are not your family members, doctors, beneficiaries, or creditors.

❑ Identify someone that you can appoint to make medical decisions if you are incapacitated.

❑ Prepare and sign your living will. Also have your witnesses sign your living will. It is recommended that your living will be notarized.

❑ Give copies of your living will to your appointed agent, your family, and your doctor.

❑ If your living will involves difficult or complex issues, you should consult an attorney.

Form 6: Living Will

1. I, _____(Maker), being of sound mind, voluntarily declare that this directive is made this _____ day of _____, 20_____ as my Living Will in accordance with the laws of the State of _____.

2. If I should have at any time an incurable condition caused by illness, disease, or injury certified to be a terminal condition by two licensed physicians, and where there is no reasonable expectation of recovery from said terminal condition, and where the application of life-sustaining methods and equipment would only prolong the moment of my imminent death, I hereby direct and request that said life-sustaining methods and equipment not be used, and that I be allowed to die naturally and not be kept alive by artificial or extraordinary means.

3. In the event that I am unable to give conscious direction regarding medical treatment or the use of said life-sustaining procedures, I direct and request that this Living Will be honored by my family, physicians and all others as the final and conclusive expression of my legal right to refuse medical treatment. I hereby appoint _____ as my true and lawful attorney in fact to act for me and make decisions concerning medical treatment, including the withdrawal or withholding of life support, in accordance with this Living Will. This power of attorney shall remain in effect in the event that I should become or be declared disabled, incapacitated, or incompetent.

4. This Living Will shall be in effect until it is revoked by me.

5. My current residence is: _____

In Witness Whereof I have signed this document as my declaration and Living Will.

_____
Maker's signature

The maker of this Living Will is personally known to me, is of sound mind, and has executed this document of his or her own free will.

Witness' Signature	Name	Address
Witness' Signature	Name	Address
Witness' Signature	Name	Address

Subscribed and sworn to before me on this _____ day of _____, 20__.

_____
Notary

7 How to Make an Organ Donor Pledge

Making a Gift of Your Body or Organ

Upon your death, you may wish to donate certain of your organs or body parts for medical or other purposes. Every state and the District of Columbia have enacted laws permitting and regulating gifts of your human body, organs, or parts thereof. These gifts can be made by your last will and testament or by any other document which gives or pledges your body or body parts.

Normally, it is the right and obligation of your spouse, children, parents, other family members, or guardian to dispose of your body after your death. However, you can direct what happens to your body in your will or pledge. These pledges can be extremely useful for medical therapy, transplantation, education, and research.

The laws governing gifts of the human body or body parts are similar in all the states. The laws generally provide that any person of sound mind and 18 years of age or more may give all or any part of his or her body for any permitted purpose. These gifts can generally be made to any hospital, doctor, medical school, university, or storage facility for the purposes of medical or dental education, research, therapy, or transplantation. The gifts can also be made to any individual for therapy or transplantation needed by him or her.

If you make a gift or pledge of your body or body parts without identifying a donee or recipient, your attending physician usually may accept the gift as donee. Your attending physician can then donate your body or parts according to his or her best judgement.

Your pledge of your body or organs supersedes the desires of your spouse, family, and others as to the disposition of your body. If you make a pledge, you should review it with your family and doctor to make your wishes known.

Your gift of your body or organs, whether by your will or other documents, takes effect only upon your death.

You can make your pledge at any time. You can make a pledge of your body, organs, or parts by including an appropriate donor clause in your will. A sample donor clause for your will is included at the end of this chapter. A discussion on how to prepare your will can be found in chapter 3.

You can also make a gift or pledge by a written document other than your will. This document spells out the nature of your gift, the donee, and the purpose of your gift. The document must be signed by you, generally in the presence of two or more witnesses. The pledge document can be prepared in the form of a card which is carried on you. Many states allow a pledge to be printed on the back of your driving license. A sample pledge form is provided on the next page.

Form 7: Pledge of Human Body, Organ, or Part Thereof

1. I, _____(Donor's name),

residing at _____(Donor's address)

am of sound mind and 18 years or more of age.

2. Effective upon my death, I hereby pledge and give to _____(Donee's name)

_____(Donee's address)

my body or parts thereof as indicated and marked below:

        ❏ my entire body.

        ❏ any needed body part or organ.

        ❏ the following named organ(s) or body part(s):_____

        _____

If the Donee named above is unable to accept or receive the above pledge, said pledge shall be given to the attending physician at my death.

3. My gift above shall be used only for the purpose(s) indicated and marked below:

        ❏ for transplant

        ❏ for therapy

        ❏ for medical research

        ❏ for medical education

        ❏ any lawful purposes

In Witness Whereof I have signed my name in the presence of the witnesses below.

_____   _____

Donor's Signature   Date

Witness' Signature   Name   Address

Witness' Signature   Name   Address

Witness' Signature   Name   Address

Subscribed and sworn to before me on this _____ day of _____, 20__.

_____

Notary

8

Transferring Your Personal Rights by an Assignment

What Is an Assignment?

An assignment is a transfer of property, or any rights or interests therein, from one person to another. Usually assignments are used to transfer title to personal property as well as contractual rights, rights to payment, rights to sue, and other rights connected with either personal property or real estate.

The person transferring or assigning rights is referred to as the "assignor." The "assignee" is the person to whom rights are transferred.

What Rights Are Assignable?

Generally all of your rights are assignable to another unless there is an agreement to the contrary or the assignment is against public policy and prohibited by law.

You can assign your right to receive payment or other benefits under a contract. This can include rights such as the rights to rental payments under a lease, payments under a promissory note, compensation under an employment agreement, royalties, dividends, and many others. Unlike your right to payment, your obligations to perform under a contract generally are not assignable, particularly if the contract is one for your personal services.

You can also assign most rights in your personal property and real estate. However, title to real estate is generally transferred by a deed rather than an assignment. Title to your personal property, such as stocks, bonds, household furnishings, equipment, and the like can be transferred by an assignment. An assignment can be evidence of the transfer of title to your automobile, but it is normally required that you transfer the Certificate of Title.

Requirements for Making a Valid Assignment

An assignment is essentially a contract. Therefore, to make a valid assignment, you generally must be of legal age and have the legal mental capacity to enter into contracts. A valid assignment must be entered into voluntarily and be free of fraud, coercion, or duress. Also, for an assignment to be enforceable, it is usually required that both the assignor and assignee give consideration or something of value under the assignment. You can make a valid assignment as a gift to the assignee. However, the assignee generally cannot enforce the assignment against you unless he or she has paid or promised you something in return. To safeguard against fraud and misunderstanding, your assignment should be in writing.

When you make an assignment, your assignee generally cannot obtain any rights or interests in the assigned property which are greater than those you may have. This simply means that you cannot transfer anything more than what you have. The assigned property, in the hands of your assignee, is still subject to all claims, liens, or other interests which existed against the property before you assigned it.

You do not avoid any liability or obligation you may have regarding a contract or other property merely because you have assigned your rights and interests therein. For example, if you finance the purchase of a car, you do not avoid your obligations to pay back your loan by assigning the car to someone else. Likewise, when you sublet an apartment, you are still obligated to pay the rent to your landlord. You are released from any liabilities and obligations in an assignment only if the assignee and all other parties involved agree or consent to your release.

Using the Sample Assignment Form
A sample assignment form is provided at the end of this chapter. The sample assignment form should be adaptable for use in all the states.

Item 1 of the assignment should identify the assignor and assignor's address. It should also clearly identify the assignee and assignee's address. This clause provides for the assignment and transfer of all of your rights, title and interests to the assigned property or other interests. The assigned property, rights, and interests should be specifically and clearly identified in the assignment.

In item 2 you should include any terms and conditions which affect or govern the assignment. For example, this could include provisions for payments, inspections, releases, consents, and the like.

Item 3 includes the effective date of the assignment. Item 4 should specify which state laws the assignment shall be governed by.

The assignment should be signed and dated by the assignor and assignee. It should also be signed by other parties who are affected by the assignment to show their consent and acceptance.

It is recommended that the assignment be notarized.

Form 8: Assignment

1. For valuable and sufficient consideration, _____(Assignor's name) _____(Assignor's address),

   hereby assigns and transfers to

   _____(Assignee's name) _____(Assignee's address),

   all of his/her rights, title, and interest in and to the following:

2. This assignment is subject to the following terms and conditions:

3. This assignment is effective on the _____ day of _____, 20__.

4. This assignment shall be governed by the laws of the State of _____.

In Witness Whereof, I have signed this Assignment of my own free will.

_____   _____
Assignor's Signature   Date

Agreed to and Accepted by:

_____   _____
Assignor's Signature   Date

Other Parties: _____   _____
Signature   Date

Subscribed and sworn to before me this _____ day of_____, 20___.

_____
Notary

9

Operating Through Someone Else by Power of Attorney

Understanding the Power of Attorney

A power of attorney is basically a written document which authorizes someone else to act on behalf of and as agent for you. If you make a power of attorney, you are commonly referred to as the *principal*. The person to whom you have given the power of attorney to act on your behalf is referred to as the *attorney in fact* or *agent*.

Your power of attorney can be a general power of attorney, which authorizes your agent to conduct your entire business and affairs. A limited or special power of attorney authorizes your agent to conduct specified business or perform a single act on your behalf.

Your power of attorney primarily serves as evidence to others of your principal-agent relationship created by your power of attorney. It also serves as an agreement between you and your agent regarding the business to be transacted under your power of attorney.

A power of attorney can be useful in a variety of situations. For example, a power of attorney could be useful when you do not have the legal capacity or the time to manage your affairs. It can also be useful if you are incapacitated, undergoing an operation, or going away for a while. You may give a power of attorney to a real estate agent to manage, lease, or sell your home or apartment.

For almost anything that you can do for yourself, you can give a power of attorney to someone to act on your behalf. This includes the power to contract, buy and sell property, sign checks, make deposits and withdrawals, settle claims, file lawsuits, and almost anything else.

By their very nature, powers of attorney are serious documents which should be given careful consideration. Particularly with the broad general power of attorney, you should make certain your agent is trustworthy and competent.

Requirements for Making a Power of Attorney

Powers of attorney are usually governed by the laws regulating agents for the state where the power of attorney is made or the acts will be performed. Generally, any person who has the legal capacity to contract or appoint an agent can give his or her power of attorney to another person, corporation, or other entities. The principal should be of legal age and mentally competent.

You can make a *durable power of attorney* which will remain valid even if you later lose the capacity to contract and appoint an agent. Your durable power of attorney must be in writing and must contain language which shows that you intend the power of attorney to remain in effect even if you are disabled or incapacitated.

Any power of attorney that you make should be in writing. It should include your name and address as the principal. It should also include the name and address of your agent. You should indicate the status of your agent as an individual, corporation, association, etc.

Your power of attorney should clearly show the scope and extent of the powers granted. It should indicate whether the power of attorney is a *general* or a *limited* one. It should include the effective date and the time period during which the power of attorney will be in effect. To the extent possible, you should list the specific acts which are to be performed by your agent.

Property which is subject to your power of attorney should be clearly described. Indicate the nature, ownership, and location of such property, whether personal property, securities, real estate, and the like.

It is recommended that a provision be included which covers the manner by which you can revoke your power of attorney. Remember that if you want your power of attorney to be a durable one you must include a provision that it shall remain in effect if you become incapacitated.

If you intend for your agent to be compensated for the agent's services, indicate the amount and manner of compensation.

Your power of attorney should be signed and dated by both you as the principal and by your agent. It is recommended that your power of attorney be notarized. Some states require that powers of attorney dealing with the sale or conveyance of real estate be recorded in the county where the property is located. Be sure to check with your county clerk or recorder of deeds for specific requirements.

A sample durable power of attorney form is provided at the end of this chapter and will be useful for most situations. You can have an attorney draft a power of attorney for you at a cost ranging from about $100 to $500 depending on complexity and location.

Form 9: Power of Attorney

1. I, _____(Principal's name)
_____(Principal's address),
being of sound mind and legal capacity, do hereby appoint _____(Agent's name)
_____(Agent's address),
as my true and lawful attorney in fact, to act for me in my name, place, and stead, and on my behalf to do and perform the following:

2. The following property, interests, or rights shall be subject to this Power of Attorney:

3. This Power of Attorney shall be effective on the date of _____,20___.

4. This Power of Attorney shall remain in effect in the event that I should become or be declared disabled, incapacitated, or incompetent.

5. This Power of Attorney shall terminate on the date of _____,20_____, unless I have revoked it sooner. I may revoke this Power of Attorney at any time and in any manner.

6. My agent shall be paid compensation for services pursuant to this Power of Attorney as follows:

7. This Power of Attorney shall be governed by the laws of the State of _____.

In Witness Whereof, I have signed this Power of Attorney of my own free will.

_____   _____
Principal's Signature   Date

Agreed to and Accepted by:

_____   _____
Agent's Signature   Date

Subscribed and sworn to before me on this _____ day of_____,20____.

_____
Notary

Chapter

10 *Buying and Selling Your Home*

Understanding Real Estate Sales

The purchase of a home or other real estate is probably the largest single expenditure you will make during your lifetime. The average home can cost between $100,000 and $200,000 (depending upon location) and, when your principal and interest payments are combined, your total costs can exceed three or four times the purchase price.

The purchase and sale of real estate such as land, a house, an apartment, or a condominium can involve many issues such as ownership, type of deed, fire and title insurance, liens, mortgage contingencies, taxes, and more. If you are buying or selling real estate of any size or magnitude, you need to be as informed as possible about the legal and financial matters involved.

It is customary for both the seller and the buyer to obtain an attorney to represent each in the transaction. The attorney can usually handle the preparation of the agreement of sale, deed, and other documents and assist in arrangements for the title search and financing. Typical attorney's fees for simple real estate transactions vary with location, but usually range from approximately $500 to $1,000.

If you are knowledgeable in real estate transactions, you may be able to save legal expenses by handling some or all of these activities yourself. You may also obtain help from your real estate broker, mortgage lender, or title insurance company.

Using a Real Estate Agent

Most real estate sales are made through a licensed real estate agent (or broker) with whom the seller has listed the property. The real estate broker is basically an agent for the seller and acts as an intermediary between buyer and seller in procuring the sale. Generally, the broker acts based upon a written listing agreement with the seller and will receive a commission if a successful sale is completed.

If you are the buyer, any services the real estate agent gives you are usually free of charge. Be aware that the agent represents the interests of the seller and not the buyer. However, if you are selling property, you typically pay a commission to your agent which can range from about five percent to seven percent of the sales price.

When you list your property with a real estate agent, you can enter into an exclusive or a nonexclusive listing. With an exclusive listing, the agent will receive his or her commission if the property is sold, even if you or someone else obtains the buyer. If the listing is nonexclusive, the broker receives a commission only if he or she actually finds the buyer. Although an exclusive listing locks you in with the agent for the term of the listing agreement, the agent is normally under a duty to use good faith efforts to find a buyer who is ready, willing, and able.

A sample listing agreement is provided at the end of this chapter. The listing agreement should include the names and addresses of the owner and the agent. It should have an address, location, and written description of the real estate property being listed for sale. Make sure the listing agreement indicates whether it is an exclusive or a non-exclusive listing. Include the agent's compensation as a percentage of the gross sales price paid to or retained as deposits by the owner. Other important provisions for you to consider are a minimum sales price, listing of any personal property to be included, a termination date, and a designation of the governing state law. Make sure that the term of the listing agreement is not too long. A term of 3 to 6 months is usually sufficient. The listing agreement is signed by both the owner and the agent. It is recommended that the listing agreement be notarized.

Making a Real Estate Agreement of Sale

The sale of real estate property ordinarily begins with the buyer and seller entering into a contract or agreement of sale. Next to the deed, the agreement of sale is perhaps the most important document covering the real estate transaction.

The agreement of sale normally must be in writing and should include the names and addresses of the buyer and seller, the sales price and manner of payment, an adequate description of the property, the extent of title to be conveyed, the date of closing, and any other important terms and conditions. The agreement of sale is a negotiated document between the buyer and seller and should be fully understood and agreed to by both. If you are the purchaser, you should consider including clauses covering inspection for termites and other physical damage, fire and building code violations, and the buyer's ability to obtain an acceptable mortgage.

The terms of the agreement of sale are very important to determine its validity and to support remedies for damages or specific performance in case of breach. Usually, the seller's promise to convey the property and

the buyer's promise to purchase for a certain price constitute valid consideration under the laws of contract. The description of the property must be sufficient to permit reference to specific property without ambiguity. It is recommended that the agreement of sale include a legal description from the prior deed as well as a street address and location. Any personal property which is included in the sale should be specifically identified in the agreement of sale.

The agreement of sale should clearly include the amount of the purchase price and the manner of payment, such as by cash, certified check, or electronic transfer. Often, the buyer will need to borrow money to pay for the property and should make the agreement of sale contingent upon the buyer obtaining an acceptable mortgage or financing. The mortgage contingency clause should specify the minimum amount of mortgage money required, the maximum acceptable interest rate, and the term of the mortgage (usually 30 years). The mortgage contingency clause should include a time period within which the buyer is required to obtain a mortgage commitment from a lending institution. The buyer is obligated to use reasonable and good faith efforts to obtain an acceptable mortgage.

The real estate agreement of sale should specify the type of title which will be conveyed to the buyer and the type of deed to be delivered (i.e. warranty deed or quitclaim deed). The agreement of sale generally implies that the seller will convey to the buyer a marketable title free of encumbrances. Such title gives the buyer an unrestricted right to transfer or dispose of the property. Marketable title is normally one which has reasonable validity, certainty, and freedom from attack in court.

The agreement of sale should state the date, time, and place of closing. If it is essential for closing to take place on the stated closing date, then the agreement of sale should indicate that time is of the essence. Both the buyer and seller should be ready, willing, and able to conclude the sale at closing. If time is made of the essence for closing, any party who is not ready and able to close will be in breach of the agreement.

Sometimes, the agreement of sale is prepared from a pre-printed form by the real estate agent. It usually starts as a signed offer from the buyer which is later accepted and signed by the seller. Both buyer and seller should feel free to consult an attorney and to modify the agreement of sale before signing by amending, adding, or deleting provisions in the agreement. The agreement of sale must be signed by both buyer and seller or their authorized representatives for the agreement to be legally enforceable.

It is customary for the buyer to pay a deposit (typically one percent to five percent of the purchase price) upon signing the agreement of sale. This deposit is usually applied toward the purchase price. However, the disposition of the deposit should be clearly spelled out in the agreement of sale. The agreement of sale may provide that any deposit will be forfeited to the seller as liquidated damages if the buyer breaches the agreement. It is recommended that the deposit be held in escrow with instructions as to its disposition should either the buyer or seller breach the agreement of sale.

After the real estate agreement of sale has been signed by both parties, the buyer normally becomes the equitable owner of the property. Unless the agreement of sale provides otherwise, the buyer assumes the risk of damages or destruction of the property after the agreement has been fully signed. The buyer is well advised to purchase insurance to protect his or her interest or to include a provision in the agreement of sale that the risks of loss or damage remain with the seller until closing. Likewise, it is recommended that the seller maintain insurance in force if the agreement of sale provides for the seller to assume the risk of loss.

A sample Real Estate Agreement of Sale is provided at the end of this chapter and is adaptable for use in most states.

Obtaining Financing for Your Real Estate Purchase

There are a number of financing arrangements and sources available to you for the purchase of real estate. Financing for the purchase of residential property is usually cheaper and easier to obtain than financing for commercial and investment properties. For example, if you are purchasing a house or other residential property, you may be able to obtain conventional, Federal National Mortgage Association (FNMA), Federal Housing Administration (FHA), Veteran's Administration (VA), purchase money mortgage, mortgage assumption, or land contract financing.

Conventional financing normally involves the borrowing of money from a regular lending institution, where the loan is not guaranteed by a third party. On the other hand, depending on your qualifications, you may be able to obtain an insured mortgage loan, such as FNMA, FHA or VA, whereby a governmental agency or private mortgage company guarantees or insures repayment of the loan if you should default. The insured financing can usually be obtained with a relatively low down payment (i.e., ten percent or less), whereas conventional financing may require as much as a twenty percent to thirty percent down payment.

Other financing options with a conventional mortgage are a fixed rate or an adjustable rate mortgage. A fixed rate mortgage has a constant interest rate over the entire term of the mortgage loan. The interest rate for an adjustable rate loan is normally adjusted up or down within certain limits and is usually based on the prime rate, consumer price index, or other common economic indicators. Conventional mortgages normally have a term of 15–30 years and provide for equal monthly installment payments for the term of the loan.

A purchase money mortgage is a type of private financing in which the seller provides the financing. The seller takes back a mortgage and promissory note for the balance of the purchase price in this situation.

A land contract is similar to the purchase money mortgage, except that the seller will generally retain title to the property until all the payments have been made under the land contract. You should seriously consider all of the various types of financing and decide on the financing arrangements which are most suitable for you.

Typically, you will apply to banks, savings and loan associations, credit unions, and other mortgage companies to secure financing for your real estate purchase. The lending institution will usually require a copy of the agreement of sale and financial and employment information on you. A nonrefundable loan application fee, which may be up to several hundred dollars, is frequently required by the lender. Most lenders will also require that you pay a loan origination fee or points if your loan is approved, which can amount to one percent to three percent or more of the mortgage amount. If your loan application is approved, a mortgage commitment letter specifying the terms of the mortgage will be given to you by the lending institution.

At closing the lender will usually require you to sign a mortgage and security agreement and a promissory note. The promissory note is essentially a negotiable document whereby you promise to pay a certain sum of money at a definite time. Generally the promissory note will be in writing and signed by you as the maker. A sample Promissory Note is provided at the end of this chapter.

Once you, the buyer, have accepted the mortgage commitment, you or your attorney may order a title search, obtain title and fire insurance, and handle other activities leading to closing. You should request from the seller copies of the seller's deed, any title insurance policies, any surveys of the property, and any other information concerning the title to the property. This information from the seller should be sent to the title insurance company which will be conducting the title search. Title insurance is generally required by the lender for

its benefit as a condition for the mortgage, but is is recommended that the buyer also obtain a buyer's policy to protect the buyer's own interests.

The seller, in preparing for closing, will clear the property of any liens or other encumbrances which are required to be satisfied. Also, the seller will usually make any necessary repairs and otherwise put the property in condition for delivery of possession to the buyer at closing.

What Happens at Closing?

The "closing" (or "settlement") is a very important step in the sale and purchase of real estate. This is usually the point when the real estate transaction is finalized, with the buyer receiving the deed and possession of the property and the seller receiving the purchase money. At closing, the buyer, seller, attorneys, real estate agents, a representative from the lending institution, and a representative from the title insurance company usually meet to review and sign all the necessary documents and proceed with closing.

The Federal Real Estate Settlement Procedures Act (RESPA) requires that the person conducting the closing (typically the real estate agent, title company, or mortgage lender) provide a settlement statement to the buyer and seller. RESPA also requires that the lender give to the buyer-borrower a good faith estimate of the closing costs when the mortgage loan application is made. RESPA applies to real estate transactions involving first mortgage loans for homes having no more than four separate units and financed by a federally related mortgage loan. This includes most residential mortgages, such as those from federally insured banks and savings and loans associations, FNMA, FHA, or VA. RESPA generally does not apply to mortgage assumptions, land contracts, second mortgages, or purchase money mortgages.

The settlement statement given at closing lists all settlement costs to be paid by buyer and seller. This settlement statement can be used by the buyer to determine how much money the buyer will actually need to bring to closing. Normally, the buyer is required to make payment at closing by certified check. The settlement statement also lets the seller know what items are being charged against the seller, such as seller's attorney's fees, real estate commissions, transfer taxes, and payoff of any existing mortgages and liens. If the seller has not taken care of the appropriate liens, encumbrances, or repairs to the property, some of the purchase money should be placed in escrow to take care of these.

At closing, the seller will have prepared a deed to the property, which will be given to the buyer. Typically, title is transferred to the buyer by a general warranty deed which carries full guarantees of title against any and all claims or by special warranty deed which guarantees title only against any claims by, through, or under the seller/grantor or seller/grantor's heirs. A quitclaim deed, on the other hand, conveys only that interest which the seller has, if any. A quitclaim deed makes no guarantees of title and is typically used when property is transferred as a gift or for nominal consideration. Remember that the agreement of sale should specify the type of deed to be delivered to the buyer at closing.

The deed generally must include the names of all the sellers-grantors and buyers-grantees, a legal description of the property, the appropriate clause granting title to the grantees, the date, and the signatures of the grantors and witnesses. Samples of a General Warranty Deed, Special Warranty Deed, and a Quitclaim Deed are provided at the end of this chapter. After closing, the buyer should have the deed recorded with the County Recorder or other appropriate office.

Once closing has concluded, the buyer receives his or her deed, title insurance policy, and possession of the property, while the seller receives the purchase money after adjustments for charges to the seller. In addition, the lender receives its mortgage agreement and promissory note from the buyer and the mortgagee's title insurance policy from the title company. The real estate agents and attorneys are usually also paid at closing. If buyer and seller have realized their expectations and have properly acted to protect their interests, the real estate transaction should close smoothly.

Checklist for Sale or Purchase of Real Estate

❑ If Seller, list property with real estate broker. Execute appropriate Real Estate Listing Agreement.

❑ Buyer and Seller sign Agreement of Sale.

❑ Include mortgage contingency clause if buyer will be obtaining a mortgage loan to purchase the property.

❑ Specify in Agreement of Sale the type of title and deed to be conveyed to Buyer.

❑ Include a closing date in Agreement of Sale. Indicate if time is of the essence.

❑ Identify in Agreement of Sale any personal property to be included.

❑ If Buyer, apply for any necessary mortgage financing and obtain mortgage commitment.

❑ If Buyer, obtain title search and title insurance.

❑ If Buyer, obtain fire and hazard insurance.

❑ Pre-closing inspection and testing for termites and other damage.

❑ If Seller, clear property of any required liens and charges and make any necessary repairs.

❑ If Seller, prepare appropriate deed to be delivered to buyer at closing.

❑ If Buyer, obtain certified check or other appropriate means for payment of balance of settlement charges at closing.

❑ Close on the real estate transaction. Buyer signs any necessary mortgage agreements and promissory notes. Buyer delivers balance of purchase price to seller or closing agent. Seller delivers deed and possession of property to buyer.

❑ Buyer records deed with County Recorder or other appropriate office.

❑ Consult an attorney if the real estate transaction involves complex or difficult issues.

Form 10: Real Estate Listing Agreement

1. This Listing Agreement is made and is effective this ____ day of _____, 20_____ by and between
_____(Owner's name)
_____(Owner's address)
and _____(Agent's name)
_____(Agent's address).

2. Owner has the legal right to enter into this Listing Agreement and has legal title to the real property located at
_____ (street address)
_____(city)_____(county)_____(state); said property being specifically described as follows:

3. Agent is a licensed real estate agent or broker in good standing under the laws of the State of _____ and is authorized by law to represent Owner as a real estate agent or broker.

4. Owner hereby grants to Agent the right to offer for sale said property described above in accordance with the terms of this Listing Agreement. This right to Agent shall be: (check one)

   ❏ (a) exclusive
   ❏ (b) nonexclusive

5. Owner shall pay to Agent on or before the date set for closing in any binding agreement with owner for the purchase and sale of said property a commission in the amount of ___ percent (____%) of the gross sale price actually paid to or forfeited to owner by a buyer, subject to the following provisions:

   (a) if Agent has an exclusive right to offer for sale said property as indicated in Item 4(a) above, said commission shall be payable in accordance with Item 5 above to Agent if any buyer executes a binding agreement with Owner for the purchase and sale of said property during the term of this Listing Agreement; and

   (b) if Agent has a nonexclusive right to offer for sale said property as indicated in Item 4(b) above, said commission shall be payable in accordance with Item 5 above to Agent only if a buyer procured by Agent executes a binding agreement with Owner for the purchase and sale of said property during the term of this Listing Agreement.

6. Agent is an independent contractor under this Listing Agreement, and Agent shall be responsible for any brokerage fees, commissions, or other compensation to other agents and employees in procuring a sale of said property pursuant to this Listing Agreement. Owner shall not be liable for any brokerage fees, commissions, or other compensation except as provided in Item 5 above.

7. Agent is given authority under this Listing Agreement only to solicit offers from prospective buyers of said property. Agent shall have no authority to accept any offers from prospective buyers or to otherwise make any binding agreements on behalf of Owner. Agent shall not list or advertise said property at a price of less than $_____. Agent shall not assign or delegate any of Agent's duties and performance under this Listing Agreement without Owner's prior written consent.

8. Owner may accept or reject any offer from any prospective buyer at Owner's sole discretion.

9. Only the personal property specifically listed below is included in the sale of the real property covered by this Listing Agreement:

10. This Listing Agreement represents the entire agreement and understanding of Owner and Agent in reference to the property covered herein. This Listing Agreement shall terminate on the _____ day of _____,20____.

11. This Listing Agreement shall be governed by the laws of the State of _____.

12. Owner and Agent hereby agree to the following additional terms and conditions:

Owner and Agent, intending to be legally bound, have signed this Agreement on the date first indicated above.

_____   _____
Owner's signature   Agent's signature

Subscribed and sworn to before me on this _____ day of _____, 20____.

_____
Notary

Form 11: Real Estate Agreement of Sale

1. This Agreement is made on this _____ day of _____, 20_____by and between

_____(Buyer's name)

_____(Buyer's address)

and _____(Seller's name)

_____(Seller's address).

2. Buyer shall purchase and Seller shall sell and convey to Buyer the property located at: _____

_____(address of property),

including the land and any and all buildings, structures, fixtures, improvements, easements, rights and privileges apper-

taining thereto; said property being legally described as follows:

3. Only the personal property specifically listed below is included in the sale of the property covered by this Agreement:

4. Buyer shall pay to Seller a total purchase price for the Property in the amount of _____

_____Dollars ($_____). The purchase price shall be paid by Buyer as follows:

(a) Buyer shall pay to Seller or Seller's agent, upon signing this Agreement, the amount of _____

_____Dollars ($_____) by cash or check as a deposit in escrow to be applied toward the purchase price.

(b) Buyer shall pay to Seller or Seller's agent, on or before the closing date of this Agreement, the balance of the purchase

price in the amount of _____ Dollars ($_____) by cash or certified check.

5. The closing date of this Agreement shall be on the _____ day of _____, 20___, at the time of_____

and at the place of _____.

Time is of the essence for the closing of this Agreement.

6. This Agreement is contingent upon Buyer obtaining a mortgage commitment by the ___ day of _____, 20___ from a regular lending institution for a mortgage loan on the following terms:

        (a) minimum amount of mortgage loan: $_____

        (b) maximum annual interest rate: _____%

        (c) maximum loan fee or points: _____%

        (d) minimum term of mortgage: _____ years

Buyer shall exercise reasonable and good faith efforts to obtain a mortgage commitment by the prescribed date on the above terms or more favorable ones. In the event that Buyer is unable to obtain such a mortgage commitment by the prescribed date, this Agreement shall be void and all obligations hereunder terminated, except that any funds paid by Buyer as deposits shall be returned to Buyer.

7. Seller shall convey to Buyer good, insurable, and marketable title to the property by _____ deed. If Seller is to convey by warranty deed, Seller warrants title to be free and clear of all liens, charges, defects, and encumbrances, except for the conditions, restrictions, reservations, and easements listed below:

8. Seller makes the following additional representations and warranties to Buyer, which shall survive the conveyance of title to Buyer:

9. Seller shall give possession of the property to Buyer at the date of closing, and the property shall be in the condition as warranted by Seller, or in the condition as of the date of this Agreement if Seller makes no warranties as to the condition of the property.

10. The risk of loss or damage to the property shall remain with Seller until conveyance of title to Buyer. The risk of loss or damage to the Property shall be with Buyer after conveyance of title to Buyer.

11. Any prepaid utilities and any real estate taxes shall be prorated as of the date of closing. Seller shall be responsible for any such utilities and taxes up to and including the date of closing and Buyer shall be responsible for any such utilities and taxes thereafter.

12. Seller shall be responsible for payment of any commission to any real estate agent or broker involved in procuring the sale of this property.

13. This Agreement shall be governed by the laws of the State of _____.

14. This Agreement shall be binding upon and inure to the benefit of Buyer and Seller and their respective heirs, successors, and assigns.

Buyer and Seller, intending to be legally bound, have signed this Agreement on the date first indicated above.

_____
Buyer's Signature

_____
Seller's Signature

_____
Witness' Signature

_____
Witness' Signature

_____
Witness' Name

_____
Witness' Name

_____
Witness' Address

_____
Witness' Address

Form 12: Promissory Note

Amount $_____

Date _____

1. I, _____(Maker's name)

_____(Maker's address),

for valuable and sufficient consideration received, promise to pay to the order of

_____(Payee's name)

_____(Payee's address)

the sum of _____ Dollars ($_____), along with interest from the date of this Note on the

unpaid principal at an annual rate of _____ percent (_____%).

2. (a) Principal and interest due under this note shall be payable as follows:

(b) Payments due under this Note shall be made at the following address or as Payee or assigns may reasonably designate:

3. Default in the payment of any amount when due as provided in this Note, or the voluntary or involuntary filing of a petition for bankruptcy of Maker, shall at the discretion of the Payee or assigns, cause the entire unpaid balance hereof to become immediately due and payable. If collection efforts have to be made to enforce payment of any amount due under this note, Maker shall pay all reasonable costs and attorney fees incurred in such collection.

4. Maker may prepay the principal balance and interest due under this note at any time in whole or in part without incurring any penalties.

5. Maker gives the following property as collateral security for the payment of this note, and shall execute any necessary documents to perfect said security interest:

6. This note shall be governed by the laws of the State of _____.

Maker, intending to be legally bound, has signed this Promissory Note on this _____ day of _____, 20___.

_____
Maker's signature

Subscribed and sworn to before me on this _____ day of _____, 20___.

_____
Notary

Form 13: General Warranty Deed

1. By this General Warranty Deed made on this ___ day of _____, 20____

I, _____(Grantor's name)

_____(Grantor's address)

hereby give, grant, transfer, and convey to

_____(Grantee's name)

_____(Grantee's address),

and Grantee's heirs and assigns in fee simple, the real property, including the land and all the buildings and structures on the land, located at _____(address of property), and legally described as:

2. This conveyance is made in consideration for the sum of _____ Dollars ($_____)
paid to and received by Grantor.

3. Grantor and Grantor's heirs hereby warrant that Grantor has good and legal title to the above-described property, that Grantor has a good right to convey, that said property is free of all encumbrances except those of record and specified herein, and that Grantor and Grantor's heirs will defend said property against every person claiming the same.

In Witness Whereof, the Grantor has signed this General Warranty Deed on the date first described above.

_____
Grantor's Signature

Witnessed By:

_____   _____
Witness' Signature   Witness' Signature

_____   _____
Witness' Name   Witness' Name

_____   _____
Witness' Address   Witness' Address

Subscribed and sworn to before me on this ____ day of _____, 20____.

_____
Notary

Deed From   **Recorded At:**

_____,
Grantor

To

_____
Grantee

Form 14: Special Warranty Deed

1. By this Special Warranty Deed made on this ___ day of _____, 20____

I, _____(Grantor's name)

_____(Grantor's address)

hereby give, grant, transfer, and convey to

_____(Grantee's name)

_____(Grantee's address),

and Grantee's heirs and assigns in fee simple, the real property, including the land and all the buildings and structures on the land, located at _____(address of property), and legally described as:

2. This conveyance is made in consideration for the sum of _____ Dollars ($_____) paid to and received by Grantor.

3. Grantor and Grantor's heirs hereby warrant that they have not done anything to destroy or otherwise affect good and legal title to the above-described property or Grantor's right to convey, that said property is free of all encumbrances except those of record and specified herein, and that Grantor and Grantor's heirs will defend said property against every person claiming the same by, through, or under Grantor and Grantor's heirs.

In Witness Whereof, the Grantor has signed this Special Warranty Deed on the date first described above.

_____
Grantor's Signature

Witnessed By:

_____   _____
Witness' Signature   Witness' Signature

_____   _____
Witness' Name   Witness' Name

_____   _____
Witness' Address   Witness' Address

Subscribed and sworn to before me on this ____ day of _____, 20____.

_____
Notary

Deed From   **Recorded At:**

_____,
Grantor

To

_____
Grantee

Form 15: Quitclaim Deed

1. By this Quitclaim Deed made on this _____ day of _____, 20_____,

I, _____(Grantor's name)

_____(Grantor's address)

hereby give, grant, transfer, convey, and quitclaim to

_____(Grantee's name)

_____(Grantee's address)

and Grantee's heirs and assigns, any and all of Grantor's rights, title, and interest in and to the real property, including the land and all the buildings and structures on the land, located at

_____(address of property),

and legally described as:

2. This conveyance is made in consideration for the sum of _____ Dollars ($_____)

paid to and received by Grantor.

In Witness Whereof, the Grantor has signed this Quitclaim Deed on the date first described above.

_____
Grantor's Signature

Witnessed By:

_____	_____
Witness' Signature	Witness' Signature
_____	_____
Witness' Name	Witness' Name
_____	_____
Witness' Address	Witness' Address

Subscribed and sworn to before me on this _____ day of _____, 20_____.

_____
Notary

Deed From   **Recorded At:**

_____,
Grantor

To

_____
Grantee

Chapter

11 *Leasing Your Home or Office*

Looking at Renting

In many cases, renting can be a reasonable alternative to buying a home or commercial property. For many young adults, renting an apartment or house may be the only means to obtain affordable housing. Likewise, renting an office or commercial space may be the only route for a young professional or small business to get started. Having a good understanding of the landlord-tenant relationship and resources available can be beneficial to both the prospective tenant and landlord.

Many resources may be available to you if you are trying to find rental property. They may also be useful if you own real estate and will be holding it as investment rental property. These sources of information and assistance include the newspapers, community agencies, business associations, rental agencies, real estate agencies, and employer personnel and relocation departments.

The rental process typically starts with the interested tenant inspecting premises which the landlord has listed or advertised for rent. It is at this time that the tenant should make a careful inspection and examination of the rental premises for suitability for his or her particular needs. If the premises are acceptable, the tenant and landlord typically negotiate and sign a lease agreement.

For many residential leases, the prospective tenant is initially required to complete an application form and give information on his or her background and financial status. Similar credit and financial information may be required for commercial leases. The tenant is required to pay a nonrefundable application fee, which can range from about $20 to $100. If the prospective tenant's credit and financial and other background are acceptable, the tenant and landlord then proceed with executing a lease agreement.

The lease agreement should always be in writing with the terms of the lease clearly spelled out. Although oral leases are generally valid, you should never rely on an oral lease. Your lease must be in writing if it has a rental period of more than one year. Even if the rental period is one year or less, the lease must still be in writing if any portion of the rental period will extend beyond one year after the lease has been fully signed. For example, if you enter into a lease agreement today for a six-month lease which will start seven months in the future, the lease generally must be in writing. Both the tenant and the landlord should always read and understand the lease before signing it.

The tenant is usually required to pay the first month's rent and a security deposit equal to one to two months' rent upon signing the lease. The security deposit (which is discussed later in this chapter) is refunded to the tenant after appropriate deductions for damages and other charges after expiration of the lease.

The tenant usually receives the keys and possession of the premises after the lease has been fully executed and the landlord-tenant relationship has begun. Legal fees for simple landlord-tenant cases typically range from about $500 to $1,000.

Understanding Landlord-Tenant Law

The landlord-tenant relationship is primarily contractual and results from a lease of real estate for a term of years, from period to period, for life, or at will. Basically, a landlord-tenant relationship exists anytime a person occupies and has possession of the premises of another person with the other's permission.

Landlord-tenant relationships are governed by concepts of both contract law and property law. A lease of real estate creates a contract between the lessor (landlord) and the lessee (tenant) in which responsibilities and obligations are imposed on both parties. The obligations under contract law are generally determined by the terms of the lease agreement.

Since a lease is a conveyance of an interest in real estate, principles of property law may come into play. A lease typically conveys to the tenant the right to exclusive possession of the premises in exchange for the tenant's obligation to pay rent. It is important that the lease refer to specific premises at a fixed location to avoid ambiguities.

Historically, property laws did not excuse a tenant from the obligation to pay rent if the landlord failed to maintain the premises or otherwise breached the lease. This situation has been changed recently in many states, where a tenant of residential property generally receives an implied warranty of habitability, which is tied to the obligation to pay rent.

Types of Landlord-Tenant Relationships

There are four basic leasehold tenancies created by the landlord-tenant relationship. These tenancies are as follows:

- Periodic Tenancy. A periodic tenancy is one for a repeated period of time that has no specific termination date. An example would be a month-to-month lease. This tenancy is automatically renewed from period to period and can only be terminated by proper notice from the landlord or the tenant. Proper notice is usually required to be at least one period under the lease. For example, for a month-to-month lease, at least one month notice of termination is normally required.

- Tenancy for Years. A tenancy for years is created by a lease for a fixed period of time and with a definite termination date. It can be for more or less than a year. Examples would be a 6-month or a 1-year lease. No notice of termination is usually required unless specified by the lease agreement. A tenancy for years automatically terminates upon expiration of the lease, unless the landlord and tenant have agreed to extend the lease. The typical residential lease is for a fixed period and may provide that the lease will be automatically extended for a similar fixed period unless notice of termination is given one to three months before expiration of the lease.

- Tenancy at Will. A tenancy at will exists when either the landlord or the tenant has the right to terminate the lease at will and at any time. The tenancy at will is not common because it offers no stability to either the tenant or the landlord. Notice of termination is required to terminate a tenancy at will. Some states may require a minimum of one-month notice of termination even for a tenancy at will.

- Tenancy at Sufferance. A tenancy at sufferance or holdover tenancy exists when the tenant fails or refuses to vacate after the expiration of the lease. In such a case, the landlord may treat the tenant as a trespasser and seek eviction or the landlord may choose to hold the tenant to a new tenancy under the old lease.

You should choose the leasing arrangement which is best for your particular circumstances. The tenancy for years or fixed period is appropriate in most residential and commercial situations. It offers stability in both duration of the lease and in the amount of rent. A month-to-month tenancy may be appropriate when the rental property is on the market for sale or when the tenant expects to relocate in the near future.

Warranty of Habitability

For hundred of years, the landlord had no duty to deliver or maintain the rented premises in a condition of habitability or fitness for any purpose, unless this duty was explicitly included in the terms of the lease agreement. Landlord-tenant law has been changed in many states to impose greater responsibilities on the landlord, especially in residential leases. Many states now require that residential premises comply with housing codes and occupancy standards and recognize that residential leases contain an implied warranty of habitability. The implied warranty of habitability does not have to be written into the lease agreement but is implied by operation of law as a required feature of residential leases.

The implied warranty of habitability requires the landlord to keep the premises in a condition that is suitable for living purposes. This usually means that the premises must comply with all housing, building, and safety codes. Minor defects in the premises do not violate the warranty of habitability. This requirement of habitability generally must be satisfied at the beginning of the lease and continues throughout the entire term of the lease. The following forty-two states have adopted the implied warranty of habitability either by legislation or court decisions:

Alaska, Arizona, California, Delaware, Florida, Georgia, Hawaii, Idaho, Illinois, Indiana, Iowa, Kansas, Kentucky, Louisiana, Maine, Maryland, Massachusetts, Michigan, Minnesota, Missouri, Montana, Nebraska, New Hampshire, New Jersey, New Mexico, New York, North Carolina, North Dakota, Ohio, Oklahoma, Oregon, Pennsylvania, Rhode Island, South Carolina, South Dakota, Tennessee, Texas, Vermont, Virginia, Washington, West Virginia, and Wisconsin.

The implied warranty of habitability generally does not extend to commercial or business-type leases.

In most cases, the tenant's obligation to pay rent under a residential lease is dependent upon the landlord's compliance with the warranty of habitability. If the landlord breaches the warranty of habitability, the tenant may terminate the lease and vacate the premises without any further obligation to pay rent. The tenant would also be entitled to recover any rent paid in advance under the lease. If the tenant chooses to remain in possession, the rent may be reduced by a percentage amount equal to that percentage of the leased premise which is in violation of the warranty of habitability. Some states also permit the tenant to remain in possession and pay rent into escrow with the court or to make the necessary repairs and deduct the costs for such repairs from the rent. In any event, the tenant usually must give notice of defects to the landlord and allow a reasonable time for the landlord to correct the defects before the tenant can withhold rent or make repairs.

The tenant can also report housing and building code violations to the proper authorities in an effort to force the landlord to make repairs. The laws typically prohibit the landlord from taking any retaliatory action against a tenant who has reported violations or withheld rent because the leased premises were uninhabitable.

It is important that good documentary evidence be maintained of communications between the tenant and landlord. Problems with maintenance and service should always be brought to the landlord's attention in writing, with the tenant keeping a copy for his or her records. Even when the tenant has discussed problems with the landlord orally or over the telephone, the tenant should follow up with a letter. The tenant should retain receipts for any repairs by the tenant to the leased premises. The tenant should also receive signed receipts from the landlord for deposits, fees, and rental payments made to the landlord. Both the tenant and the landlord should each keep a copy of the lease agreement for their respective files.

Other Landlord-Tenant Obligations

In addition to maintaining the leased premises in a habitable condition, the landlord must live up to all other requirements and conditions specified in the lease agreement. The landlord must also exercise reasonable care to keep the premises secure and free of hazards. In many states, a lease's exculpatory clauses exempting the landlord from liability for damages and injuries resulting from the landlord's negligence are invalid.

Federal and state laws generally prohibit discrimination in leases. The Federal Fair Housing Act makes it illegal to refuse to sell or rent a dwelling on the basis of race, color, religion, sex, familial status, or national origin. The "familial status" prohibition was designed to eliminate discriminating against families with children, except when the housing is intended for elderly residents. A prospective tenant can bring legal action in federal or state court against the landlord for violating the Fair Housing Act.

The tenant also has obligations under a lease. The primary obligation of the tenant is the timely payment of rent. The amount, time, and place for payment of rent is usually spelled out in the lease agreement. The lease agreement may also impose additional obligations and restrictions on the tenant, such as restricting use of the premises to either residential or commercial, requiring fire insurance, restricting the number of occupants, prohibiting pets, restricting alterations to the premises, requiring tenant to maintain the premises in a clean and safe condition, prohibiting illegal activities, and complying with housing codes and zoning laws.

If the tenant breaches important and material obligations under the lease agreement, the landlord may be able to terminate the lease. Most states provide for relatively quick judicial proceedings (typically two to four weeks) for evicting a tenant who has violated material provisions of the lease. The most common ground for termination of the lease and eviction of the tenant is nonpayment of rent. Other grounds for eviction frequently include illegal use of the leased premises, failure to maintain the premises in the condition required, unauthorized pets, and failure to comply with building and zoning regulations. The landlord may also bring legal action to collect rents and damages if the tenant has violated the lease.

The tenant also has various remedies when the landlord has violated the lease. Many of these remedies, such as termination of the lease, withholding of rent, payment of rent into escrow, reduction in rent, and deductions for repairs, were discussed earlier with respect to when the landlord has breached the warranty of habitability. The tenant may also bring legal action to recover monetary damages.

Security Deposits

It is common in both residential and commercial leases for the landlord to require that the tenant pay a security deposit. This security deposit serves as a source of funds for the landlord to resort to in case the tenant breaches the lease agreement or otherwise causes damage to the leased premises. The security deposit is normally paid to and held by the landlord until expiration of the lease.

The amount of the security deposit usually ranges from about one to three months' rent. Some states limit the amount of security deposit to no more than two months' rent. The landlord is normally free to hold the security deposit without paying any interest to the tenant. However, some states, such as New Jersey, require that the landlord keep the security deposit in a separate interest-bearing account.

Many states have passed laws designed to help the residential tenant collect the security deposit after termination or expiration of the lease. Laws governing security deposits have been enacted in Alaska, Arizona, California, Connecticut, Delaware, Florida, Hawaii, Illinois, Iowa, Kansas, Kentucky, Louisiana, Maryland, Massachusetts, Michigan, Montana, Nebraska, New Jersey, New Mexico, New York, Oregon, Pennsylvania, Rhode Island, South Carolina, Tennessee, Texas, and Virginia.

These laws typically provide that the landlord must return the security deposit to the tenant within thirty to sixty days after the end of the lease.

If the tenant has damaged the leased premises, the landlord may keep part or all of the security deposit to cover the amount of damage. In such a case, the landlord must send an itemized list of damages and deductions to the tenant. Damages to the leased premises do not include normal wear and tear but may include cleaning and painting. The tenant can usually recover double or triple the security deposit if the landlord fails to refund the security deposit within the specified time.

Assignment and Subletting

Unless prohibited by the lease agreement, the tenant may assign all or part of his or her interest in the lease. A complete transfer of all of the tenant's remaining interest in the lease is generally considered an assignment. If the tenant transfers only a part of his or her remaining interest in the lease, the transfer is a sublease.

In an assignment, the original tenant gives up possession of the entire leased premises for the full remainder of the lease period to the new tenant/assignee. Although the new tenant/assignee becomes liable to the landlord for the payment of rent, the original tenant also remains liable unless the landlord has definitely released the original tenant from the obligation to pay rent. If the original tenant is required to pay any rent to the landlord after an assignment of the lease, the original tenant may recover that rent from the new tenant/assignee.

A sublease is essentially a partial assignment where the new tenant/sublessee either leases a part of the leased premises, or leases the entire premises for only a part of the lease period before it reverts back to the original tenant. In a sublease, the new tenant/sublessee is not personally liable to the landlord for the payment of rent. Rather, the payment of rent remains the primary responsibility of the original tenant. However, the new tenant/sublessee is obligated to pay rent to the original tenant.

For practical reasons, most commercial tenants bargain to include the right to assign or sublet in the lease. Typically the consent of the landlord is required but must not be unreasonably withheld. The ability to assign and sublet may also be important in a residential lease if the tenant may need to move or relocate. The landlord almost always has the ability to assign the right to rental payment under a lease. The landlord may also sell the leased premises and the new owner takes the property subject to any existing lease.

Basic Provisions of a Lease Agreement

It is the lease agreement, more than anything else, which governs the relationship between landlord and tenant. The lease agreement should always be in writing. It should be carefully drafted and reviewed by both the landlord and tenant to include all important terms and conditions and to avoid ambiguities and uncertainties. Once the lease agreement is signed by the landlord and tenant, it becomes a legally binding contract.

The lease agreement should include the names and addresses of the landlord and tenant. It should include a clear and definite description of the leased premises, including address, location, size, and physical characteristics of the property. Also identify any personal property, appliances, equipment, and fixtures which are included with the leased premises.

The lease agreement should indicate the purpose of the lease and the use which the tenant is to make of the leased premises. If the lease is for residential purposes, the lease agreement will preferably include the number of or names of the people who will be occupying the premises. A commercial lease should identify the specific type of commercial or business activity which will be conducted on the leased premises.

The lease agreement should include a term or lease period, which usually specifies a beginning date and an ending date. The lease agreement should include the amount and frequency of rent payments and the total amount of rent due during the term of the lease. The standard rental arrangement is the flat rate which provides for a fixed amount each month for the entire term of the lease. The lease agreement should also indicate when and where rent payments are to be made. Provisions should also be included for penalties and charges for late payment of rent.

Other provisions which are customarily included in a lease agreement include responsibilities for utilities, trash removal, maintenance and repairs, heating and air-conditioning, and insurance. Also included are provisions concerning security deposits, alterations, access to the premises, assignment and subletting, condemnation by eminent domain, and indemnification of the landlord or tenant for any damages or liabilities incurred because of the other party. These provisions can be drafted in clear and simple terms to fit your particular situation.

The lease agreement is signed by both the landlord and tenant. It is recommended that the lease agreement be notarized.

A sample lease agreement is provided at the end of this chapter.

Checklist for Making a Lease

❏ Inspection of premises by tenant.

❏ Application to enter into lease. Application fee?

❏ Background and credit check on tenant.

❏ Preparation of lease agreement:

- identification of landlord and tenant
- location and description of premises, including any fixtures, equipment, appliances, and personal property
- purpose of lease and restrictions on use
- term of lease, with beginning and ending dates
- amount of rent and time and place of payment
- utilities
- maintenance and repairs
- security deposits
- prepaid rents
- assignment and subletting
- alterations and modifications to premises
- heating and air conditioning
- trash removal
- insurance
- access to premises by landlord
- condemnation and eminent domain
- indemnification

❏ Signing of lease agreement by landlord and tenant.

❏ Delivery of possession of the leased premises to tenant.

❏ Move-in inspection by tenant and written report of any defects and damages to landlord.

❏ Consult an attorney if the leasing arrangement involves difficult or complex issues.

Form 16: Lease Agreement

1. This Lease Agreement is made this _____ day of _____, 20_____ by and between

_____(Landlord's name)

_____(Landlord's address)

and _____(Tenant's name)

_____(Tenant's address).

2. Landlord leases and transfers possession to Tenant, for the term of this Lease Agreement, of the premises located at

_____ _____ (Address of premises);

said premises being specifically described as follows:

3. The premises leased under this Lease Agreement shall be used by Tenant solely for the purpose of:

4. The premises leased under this Lease Agreement shall be used and occupied, in accordance with Item 3 above, only by the parties listed below:

5. This Lease Agreement shall be effective for a term of _____ months, beginning on the _____ day of _____,20_____, and ending on the _____ day of _____,20_____.

6. In consideration for this Lease Agreement and the rights hereunder, Tenant shall pay rent to Landlord during the term of this Lease Agreement in the amount of _____Dollars ($_____) per _____; for a total rent for the term in the amount of _____ Dollars ($_____).

7. Rent payments hereunder are due on _____ and shall be paid at _____ or as the Landlord may designate. If any rent due and payable hereunder is not made within _____ days after said rent shall become due, Tenant shall pay to Landlord additional charges equal to _____ Dollars ($_____) for each _____ said rent remains unpaid.

8. On or before the start of the term of this Lease Agreement, Tenant shall deposit with Landlord the sum of _____ Dollars ($_____) as a security deposit for the compliance with and performance of the terms and provisions of this Lease Agreement. If Tenant should default or breach any of the terms and provisions of this lease, or has otherwise caused damage to the leased premises except for normal wear and tear, Landlord may apply, use, or keep all or part of said security deposit to the extent required to correct such default, breach, or damage.

9. The following equipment, appliances, or other personal property is included and forms a part of the leased premises under this Lease Agreement:

10. Landlord shall provide and be responsible for, at no additional cost to Tenant, the following services and utilities for the leased premises:

11. Tenant shall provide and be responsible for, at no additional cost to Landlord, the following services and utilities for the leased premises:

12. This Lease Agreement shall terminate if all or any part of the leased premises should be acquired or condemned by Eminent Domain.

13. Landlord shall have the right to enter the leased premises at reasonable times and after giving reasonable notice to Tenant to inspect, repair, or improve the leased premises or to respond to any emergency.

14. Tenant shall not assign or sublet Tenant's interest under this Lease Agreement without the prior written consent of Landlord, which consent shall not be unreasonably withheld by Landlord.

15. Landlord and Tenant agree to the following additional covenants, rules, and conditions:

16. The terms, provisions, and covenants contained in this Lease Agreement shall be binding on and inure to the benefit of Landlord and Tenant and their respective successors, heirs, and assigns.

17. This Lease Agreement shall be governed by the laws of the State of _____.

Landlord and Tenant, intending to be legally bound, have signed this Lease Agreement on the date first indicated above.

_____
Landlord's Signature

_____
Tenant's Signature

_____
Witness' Signature

_____
Witness' Signature

_____
Witness' Name

_____
Witness' Name

_____
Witness' Address

_____
Witness' Address

Subscribed and sworn to before me on this _____ day of_____,20_____.

_____
Notary

Chapter

12 *Personal Property for Sale*

Buying and Selling Personal Property

Tangible personal property, such as automobiles, boats, equipment, furniture, and appliances, is bought and sold all the time. When major items such as these are purchased from a regular business establishment they are usually accompanied by a sales receipt, invoice, or other evidence of the sale. This evidence of sale can be very important in proving ownership and for insurance purposes. It is recommended that you keep these for your records during the useful life of the property.

Likewise, when you buy and sell personal property in an informal and nonbusiness context, this transaction should be evidenced by a "bill of sale" or other appropriate documentation. A bill of sale is basically a written document which shows that a sale has taken place. It may also include important terms and conditions of the sale.

The bill of sale should identify the seller and buyer and give their respective addresses. It should contain a description of the property which is sufficient to specifically identify the property. The description should include the manufacturer's name, serial number, and date or year of manufacture, if available. The amount that the property is being sold for should also be in the bill of sale. This figure could be useful in establishing the value of the property for an insurance

claim or tax loss. The bill of sale should be signed and dated by the seller. It should also be accepted and signed by the buyer.

Other provisions that you may want to put in the bill of sale are any warranties or guarantees, terms of payment, time and place of delivery, insurance, storage, and terms for return or credit. If the seller is financing the purchase of the property, the buyer may be required to sign a promissory note. A sample promissory note is provided at the end of chapter 10 and is useful and handy anytime you lend money or extend credit to someone.

It is common for property to be sold among family, friends, and other individuals without any warranties or guarantees. If the property is sold without any warranties, the bill of sale should indicate that it is being sold "as is" or other similar language. If the seller offers a warranty, it should be expressly written into the bill of sale with all its terms and conditions. It is common for the bill of sale to include a warranty that the seller owns good title to the property and has the lawful right to transfer title.

Remember that you can only sell what you own. If you are selling property which is covered by a mortgage or security interest, your buyer generally acquires the property subject to these existing claims. If you own the property jointly with other people, these people must also sign the bill of sale to transfer complete title and ownership.

A sample bill of sale is provided at the end of this chapter. This bill of sale should be useful in any state to transfer ownership of most tangible personal property. Some property, such as an automobile, has an official Certificate of Title issued by the state where it is registered. In most cases this Certificate of Title must be transferred to the new owner. A bill of sale can also be used along with the Certificate of Title to include important terms and conditions.

Form 17: Bill of Sale

1. By this Bill of Sale made on this _____ day of _____, 20_____,

_____(Seller's name)

_____(Seller's address)

hereby sells and transfers to _____(Buyer's name)

_____(Buyer's address),

the property described below:

2. The purchase price of the property is _____ Dollars ($_____),

which shall be paid by Buyer as follows:

3. Seller warrants that Seller has good title to the property and the lawful right to sell and transfer the property to Buyer, and that the property is free of all liens and encumbrances, except the following:

4. Seller makes no warranties as to the condition of the property, including no **warranty of merchantability** and no **warranty of fitness for a particular purpose**, except for any warranties expressly indicated below:

5. Additional Terms and Conditions:

Buyer and Seller, intending to be legally bound, have signed this Agreement on the date first indicated above.

_____   _____
Seller's Signature   Buyer's Signature

Subscribed and sworn to before me on this _____ day of _____,20_____.

_____
Notary

Chapter

13 Contracting for Repairs and Services

Entering into a Contract for Services

It is common for contracts to be entered into for performing a variety of personal services, such as home repairs, landscaping and gardening, equipment repairs, child care, legal services, catering, management and sale of real estate, and many others. Whether you are the provider or the recipient of these services, you should put the contract in writing to spell out clearly the obligations and terms of performance.

Although most orally agreed-upon contracts can be valid, there are some instances in which the contract must be reduced to writing in order to be enforced. For example, a contract that cannot be completed within one year of the agreement must be in writing to be enforceable. However, it is generally adviseable to reduce all contractual agreements to writing. This is important because when a dispute arises over the terms of an oral contract, it is not surprising to find that all parties involved have different memory recollections regarding the terms of the contract

In chapter 2, a lawyer's retainer agreement is reviewed, along with other considerations for hiring a lawyer. Also, a real estate listing agreement is discussed in chapter 10 for using a real estate agent or broker in selling real property. Many of the considerations in hiring a lawyer or real estate agent are applicable in contracting for other services.

Typically, a decision has to be made whether the person to perform services will be an employee or independent contractor. It is usually less complicated and less expensive to contract for the services of an independent contractor rather than an employee. This is because an employer may be required to pay federal social security taxes and state workers' compensation insurance, withhold federal and state income tax, and provide other benefits such as health care and vacation to employees. In an employer-employee relationship, the employer may also be liable to others for any damage or injury caused by the employee during the course of the employment. For example, if you hired a landscaper as an employee and he or she negligently caused a tree to fall, damaging a neighbor's property, you could be held personally liable for the damage.

Most of these problems can be avoided by contracting with an independent contractor. Therefore, a contract for the services of an independent contractor should clearly indicate that the person performing the services is an independent contractor and not an employee. The contract should identify the contractor along with the contractor's address. It should also include the customer's name and address.

The contract should include a complete description of the work and duties which are to be performed by the independent contractor. The contract should further list any type of agreed-upon specific materials or supplies to be used or installed. Be sure to include the time period within which the services of the contractor are to be completed. If the time for completing the work is of critical importance, then the contract should explicitly provide that time is of the essence.

The contract should include the amount and manner of compensation to be paid to the independent contractor. This can be a fixed amount—typically payable in installments during the course of the work—or a total sum to be paid when the work is completed. If you enter into an agreement with a contractor for multiple services, you should enter into a series of separate contracts or specify that the single contract is divisible. Many contractors may charge an hourly or daily rate for their services. In any event, try to put in the contract a good faith estimate of costs and indicate whether this includes any materials and expenses as well as services.

Include in the contract any warranties and guarantees of performance from the contractor. The contractor should be responsible for hiring any assistants needed and should indemnify the customer for liability caused by the contractor, assistants, or the contractor's subcontractors (if any). You should also inquire into whether the contractor is insured or bonded. Before entering into a contract for extensive home repairs or remodeling, an individual should verify the contractor's former customers and possibly contact the local Better Business Bureau. It is also recommended that some provision be included in the contract for termination.

It is common for the contract to be terminated by the customer for nonperformance or breach by the contractor. The contractor typically can terminate the contract for nonpayment or noncooperation.

Other provisions may be included in the contract for services, such as delegation and assignment, penalties for nonperfor-

mance, insurance, and other restrictions and requirements. Finally, the contract should be signed by both the contractor and the customer. However, even if both parties do not sign the contract, the contract can still generally be enforced against the party that did sign the contract.

One commonly overlooked aspect of service contracts is the ability of parties to assign or transfer their rights. It is a general principle of contract law that all contractual rights may be assigned unless the contract specifies that it is not assignable. Therefore, if you entered into an agreement with a specific contractor to paint your house, that contractor is legally entitled to have another contractor paint your house. One of the few exceptions to this rule is where the nature of the personal services is unique (e.g., services involving either a doctor or lawyer) rather than ordinary or routine.

A sample Contract for Services is provided at the end of this chapter. Attorneys' fees for drafting a simple contract range from about $200 to $500 depending on complexity and location.

Form 18: Contract for Services

1. This Contract for Services is made on this _____ day of _____,20_____ by and between
_____(Contractor's name)
_____(Contractor's address)
and _____(Customer's name)
_____(Customer's address).

2. Contractor shall perform the following work, duties, or services on behalf of Customer in a professional and workmanlike manner:

3. Customer shall pay to Contractor, for the work, duties, or services performed under this contract, compensation in the amount of and at the time as provided below:

4. The work, duties, or services to be performed by Contractor under this Contract shall commence on the _____ day of _____,20____ and shall be completed on the _____ day of _____,20___. Time is of the essence for the performance under this Contract.

5. Contractor is and shall remain an independent contractor at all times under this Contract. Contractor shall be responsible for hiring any assistants or subcontractors needed in performing under this Contract at no additional cost to Customer. Contractor shall indemnify Customer for any and all damages and liabilities caused by Contractor or Contractor's subcontractors or assistants in their performance under this Contract.

6. This Contract can be terminated as provided below:

7. This Contract shall be binding on and inure to the benefit of Contractor, Customer and their respective heirs, successors, and assigns.

8. This Contract shall not be assigned, nor any performance hereunder delegated by Contractor or Customer, without the express written consent of the other, which consent shall not be unreasonably withheld.

9. Additional Terms and Conditions:

10. This Contract shall be governed by the laws of the State of _____.

Contractor and Customer, intending to be legally bound, have signed this Contract as of the date first set forth above.

_____   _____
Contractor's Signature   Customer's Signature

Subscribed and sworn to before me on this _____ day of _____,20_____.

_____
Notary

14 Handling a Simple Divorce or Separation

What to Do When Relationships Don't Work

Practically everyone has been in a personal romantic relationship of some type that has not worked out. Typically these relationships end on a bitter note because of inflamed emotions, disappointments, accusations of fault, and other conflicts. However, relationships do not have to end in such a negative fashion, if you and your partner work at conciliation and compromise for a positive resolution.

Many times in a personal relationship, your emotions may cloud your judgment and your ability to settle issues on an amicable basis. Most people just never learn how to manage their personal relationships or how to plan in the event that they come to an end. Rather, we spend most of our lives focusing on our jobs and careers and so little time focusing on our personal relationships. Although there is no magic formula for a happy marriage or relationship, or a happy ending to one, you can typically foster such positive results by communication, compromise, and planning.

If the relationship is important to you, try sincere efforts to make it work. Talk over problems with your spouse or partner. Ask close friends and family for advice and counseling without making your friends and family an issue in the relationship. Consider obtaining the help of a marriage counselor or other professional mediator to help the two of you identify problems and potential solutions.

It is important that you be fair and honest to yourself and your spouse or partner. Realize that relationships don't always last despite your best efforts to make the relationship survive. Talk to each other about what should happen if the relationship ends. Don't focus on fault and blame, as this can be counterproductive. Rather, look at what can be a win-win situation for both of you. Also consider what's best for any children involved. Both of you can learn and grow from even a failed relationship.

Property Settlement and Other Agreements

Many times, a fair and equitable separation, property settlement, or prenuptial agreement can be helpful in making a break-up amicable. These agreements have been frequently criticized because it is said that they take the romance out of the relationship. But these agreements can do much to relieve tension and promote harmony in the relationship.

A prenuptial agreement is basically a property settlement agreement, entered into by prospective spouses prior to marriage, which provides for the property rights of one or both of the prospective spouses and/or any children. These agreements are recognized and enforced in many, but not all, of the states. Generally, a prenuptial property settlement agreement must be in writing and signed by both parties. A prenuptial agreement can define the rights and obligations of each of the parties in any of the property of either of them, whenever and wherever acquired or located. You can also agree to your rights to buy, sell, use, transfer, or otherwise manage and control property. You can provide for the disposition of property upon separation, marriage dissolution, death, or the occurrence or non-occurrence of any other event. Additionally, you may eliminate or modify any obligations of spousal support.

A sample property settlement agreement is provided at the end of this chapter. This agreement may be useful as a prenuptial agreement in contemplation of marriage to settle property, support, custody, and other issues. You may also find the property settlement agreement useful if you are going through a separation or divorce.

It may even be beneficial for couples who will only be living and cohabiting together to enter into a property settlement agreement. Oftentimes couples living together contribute jointly to the acquisition of furniture, household items, and other assets. It is recommended that couples living together enter into a property settlement agreement to address ownership of property and other rights. The sample property settlement agreement provided at the end of this chapter is also useful for couples who plan to live together.

Going Through a Divorce

Going through a divorce is never easy. But if your marriage is irretrievably broken, a divorce may be the best way to terminate the relationship and start life anew.

Many states now allow a divorce based on consent and commonly called "no fault" divorce. This approach can foster an amicable divorce in which both spouses agree that the marriage has broken down. Some states allow a divorce when there has been a separation and the husband and wife have lived apart for a specified period of time.

You can also obtain a divorce based on fault, but these tend to be complicated and unfriendly. It is recommended that you obtain legal counsel if you are undergoing a complicated or contested divorce. Typical legal fees for a simple divorce range from about $500 to $1,000, depending on complexity and location.

Typical grounds for a divorce based on fault include adultery, willful desertion, physical cruelty, insanity, habitual drunkeness, and conviction of a felony. Adultery is usually defined as a voluntary sexual relationship with another person other than a spouse and without the spouse's consent. Desertion is the intentional abandonment of marital cohabitation by either spouse without cause or justification and without the consent of the abandoned spouse. Physical cruelty involves personal violence and physical treatment that endangers life, limb, or health and renders cohabitation unsafe.

Habitual drunkenness typically involves a frequent state of intoxication for a specific period to time such as one or two years. Insanity generally requires a mental disease, defect, or failure of the mind such that a spouse does not have the capacity to conduct his or her own affairs. The felony conviction as a basis for divorce typically requires a prison sentence for a specified period of time.

Basically, a divorce is the legal termination of a marriage resulting from a court decree. Divorce laws may vary significantly from state to state. Be sure to check the specific rules and requirements for your particular state.

A divorce differs from an annulment. A divorce terminates a valid marriage. An annulment declares the marriage completely void because of some defect or disability, so from a legal viewpoint the marriage never took place.

Most states require specific periods of residence in the particular state before its courts can grant a divorce. These residency requirements may be as long as one year. Again, check the requirements in your state.

A state has jurisdiction to grant a divorce to a resident even if the other spouse lives outside that state. However, if the court does not have personal jurisdiction over the nonresident spouse, the divorce decree normally may not provide for alimony payments or division of property.

A divorce properly obtained in one state must be honored and given full faith in other states. This recognition of out-of-state divorces is required by the federal Constitution. No such recognition and full faith is required for divorces granted in foreign countries. However, most states recognize divorces of foreign countries if at least one spouse resided in the foreign country.

An action for divorce is commenced by one spouse filing a complaint for divorce with the court. Divorce actions are typically brought in the family court for your jurisdiction. A sample Complaint for Divorce is provided at the end of this chapter. This complaint should be useful in most states, particularly in filing for a "no fault" or "mutual consent" divorce.

The Complaint for Divorce identifies the plaintiff (spouse filing for divorce) and defendant (spouse who is being sued) in the left caption. The court and docket number are usually placed in the right caption. The complaint must generally include specific allegations as to jurisdiction, residence, date and place of marriage, and basis for divorce. Other declarations and requests may be included concerning other court actions, children, custody, visitation, property settlement agreements, support, and alimony. The complaint concludes with a request for a judgment dissolving the marriage and any further relief sought. The complaint typically must be signed and dated by the plaintiff.

It may be required that the Complaint for Divorce be verified by a sworn affidavit signed by the plaintiff. Some states may also require that an affidavit of consent, signed by both spouses, be filed with the complaint for "no fault" or "mutual consent" divorces. A sample Affidavit of Consent is provided at the end of this chapter. Some states, such as Pennsylvania, may also require that special notices to defend and claim rights be filed.

You file a divorce complaint and other required documents with the appropriate court in your jurisdiction. An original copy of your marriage license should be attached to the complaint. Filing fees are typically required and vary for each jurisdiction. Always keep a copy of the complaint for your records and obtain the docket number for your case from the court clerk.

A copy of the complaint must generally be served on the defendant. Service of the complaint upon your defendant spouse is normally accomplished by you or the court through personal service or by certified mail. If the defendant's address and location are unknown, you may be required to advertise the divorce action in the newspaper at your locality and the last known locality of the defendant.

The court normally sets a date for a hearing in the case, which usually must be attended by you and the defendant or legal counsel. If the defendant spouse fails to respond or appear, after proper service of the complaint, the court may nevertheless grant a divorce decree by default. If you, the plaintiff, fail to appear, the court may dismiss the case.

If the court is satisfied that all legal requirements have been met, it will issue a decree for divorce and other appropriate relief.

Checklist for Filing for a Simple Divorce

❏ Try efforts at reconciliation, if possible.

❏ Negotiate a property settlement agreement, if possible.

❏ Prepare Complaint for Divorce.

❏ Attach original copy of marriage license.

❏ Attach a copy of property settlement agreement, if any.

❏ Check residency requirements for your state.

❏ Prepare an Affidavit of Consent if required in your state for "no fault" or "mutual consent" divorces.

❏ Check with Court Clerk for filing fees and requirements in your state.

❏ File Complaint for Divorce and any accompanying documents with court clerk. Obtain docket number from court clerk.

❏ Serve complaint on defendant spouse.

❏ Attend hearings as required by the court.

❏ Consult an attorney if your divorce involves complex or complicated issues.

Form 19: Property Settlement Agreement

1. This Agreement is made this _____ day of_____,20_____
by and between _____(First Party's Name)
_____(First Party's Address)
and _____(Second Party's Name)
_____(Second Party's Address).

2. For and in consideration of the mutual covenants, promises, and acts to be performed by each party hereunder, the parties hereby agree to the terms and conditions of this Agreement, and that this Agreement shall be binding as the final disposition of any and all property, spousal, marital, parental, and custody rights and obligations between the parties.

3. The First Party shall have exclusive rights to and ownership of the property listed below whenever and wherever acquired or located:

4. The Second Party shall have exclusive rights to and ownership of the property listed below whenever and wherever acquired or located:

5. Except as otherwise provided in this Agreement, each party may dispose of his or her property in any way, and each party hereby waives and relinquishes any and all rights to share in the property or the estate of the other as a result of marriage, cohabitation, joint tenancy, or any other relationship.

6. The First Party shall have the obligations of and be responsible for the following:

7. The Second Party shall have the obligations of and be responsible for the following:

8. The custody of any minor children of the parties shall be as follows:

9. Each of the parties shall, at the request and expense of the other party, acknowledge, execute, sign, and deliver to the other party any documents which may be required to bring into effect the property rights and other interests and provisions of this Agreement.

10. The parties agree to the following additional terms and conditions:

11. This Agreement contains the entire understanding and agreement between the parties, and shall be binding on and inure to the benefit of the parties and their respective heirs, successors, and assigns.

12. This Agreement shall be governed by the laws of the State of _____.

13. This Agreement shall remain in effect until expressly terminated in writing by mutual agreement of the parties.

The First Party and Second Party, intending to be legally bound, have signed this Agreement below of their own free will as of the date first set forth above.

_____   _____
First Party's Signature   Second Party's Signature

Subscribed and sworn to before me on this _____ day of _____, 20_____.

_____
Notary

Form 20: Complaint for Divorce

_____
Plaintiff

v.

_____
Defendant

Court _____

Docket No. _____

The plaintiff, _____, respectfully declares the following:

1. Plaintiff currently resides at the following address: _____

_____

2. Plaintiff has been a resident of the State of _____ for a period of _____ months.

3. Defendant currently resides at the following address: _____

_____

4. Plaintiff and Defendant were married on the _____ day of _____, 20_____, and at the place of
_____(city) _____(county) _____(state). A copy of the
marriage license is attached hereto.

5. Plaintiff seeks a divorce from Defendant based on the following:

6. There have been no previous actions for divorce or annulment between Plaintiff and Defendant except:

7. The marriage between Plaintiff and Defendant is irretrievably broken and efforts at reconciliation have not been successful.

8. Plaintiff and Defendant ___ have (copy attached) ___ have not entered into a Settlement Agreement.

9. Other declarations:

Wherefore, Plaintiff requests judgment dissolving the marriage between the parties and such further relief as Plaintiff may have requested herein.

Verification

I, being of full age and mind, hereby certify that I am the Plaintiff in the foregoing Complaint for Divorce, that all declarations are true to the best of my knowledge and belief, and that said Complaint is filed in good faith and without collusion. I am aware that perjury and willful false statements will subject me to punishment under the law.

_____   _____
Plaintiff's Signature   Date

_____   _____
Address   Telephone

Subscribed and sworn to before me on this ____ day of_____, 20_____.

_____
Notary

Form 21: Affidavit of Consent

_____
Plaintiff

v.

_____
Defendant

Court _____

Docket No. _____

1. A Complaint for Divorce was filed between Plaintiff and Defendant on the _____ day of _____, 20_____.

2. The marriage between Plaintiff and Defendant is irretrievably broken and efforts at reconciliation have failed.

3. I, _____, consent to the entry of a final judgment dissolving the marriage between Plaintiff and Defendant and such further relief as requested in the Complaint for Divorce.

4. I hereby certify that all statements made in this Affidavit of Consent are true to the best of my knowledge and belief. I am aware that perjury and willful false statements will subject me to punishment under the law.

_____
Signature

_____
Date

Subscribed and sworn to before me on this _____ day of _____, 20_____.

_____
Notary

15 *Getting a New Name*

What's in a Name?

Your name is the designation by which you are known in the community in which you live and work. It is what distinguishes you from other people. At law, it is also the designation by which you become bound in contracts and other legal documents.

A legal name basically consists of a given first name (such as Dyan) and a surname (such as Bryson). This name is generally given at birth and may include one or more middle names or initials. Middle names and initials may not be recognized as part of the legal name in some states. Likewise, designations such as Sr., Jr., Dr., Mr., or Mrs. do not normally constitute a part of a legal name.

A name must normally consist of words and letters. Numerals, such as 1, 2, or 3, generally are not included as part of a name.

A married woman normally retains the right to use her maiden name and she is not required to adopt the name of her husband. This may be important to a woman who has developed a longstanding professional use of her maiden name. Thus, a married woman may adopt her husband's surname as a matter of custom rather than as a matter of law.

Historically, a person was free to adopt and use any name he or she desired as long as it was not done for fraud and did not interfere with the rights of others. The person would be legally bound by any contract or other agreement into which he or she entered under the adopted name. Also, the person could normally sue and be sued in the adopted name.

Your signature is any mark used to represent your name and intended to operate as your signature. Your signature does not have to be a full expression of your legal name, but can include abbreviations, initials, nicknames, or any other mark intended by you as your signature.

Changing Your Name

At common law, you could change your name at will merely by using a new name. However, most states have enacted laws which provide rules and procedures for officially changing your name. These laws typically require that you file an application or petition for a name change with the proper court.

The petition to change your name must generally be in writing and filed with the court in the county where you reside. The petition normally includes your name, address, age, place of birth, marital status, and your proposed new name. You may also be required to include all names you have used in the past five to ten years, any pending legal actions and outstanding judgments, any criminal convictions, and the names and addresses of any creditors. The petition usually includes reasons for the change of name, which can be any lawful purpose. It is normally a sufficient reason that you like the new name better because of social, religious, or any other reason that you feel is a benefit. The petition usually must be signed by you as the petitioner and may require a sworn verification as to the truth of any statements made in the petition.

You can also file a petition to change the name of any of your minor children. Some states require that if both parents are living, both must sign the petition to change the name of a minor child. However, some states allow a single parent to petition for a name change for a child without the other parent's consent. Courts usually look at what would be in the best interests of the child in granting a petition to change the child's name.

A sample Petition to Change Name and Petition to Change Name of Minor Child are provided at the end of this chapter. The petition should be filed with the appropriate court along with any required filing fees. In most cases you are required to publish notice of your petition for a name change in a newspaper of general circulation in your area. Check with the court clerk in your jurisdiction for specific requirements.

After the petition has been filed, the court will normally schedule a hearing to decide the issue. Generally, the court will grant the petition to change the name unless someone has a justifiable objection, the legal requirements have not been met, or the petition was filed with intent to defraud or other unlawful purposes. After the petition for a name change has been granted, you generally must be known and referred to by the new name only.

You should consult an attorney if your name change involves difficult or complex issues. Typical legal fees for a simple name change range from about $300 to $1,000.

Checklist for
Filing Petition to Change Name

❏ Choose the new name.

❏ Prepare Petition to Change Name. If you are seeking to change the name of a minor child, prepare Petition to Change Name of Minor Child.

❏ Attach a copy of your birth certificate to petition. For a minor child, attach a copy of the child's birth certificate to the petition.

❏ Attach a Consent to Name Change signed by the other parent or child, if required.

❏ Sign and date the petition. Include a Verification, if required.

❏ Check with court clerk for filing fees and other requirements.

❏ File petition and other required documents with the court. Obtain docket number from court clerk.

❏ Publish notice of petition to change name in local newspaper.

❏ Attend hearings as required by the court.

❏ Court grants your petition to change name.

❏ Start using your new name only.

❏ Consult an attorney if your name change involves difficult or complex issues.

Form 22: Petition to Change Name

Petitioner's Name _____   Court _____

Docket No. _____

In re: Name Change From: _____

To: _____

Petitioner hereby declares the following:

1. Petitioner resides at the following address: _____

_____

2. Petitioner has resided at the above address for _____ months.

3. Petitioner was born on the ____ day of _____, 20___. at the place of _____(city) _____(county)_____(state). A certified copy of petitioner's birth certificate is attached hereto.

4. Petitioner was named _____ at birth and had always been known by that name, except for the following:

5. The name of petitioner's father is _____, who resides at the following address _____

6. The name of petitioner's mother is _____, who resides at the following address _____

7. Petitioner desires a change of name to _____ for the following reason(s):

8. Other declarations:

Wherefore, petitioner requests the court to issue an order changing petitioner's name

from _____

to _____

Verification

I, _____, hereby certify that I am the petitioner in the foregoing Petition to Change Name and that all statements made herein are true to the best of my knowledge and belief. I am aware that perjury and willful false statements will subject me to punishment under the law.

_____   _____
Petitioner's Signature   Date

_____   _____
Address   Telephone

Subscribed and sworn to before me on this _____ day of _____, 20_____.

_____
Notary

Form 23: Petition to Change Name of Minor Child

Petitioner's Name(s) _____   Court _____

_____   Docket No. _____

In re: Name Change of Minor Child

From: _____

To: _____

Petitioner(s) hereby declare(s) the following:

1. Petitioner(s) reside(s) at the following address _____

2. Petitioner(s) has/have resided at the above address for _____ months.

3. On the _____ day of _____, 20_____, a minor child named _____
was born to petitioner(s). A certified copy of the birth certificate of said minor child is attached hereto.

4. Said minor child resides at the following address _____

5. Petitioner(s) desire(s) to change the name of said minor child from _____ to
_____ for the following reason(s):

6. Other declarations:

Wherefore, petitioner(s) request(s) the court to issue an order changing the name of said minor child

from _____

to _____

Verification

I/We hereby certify that all statements made in the foregoing Petition to Change Name of Minor Child are true to the best of my/our knowledge and belief. I/We am/are aware that perjury and willful false statements will subject me/us to punishment under the law.

_____   _____
Petitioner's Signature   Date

_____   _____
Address   Telephone

Subscribed and sworn to before me on this _____ day of _____, 20_____.

_____
Notary

Form 24: Consent to Name Change

Petitioner's Name(s) _____   Court _____

_____   Docket No. _____

In re: Name Change of Minor Child

From: _____

To: _____

I hereby declare the following:

1. My name is _____ and I currently reside at the following address :

_____

2. I consent to the Petition to Change Name of Minor Child

from _____

to _____

3. I understand the legal effect of such a change of name, and I have no objections to this court issuing an order to effect said change of name.

Verification

I hereby certify that all statements made in the foregoing Consent to Name Change are true to the best of my knowledge and belief. I am aware that perjury and willful false statements will subject me to punishment under the law.

_____   _____
Signature   Date

Subscribed and sworn to before me on this _____ day of _____,20____.

_____
Notary

16 Being Successful in Small Claims Court

Knowing about Small Claims Court

Small claims courts have been set up in most states to provide an easy procedure for you to assert legal rights. These small claims courts are special courts which are designed to provide speedy, informal, and inexpensive adjudication of small amounts. Small claims court is an ideal forum for self-representation. Legal representation by an attorney is not required and usually not needed. With sufficient documentation, witness testimony, or other proof, and a general understanding of the relevant law, you can adequately present or defend your own case.

Cases in small claims court are civil actions in which one party is suing another party to recover money. If you filed the lawsuit, you are the plaintiff. You have the burden of proving the basis for your claim and the amount of your damages. On the other hand, the defendant is the party against whom the case is brought, and who is summoned to court to defend against the lawsuit.

Small claims courts typically have limits on the types and dollar amounts of cases which can be decided. Cases in small claims court are normally restricted to the collection of small debts, accounts, property damages, damages for physical injuries, security deposits, damages for breach of contract, or other monetary damages. These courts usually cannot be used to bring actions for libel, slander, profes-sional malpractice, assigned claims, punitive damages meant as punishment or a penalty for wrongful conduct, injunctions to stop some activity or conduct, or other complex issues.

Small claims courts tend to be limited to cases involving claims not exceeding amounts ranging from about $1,000 to $5,000. In many small claims courts you can waive the amount of your claim which exceeds the dollar limitation and still bring your case in small claims court. However, you cannot recover more than the dollar limit.

Your costs for bringing a case in small claims court, without an attorney, will usually consist of only the basic filing fee. The filing fees generally range from about $10 to $50, depending on your particular jurisdiction. Check with your small claims court for specific filing fees, dollar limits on your claim, and other requirements.

Typical attorney's fees for cases in small claims court range from about $500 to $1,000, depending on location and the complexity of the case.

Should You Go to Court?

Going to court should be your last resort in resolving claims and other disputes. This is because litigation can involve a lot of time, money, and effort. Also, most regular court schedules are overcrowded, and it could take 2–3 years or longer before your civil action comes to trial.

You should always look for ways to settle your case out of court, if possible. Try to negotiate a reasonable settlement with the defendant. Consider alternative dispute resolution procedures, such as arbitration or mediation where an independent third party hears both sides and decides the case out of court. Private and governmental consumer agencies can be helpful in settling disputes over goods and services. Also, the Better Business Bureau in your area may offer a consumer arbitration program for settling consumer business disputes.

Before you file suit in court, be aware that the law may not provide a remedy for every wrong or harm done to you. For example, if your neighbor's tree fell on your car you may not have a claim against your neighbor unless you can show that he or she was negligent. Likewise, if someone broke a promise to do something for you, he or she would not be liable to you unless you have an enforceable contract. Usually, before you can recover in court, you must show that you have suffered some damages and that the defendant legally caused those damages through intent, negligence, or breach of contract.

The law of negligence protects people from the unreasonable risks of harm caused by others. A person is considered negligent when he or she fails to conduct him- or herself as the average reasonable person would have done under the circumstances. You must generally prove all of the following elements to win a case in court based on negligence:

- violation of a recognized duty of care by the defendant,
- actual and legal cause of the resulting harm by the defendant, and
- damages or injuries suffered by you which are recognizable and measurable.

The violation of the duty of care can result from something that the defendant did or something that he or she failed to do. The required duty of care is always that which the average reasonable person would have exercised under the circumstances. The standard of care for adults is that of a reasonable adult. The standard of care required of children is that of a child of similar age, intelligence, and experience. If a person has special professional skills, such as a lawyer or doctor, he or she is held to the standard of care normally exercised by members of that profession or trade. If a professional has violated his or her duty of care, it is commonly called malpractice. Malpractice cases can be very complex and usually require expert testimony from members of the profession to prove the required standard of care.

To win a negligence lawsuit, you must prove that the defendant's conduct was the actual and legal cause of your harm. You must typically show that you would not have been injured but for the defendant's act. You must also show that the harm caused to you was reasonably foreseeable by the defendant.

The damages that you can normally recover for negligence in small claims court can be medical expenses, lost wages, and property damage. In a regular lawsuit, not brought in small claims court, you may also recover for pain and suffering and disabilities which will prevent or diminish your future ability to work.

Your conduct is also important if you sue someone for negligence. In many states you will not be able to recover if you have been contributorily negligent in causing your own harm or if you have assumed the risks of any harm suffered. Other states may allow a partial recovery based on the percentage of the defendant's negligence. For example, if the defendant is 60 percent negligent in causing your harm, you may only recover 60 percent of your damages.

You can bring an action in small claims court for breach of contract. You must be able to show the existence of a valid contract by a written document or testimony. A valid contract requires that there be an offer, acceptance, and sufficient consideration.

An offer is a proposal to enter into a contract with someone. An acceptance is the indication by the other party that he or she agrees to the terms of your offer. A contract is formed once the offer has been accepted.

A true contract contains at least one promise that is exchanged for something. The promise can be exchanged for another promise, for some act, or for a forbearance from exercising a legal right. The exchange of promises or other things in a contract is consideration. The consideration must have some value in order to be legally sufficient. In other words, if you promise or give nothing under a contract, you cannot enforce the contract because it lacks consideration.

All of your contracts should be in writing and signed by you and the other contracting party. This makes it easy to prove both the existence of a contract and the specific terms and conditions thereof. Certain contracts are generally required to be in writing to be enforceable. These typically include the following:

- A contract for the sale, lease, or mortgage of any interest in land;
- A contract to answer for the debts of another, such as a cosigner or guarantor;
- A contract that, by its terms, cannot be performed within one year after the date of its making;
- A contract for the sale of goods having a price of $500 or more; and
- A contract for the sale of stock and other securities.

Minor children and mentally incompetent persons normally do not have the capacity to enter into a binding contract. A minor can void any contract that he or she has entered into except contracts for necessities such as food, clothing, or shelter. If a person has been declared mentally incompetent by a court, then any contract that person enters into is completely void. For a person who is mentally incompetent but who has not been so declared by a court, his or her contracts can be voided if he or she so desires. With these points in mind, always try to find out as much as possible about the legal capacity of the other party before you enter into a contract.

When you sue someone for breach of contract, you can normally recover any damages caused by the breach. You may also be able to recover any money or property you may have given under the contract or the value of any services you may have rendered. It is also common to request that the court award you any court costs, expenses, and legal fees you have incurred in bringing the lawsuit.

You should only go to court if your dispute cannot be settled outside of court, and only if you have a valid claim or cause of action. Courts do not welcome frivolous lawsuits. Some courts may even impose penalties on you for bringing a trivial and groundless lawsuit.

Bringing Your Case in Court
Your court case starts by you filing a civil complaint with the proper court. Most small claims courts have preprinted forms for filing your complaint. These forms vary from state to state, but typically require you to fill out your name and address, the defendant's name and address, a statement giving the basis of your claim, and the amount being sued for. The complaint form is signed by you and may require a verification or declaration under penalty of perjury. Check with the court clerk at your small claims court or other appropriate court for filing forms, procedures, fees, and other requirements.

A sample civil complaint form is provided at the end of this chapter. This form should be adaptable for use in most states. You complete the sample form with your name, as the plaintiff, and the name of the defendant. Identify the court and the nature of your complaint, such as "Complaint for Breach of Contract" or the like. The complaint includes declarations as to your address, the defendant's address, and facts to make out your cause of action. The complaint concludes with a request for a judgement against the defendant, a verification, and your signature.

Your complaint should give the nature of the defendant's identity, such as an individual, partnership, or corporation. If you are suing more than one defendant, be sure to separately identify each one. When suing a business, the defendants should be the business owners, whether a proprietor or partners. Corporations should be sued in their legal names. It is important in many states that you include the correct and exact name of the defendant or any judgment that you win may be defective.

You must file your case in court before the statute of limitation has run. Check the specific time periods for your state at the court clerk's office or your local library. The statute of limitation for contract actions is typically four years from the date of breach or default. Negligence cases normally have a two-year statute of limitation.

After your complaint is filed with the court, it is typically served on the defendant by certified mail or personal service. The defendant is given a specified time period (usually 2–4 weeks) to file an answer to your complaint. The court then sets a date for a hearing to decide the case.

It is important that you prepare your case using good documentary evidence and witnesses, if possible. The presentation of your case in small claims court is very informal. Nevertheless, you should do your best to present a strong and logical case. Bring copies of any necessary documents to court with you, such as contracts, police reports, medical bills, and receipts for repairs and damages. Ask witnesses to accompany you to court to give their testimony. However, if they cannot appear, have them prepare and sign affidavits which contain their testimony. Photographs can also be useful to show the extent of damages or the existence of any unsafe conditions. Your own testimony is also extremely important in proving your case in court.

Likewise, if you are a defendant in a lawsuit, you should adequately prepare to defend against the lawsuit. In many states you must file a written answer to the complaint before the case goes to trial. You may deny any fault or liability on your part, or challenge the amount of the plaintiff's claim. You can also counterclaim against the plaintiff for any loss or damages to you caused by the plaintiff.

Using Affidavits to Help Prove Your Case

In some cases you will be unable to get important witnesses to attend your trial and give testimony. Even if you were to subpoena a witness, he or she might be unfriendly and unwilling to testify favorably for your case. Although it is usually better to have witnesses appear in person to testify, you may be able to use an affidavit when the witness will be unavailable or unwilling to appear in court.

An affidavit is a sworn statement used to verify or prove statements of facts or allegations. The affidavit is written and signed by the witness or declarant under oath before an officer authorized to administer oaths. These officers are typically judges, magistrates, or notaries. Affidavits may be useful in court and out of court for various limited purposes, such as evidence, proof of service, and proof of the existence of a witness. Because affidavits constitute hearsay, they are not normally admissible in regular civil cases as proof of the statements contained therein. However, formal rules of evidence may not be strictly followed in small claims courts. So, affidavits may be extremely helpful in proving your case in small claims court.

Anyone who is competent to testify in court and who has knowledge of the facts can make an affidavit. A legally sufficient affidavit must include:

- the declarant's name and address,
- statement that the declarant was duly sworn under oath,

- statement of facts,
- signature of declarant and date,
- statement that the affidavit was made before a duly authorized officer, and
- signature and title of the officer.

A sample affidavit form is provided at the end of this chapter. You should check the specific requirements for affidavits in your state.

Winning and Collecting a Judgment

Most cases brought in small claims court are lost by the defendant because the defendant failed to show up for the trial or hearing. In such a situation, the plaintiff usually wins a default judgement for everything asked for in the complaint. If the plaintiff fails to appear at trial, the court may decide the case based on the defendant's evidence or dismiss the case all together. If both the plaintiff and defendant show up for trial and present their cases, a magistrate, judge, or arbitrator will decide the issues and render a judgement.

Winning a judgement against the defendant in court is merely an announcement that you have won. After winning, you still have to collect on your judgement. The defendant may pay you outright, but more often you have to make efforts to collect your award. The court clerk or judge may tell you what collection procedures you can follow for your state. Typically, you will need to get an order or writ of execution on the judgement from the court. This is then given to your sheriff, who will attach and sell property of the defendant to satisfy your judgement. You must normally locate the defendant's property and assets and provide this information to your sheriff. If the defendant has no property or assets, or these can not be located, you may not be able to collect your judgement now. However, judgements are usually good for a period of five years or longer and they can be renewed thereafter.

Checklist for Bringing a Civil Case in Court

❏ Do you have a valid claim? (i.e., Have you suffered any damages? Was someone else at fault?)

❏ Obtain names and addresses of all parties who have caused you damages.

❏ Notify each party of your claim and try to settle the matter out of court, if possible.

❏ Check statute of limitation in your state for your case.

❏ Check with your court clerk for filing procedures, filing fees, and other requirements.

❏ Prepare a civil complaint against the defendant(s). Specifically set forth the facts and basis for your claim. Attach any relevant documents, such as contracts, receipts, affidavits, etc. Sign and verify your complaint.

❏ File your complaint with the appropriate court. Obtain a docket number for your case from the court clerk.

❏ Serve a copy of the complaint on defendant(s).

❏ Prepare your case for trial by organizing your presentation, gathering witnesses, and obtaining any other necessary documents or information.

❏ Attend the trial or hearing and present your case.

❏ Receive a judgement from the court deciding your case.

❏ If the judgement is favorable to you, collect on the judgement from the defendant(s). If you are unable to collect from the defendant(s), obtain an order or writ of execution on the judgement, locate the property or assets of the defendant(s), and have your sheriff execute the judgement.

❏ If the judgement is adverse to you, consider filing an appeal if you believe the court has made errors of law. Check with your court clerk for the procedures and requirements for filing an appeal.

❏ Obtain legal counsel if your case involves difficult or complex issues.

Form 25: Civil Complaint

_____ ,

Plaintiff

v.

_____

Defendant

Court _____

Docket No. _____

Civil Action _____

Complaint For_____

Plaintiff hereby declares the following:

1. Plaintiff resides at the following address _____

2. Defendant is: (check one)

   ❏ **a)** An individual residing at the following address _____

   ❏ **b)** An individual doing business as _____ ,
       located at the following address _____

   ❏ **c)** A corporation having a place of business at the following address:
       _____

   ❏ **d)** Other:

3. Plaintiff has a claim against the defendant based on the following:

4. Plaintiff has suffered damages caused by the defendant in the total amount of _____ Dollars ($_____). These damages are specifically listed and described below:

5. Other declarations:

6. Wherefore, Plaintiff requests the court to issue a judgement for Plaintiff and against Defendant in the amount of _____ _____ Dollars ($_____), plus costs, and such further relief as the court deems equitable and just.

Verification

I hereby certify that all statements made in the foregoing civil complaint are true to the best of my knowledge and belief. I am aware that willful false statements can subject me to punishment under the law.

_____   _____
Plaintiff's Signature   Date

_____   _____
Plaintiff's Address   Plaintiff's Telephone

Subscribed and sworn to before me on this _____ day of _____ 20_____.

_____
Notary

Form 26: Affidavit

I, _____,

being of full age, and being duly sworn according to law, upon my oath, state the following:

1. My current residence is as follows:

2. I declare that:

I do solemnly swear and certify that the foregoing statements are true to the best of my knowledge and belief. I am aware that willful false statements can subject me to punishment under the law.

_____   _____
Signature   Date

_____   _____
Address   Telephone

Subscribed and sworn to before me on this _____ day of _____20_____.

_____
Notary

17 *Using Releases to Settle Legal Claims*

Releasing Someone from a Claim

It is common to settle legal disputes without resorting to court action. In many cases, the party at fault pays an agreed sum and receives in exchange a release. A release is an agreement by which you discharge or excuse someone from liability arising out of some specific set of circumstances. When you execute and deliver a release to someone, you give up your right to pursue the released claim against that person.

Releases can be used to settle any existing claim or right. This includes rights to enforce a contract, causes of action for negligence, liens, accounts, debts, covenants, rents, and many other legal rights or remedies. In many states, a release which discharges someone from liability for his or her future negligence may be invalid. In other states, the language of the release must be clear and specific to discharge liability for future injuries and disabilities.

A release is like a contract and should be in writing and supported by valuable consideration. The consideration may be payment of money or performance of some act by the party being released. Your release and waiver of your claim is sufficient consideration on your part. To be effective, your release must be signed by you and delivered to the party being released.

It is common for you to sign a release in settling accident and insurance claims. Settling these claims can be relatively simple and easy for you to handle without hiring a lawyer. The following steps may be helpful to you in settling an accident or insurance claim.

If you are involved in an automobile or other accident, gather as many details and facts as possible. Get the owner's name, address, and any insurance information of any other vehicles involved. Get names, addresses, and telephone numbers of all witnesses and of the drivers and passengers of any automobiles involved. If the police were called, ask for a copy of any police reports regarding the accident. Draw a sketch of the scene indicating where the accident happened. Take photographs of the accident if possible.

Whether you think you are injured or not, go to a doctor. You may be injured and not know it. The doctor or hospital visit will confirm any injuries and produce important medical records. Regular visits to the doctor may be necessary if your injuries are severe.

You should write a letter to your insurance company and the insurance companies of any parties at fault. Inform the insurance companies of the date, place, and other details of the accident. The insurance companies will normally give you a claim number and the name of an insurance adjuster who will be handling your case.

Gather all of your doctor bills, medical expenses, and other expenses associated with your injury. Ask your doctor for a typewritten medical report signed by the doctor. Send copies (keep originals for your file) of these documents to the insurance company of the party at fault, along with a letter demanding a certain amount as settlement of the claim. Be sure to include in your claim an amount for lost wages and pain and suffering.

You seek to negotiate a settlement with the insurance company which is fair and reasonable to you. If a settlement is reached, you will be asked to sign a release in exchange for payment of the settlement amount. You should consult an attorney if your claim involves complex issues. Attorneys typically handle personal injury cases on a contingency basis for one-third to one-half of any recovery.

A sample release form is provided at the end of this chapter. The release should include the name and address of the party being released (i.e., debtor or defendant). It should also include the name and address of the party giving the release (i.e., claimant). A description of the claim being released should also be included, as well as a description of the consideration to be paid or exchanged for the release. The release should settle all claims arising from the dispute, transaction, or situation, and it should be binding on all parties and their heirs and assigns. Include any additional terms and conditions that may be applicable. The release must be signed by the party giving the release and should be signed by the released party to indicate his or her acceptance.

Form 27: Release

1. This Release is made and delivered on this ____ day of _____20_____ by and between

_____(Claimant's name)

_____(Claimant's address)

and_____(Debtor's name)

_____(Debtor's address).

2. Claimant hereby discharges and releases Debtor from all claims, actions, damages, and liabilities whatsoever, including those currently known and those which may arise in the future, resulting from or arising out of the following transactions, events, or circumstances:

3. In consideration for this Release, Debtor hereby agrees to pay to Claimant the sum of _____

_____Dollars ($_____) or to perform the following:

   The above consideration shall be paid or given by Debtor on or before the ____ day of _____20___.

4. This Release shall be binding on and inure to the benefit of Claimant and Debtor and their respective heirs, assigns, successors, and legal representatives.

5. Other Terms and Conditions:

6. This Release shall be governed by the laws of the State of _____. This Release is executed and delivered voluntarily as a fair settlement of the foregoing claim(s).

Claimant and Debtor, intending to be legally bound, have signed this Release on the date first indicated above.

_____
Claimant's signature

_____
Debtor's signature

Subscribed and sworn to before me on this _____ day of _____20_____.

_____
Notary

18 *How to Be a Smart Consumer*

The Consumer Must Be Aware

A missing ingredient in many business transactions is trust and good faith. Wouldn't it be nice if everything you purchased, every contract you entered into, every transaction you made, was between you and a person you trusted? There would be less need for receipts, records, and lawyers. Since this will never happen, there is only one thing you can do to keep from being taken advantage of—be an informed consumer.

The market place offers an endless line of products and services. You need to be a smart consumer and do some rational thinking both before and after you make a purchase. Before you make any significant purchase, think about what you really need and what features are important to you. Do comparison shopping among different brands and different stores. For major purchases look for expert product comparison reports. See if your local library has magazines or other publications that compare products and services. Check with your local consumer protection agencies or Better Business Bureau to find out the reputation and complaint record of prospective suppliers of goods and services.

Be sure to read and fully understand the terms of any contract before you sign it. Read the warranties to understand what steps you must take, and what the manufacturer must do, if you have a problem. Know the return and exchange policy.

After your purchase keep all sales receipts, contracts, warranties, and instructions. Read and follow the instructions on how to use the product, and use the product only for the purposes stated in the manufacturer's instructions. If you have problems, report them to the seller or manufacturer. Do not try to fix the product yourself, because this might cancel any warranties on the product.

As a consumer you have the right to receive good quality products and services for your money. Oftentimes you do not. However, if trouble develops with a product or service, there are some things you can do to resolve the problems. Begin by contacting the business from which you bought the product or service. Remain calm and explain the nature of your problem and what action you would like taken. Decide if you want the product repaired or replaced or your money back.

If you are unsuccessful in resolving your complaint with a salesperson or manager at the local level, call or write a letter to the company headquarters. Keep a file of your efforts to resolve your complaints, including the dates and names of the people that you talk with. Also keep in your complaint file copies of your receipts, warranties, and complaint letters. Always retain original copies for your file and never send out documents you cannot replace.

It is important that you complain when you are dissatisfied with a purchase. It is estimated that there are about 80 million customers dissatisfied with purchases each year in this country. Yet, only about five percent of the dissatisfied customers ever complain to the seller about their disappointment. Remember, a manufacturer is unlikely to improve goods and services unless you complain when you are dissatisfied.

It is recommended that you make your complaint letter formal by sending the letter to the seller or manufacturer by certified or registered mail. Again, the letter should be specific in describing your problem and the action you would like taken.

Your Rights with "Door-to-Door" Sales

A major consumer right with "door-to-door" sales is known as the "cooling off rule." This is a rule of the Federal Trade Commission (FTC), which gives a consumer who makes a purchase of $25.00 or more through a "door-to-door" sales person three business days to change his or her mind and cancel the purchase. A door-to-door sale is typically any sale made at the buyer's home or anywhere away from the seller's place of business.

The FTC's three-day cooling-off rule does not apply to sales that are:

* under $25;
* made entirely by phone or mail;
* initiated by the purchaser for repair of personal property;
* for real estate, insurance, or securities;
* for emergency home repair if the right to cancel is waived; or
* made at the seller's normal place of business.

The FTC requires door-to-door sellers to inform you of your cancellation rights. Any contract that you sign for a door-to-door sale must provide information about your right to cancel. You should be given a cancellation form which shows the date, name, and address of the seller and the date by which you may cancel. You can cancel your door-to-door purchase by mailing a cancellation notice to the seller's address at any time before midnight of the third business day after the date of the contract. Sundays and holidays are not counted in measuring the three-day cancellation period.

Within ten days after you have canceled your door-to-door purchase, the seller must refund any money you paid or any property that you used as a trade-in. The federal law provides for penalties against the seller if he fails to do what the law requires. If you have sent a cancellation notice within three days and the seller still refuses to return your money, contact your local consumer protection agency, your state attorney general's office, or the Federal Trade Commission. The addresses for these agencies are given in the Appendix.

There are some things you can do to protect yourself from unscrupulous salespeople:

* Get as much information on the salesperson knocking on your door as possible. Ask for identification; ask what company the salesperson represents. Watch out for scams and con artists.
* Don't pay for items you want right away. Note the price and hold out a few days; shop around for a better deal. Most likely the product or service you want to purchase is being sold by someone else. Compare prices before you buy.
* Don't sign anything unless the following questions are answered to your satisfaction: Exactly what will you receive? Exactly how much are you going to have to pay (including tax, interest, and other charges)? How do you go about getting the product serviced? Will you have to take it or ship it somewhere? Is there a warranty and exactly what is covered by the warranty? How long does the warranty last? Does the company

allow refunds and exchanges? Are you going to get the name, address, and phone number of seller or company official? Does the sales contract conform with the words of the seller? Are the terms, warranty, price, and interest rate clearly stated in the contract?

- Make sure everything promised to you is put into writing.
- Insist upon a copy of the contract and any other documents you sign.

Buying Through the Mail

Millions of consumers order products through the mail each year. If you shop by mail, you have the entire world as a shopping center. Home shopping can offer convenience, wider selection of merchandise, better prices, and accessibility to products that are difficult to find. Shopping from catalogs and magazines gives you plenty of time to make a decision on your purchase without the influence of high-pressure sales tactics.

However, the convenience of mail order shopping can become a great disappointment if there are lengthy delays in getting your merchandise, if it is not what you wanted, or if you never receive it at all. You can protect yourself when shopping by mail by understanding your rights as a mail order shopper and being a cautious consumer.

Always try to deal with reliable and reputable companies. Check with the Better Business Bureau or your consumer protection agency to find information about the company (see the Appendix for addresses). Pay careful attention to the advertisement and other information provided about the product. Do not rely solely on the picture of the item, because it could be misleading. Write to the company for additional information if you need more details.

Never pay for a mail order by cash. Rather, use a credit card (preferable), or pay by check or money order so that you will have a record of payment. Also, keep a copy of your order and any information you have on the product.

The Federal Trade Commission and the U.S. Postal Service enforce laws and regulations which are designed to protect mail order shoppers. The FTC Mail Order Rules provides you with these legal rights when buying by mail:

- Seller must see that you receive the goods no later than the date he promised you would receive them.
- Seller must ship the goods within thirty days of the date he receives your properly completed order, unless the advertisement states the contrary.
- If the seller is unable to meet the shipping deadline, he must notify you when the order will be shipped. If the new shipping date is more than thirty days past the original shipping date, you may, in writing, either accept the new shipping date or cancel the order in writing. However, if you do not cancel, this means that you accept the delay.
- If you cancel the order, you are entitled to a full refund within seven business days after the seller receives your cancellation.
- If you paid the bill by charge account and a refund is required, the seller must take no more than one billing cycle to adjust your account. Federal credit laws provide that if adjustments in this area take longer, you can stop payment on the charge by notifying the credit card company in writing.

The Mail Order Rule does not cover orders for photo development, seeds, growing plants, book and record club merchandise, magazines (after the first issue), and payment by C.O.D. Neither does it cover orders you charge directly to your credit card using an "800" number. Orders which are charged to your credit card only after the merchandise is sent also are not governed by the Mail Order Rule.

You should not accept merchandise shipped to you which is damaged. If the merchandise is visibly damaged when delivered to you, do not open it. Rather, write "Not Accepted" or "Refused" on it and return it to the seller. New postage is usually not required, unless you have signed for a C.O.D., registered, certified, or insured package.

Merchandise sent to you in the mail that you did not order is yours to keep. This includes any extra merchandise sent with items you did order. You do not have to send it back, and you can not be made to pay for it. Under the law, this is considered a gift. Enjoy it.

If a private delivery service, such as United Parcel Service, brings you merchandise that you did not order, you must do two things before you can legally keep the merchandise:

(1) you must alert the sender (preferably in writing) that you received goods that you did not order;

(2) you must allow the sender a reasonable amount of time to pick the merchandise up at the sender's expense. You should tell the sender what you intend to do with the merchandise if he fails to pick it up.

Checklists for Being a Smart Consumer

The most important steps to being a smart consumer are knowing your legal rights and taking measures to protect them. The U.S. Office of Consumer Affairs, Washington, D.C. 20233 compiles a *Consumer's Resource Handbook* which provides useful information on how to be a smart consumer. Information from this *Handbook* was used to prepare these helpful consumer checklists.

Home Shopping Checklist

Today, there are many ways to buy products or services. Some consumers buy items through mail order, telephone, or even television shopping programs. Keep the following tips in mind:

❑ Be suspicious of exaggerated product claims or very low prices and read product descriptions carefully. Sometimes, pictures of products are misleading.

❑ If you have any doubts about the company, check with the U.S. Postal Service, your state or local consumer protection agency, or Better Business Bureau before ordering.

❑ Ask about the firm's return policy. If it is not stated, ask before you order. Is a warranty or guarantee available?

❑ If you buy by telephone, make clear exactly what you are ordering and how much it costs before you give your credit card number; watch out for incidental charges.

❑ Keep a complete record of your order, including the company's name, address, and telephone number, price of the items ordered, any handling or other charges, date of your order, and your method of payment. Keep copies of canceled checks and/or statements. If you are ordering by telephone, get the names of any company representatives with whom you speak.

❑ If you order by mail, your order should be shipped within thirty days after the company receives your completed order, unless another period is agreed upon when placing the order or is stated in an advertisement. If your order is delayed, a notice of delay should be sent to you within the promised shipping period, along with an option to cancel the order.

❑ If you want to buy a product based on a telephone call from an unfamiliar company, ask for the name, address, and phone number where you can reach the caller after considering the offer. It is best to request and read written information before deciding to buy.

❑ Never give your credit card, bank account, or social security number over the telephone as proof of your identity unless you placed the call or have an account with the company you are calling.

❑ Postal regulations allow you to write a check payable to the sender, rather than the delivery company, for cash on delivery (C.O.D.) orders. If, after examining the merchandise, you feel there has been misrepresentation or fraud, you can stop payment on the check and file a complaint with the U.S. Postal Inspector's Office.

❑ You can have a charge removed from your credit card bill if you did not receive the goods or services or if your order was obtained through misrepresentation or fraud. You must notify the credit card company in writing, at the billing inquiries/ disputes address, within sixty days after the charge first appeared on your bill.

Checklist for Warranties and Guarantees

An important feature to consider before buying a product or service is the warranty that comes with it. When reviewing warranties, use the guidelines below:

❑ Do not wait until the product fails or needs repair to find out what is covered in the warranty.

❑ If the product costs $15 or more, the law says that the seller must let you examine any warranty before you buy, if you ask to see it. So use your rights to compare the terms and con-

ditions of warranties (or guarantees) on products or services before you buy. Look for the warranty that best meets your needs.

❑ When purchasing a product or service, ask these questions:
— How long is the warranty, and when does it start and end?
— What is covered? Which parts? What kinds of problems?
— Will the warranty pay for 100 percent of repair costs, or will it pay for parts, but not the labor to do the repairs? Will it pay for testing the product before it is repaired? Will it pay for shipping and/or a loaner?
— Who offers the warranty—manufacturer or retailer? How reliable are they?

❑ Keep sales receipts and warranties in a safe place.

❑ Some states have additional warranty rights for consumers. Check with your state or local consumer protection office to find the laws in your state.

Credit Card Checklist

The following suggestions can help you when selecting a credit card company or using your credit cards.

❑ Keep in a safe place a list of your credit card numbers, expiration dates, and the phone number of each card issuer.

❑ Credit card issuers offer a wide variety of terms (annual percentage rate, method of calculating the balance subject to the finance charge, minimum monthly payments, and actual membership fees). When selecting a card, compare the terms offered by several card issuers to find the card that best suits your needs.

❑ When you use your credit card, watch your card after giving it to a clerk. Promptly take back the card after the clerk is finished with it and make sure it's yours.

❑ Tear up the carbons when you take your credit card receipt.

❑ Never sign a blank receipt; draw a line through any blank spaces above the total when you sign receipts.

❑ Save your purchase receipts until the credit card bill arrives. Then, open the bill promptly and compare it with your receipts to check for possible unauthorized charges and billing errors.

❑ Write the card issuer promptly to report any questionable charges. Telephoning the card issuer to discuss the billing problems does not preserve your rights. Do not include written inquiries with your payment. Instead, check the billing statement for the correct address for billing questions. The inquiry must be in writing and must be sent within sixty days to guarantee your rights under the Fair Credit Billing Act.

❑ Never give your credit card number over the telephone unless you made the call or have an account with the company calling you. Never put your card number on a postcard or on the outside of an envelope.

❑ Sign new cards as soon as they arrive. Cut up and throw away expired cards.

If any of your credit cards are missing or stolen, report the loss as soon as possible to the card issuer. Check your credit card statement for a telephone number for reporting stolen credit cards. Follow up your phone calls with a letter to each card issuer. The letter should contain your card number, the date the card was missing, and the date you called in the loss.

❑ If you report the loss before a credit card is used, the issuer cannot hold you responsible for any future unauthorized charges. If a thief uses your card before you report it missing, the most you will owe for unauthorized charges is $50 on each card. A special note of warning: if an automatic teller machine (ATM) card is lost or stolen, the consumer could lose as much as $500 if the card issuer is not notified within two business days after learning of the loss or theft.

❑ When writing checks for retail purchases and to protect yourself against fraud, you may refuse to allow a merchant to write your credit card number of your check. However, if you refuse, the merchant might legally refuse to sell you the product. There is probably no harm in allowing a merchant to verify that you hold a major credit card and to note the issuer and the expiration date on the check.

❑ If a merchant indicates he or she is using credit cards as back-ups for bounced checks, or refuses your sale because you refuse to provide personal information (including your phone number) on the bank card sales slip, report the store to the credit card company. The merchant might be violating his or her agreement with the credit card companies. In your letter to the credit card company, provide the name and location of the merchant.

Checklist for Selecting a Financial Institution

Finding the right bank, savings and loan, or credit union means figuring out your own needs first. Answering the following questions should help you identify your "banking personality" and make choosing a financial institution a bit easier.

- ❏ What is your goal in establishing a banking relationship? Answers might include "to save money," "to have a checking account," "to get a loan," or all of the above.

- ❏ How much money can you keep on deposit each month and how many checks will you write? Knowing this will help you judge how complex or simple an account you need.

- ❏ Will you be buying a home or car or making another large purchase in the near future? If so, you will want to find out about the types of loans offered by the institutions you are considering.

- ❏ If you hope to save for a big expense or toward your child's (or your own) future education, you will also want to find out how many different savings programs are offered.

- ❏ What time of day do you prefer to do your banking? Do you like the convenience of automated teller machines (ATMs) or do you prefer to deal with live tellers? Answering these two questions will help you determine if you'd be happier at a financial institution with regular, evening, or weekend hours or one with a wide network of ATMs.

- ❏ What does the financial institution charge for services like cashier's checks, safe deposit boxes, and stop payment orders? Is there a charge for using an automated teller machine? Is there a monthly service charge, or must you maintain a minimum balance in your account to avoid a charge?

- ❏ Narrow your options to specific financial institutions. Phone or visit several near your home or office, because they are likely to be the most convenient. Take your answers to the above questions with you and find out which accounts and services are most likely to match your needs. Then compare fees and service charges, as well as deposit and loan interest rate.

- ❏ Price might not be the most important factor in your banking personality, so you also should take a minute to think about how comfortable you feel at each institution. For example, are your questions answered quickly and accurately? Do customer service personnel offer helpful suggestions?

- ❏ Remember, you can and should choose more than one financial institution to provide you with different banking services.

- ❏ Before making your final choice, make sure the institutions you're considering are federally insured. This means your deposits will be protected up to $100,000. All federally insured financial institutions are required to display a federal deposit insurance sign at each teller's window or teller station.

Home Improvement Checklist

Hiring a contractor to renovate your home, add a room, or make some other improvement can be a confusing maze of contracts, licenses, permits, and payment schedules. The suggestions listed below can help guide you through that maze.

- ❏ Compare costs by getting more than one estimate or bid. Each estimate should be based on the same building specifications, materials, and time frame.

- Before choosing a contractor, check with state, county, or local consumer protection agencies to see if any complaints have been filed against the contractor. Ask about information on unresolved cases and how long a contracting company has been in business under its current name.

- Ask a potential contractor for a list of previous customers whom you could call to find out about work quality and if they would hire that contractor for future work.

- Check with your local building inspections department to see if licensing and/or bonding are required of contractors in your area. If so, ask to see the contractor's license and bonding papers.

- Before signing a written contract, be sure it includes the contractor's full name, address, phone number, and professional license number (where required), a thorough description of the work to be done, grade and quality of materials to be used, agreed-upon starting and completion dates, total cost, payment schedule, warranty, how debris will be removed, and any other agreement information. Never sign a partially blank contract. Fill in or draw a line through any blank spaces.

- Most contractors have liability and compensation insurance to protect the customer from a lawsuit in the event of an accident. Ask to see a copy of the insurance certificate.

- If the work requires a building permit, let the contractor apply for it in his name. That way, if the work does not pass inspection, you are not financially responsible for any corrections that must be made.

- When you sign a nonemergency home improvement contract in your home and in the presence of a contractor (or contractor's representative), you usually have three business days in which to cancel the contract. You must be told about your cancellation rights and be provided with cancellation forms. If you decide to cancel, it is recommended that you send a notice of cancellation by telegram or certified mail, return receipt requested.

- For a remodeling job involving many subcontractors and a substantial amount of money, it is wise to protect yourself from liens against your home in case the contractor does not pay subcontractors or suppliers. If state law permits, add a release-of-lien clause to the contract or place your payments in an escrow account until the work is completed.

- If you cannot pay for a project without a loan, add a clause to your contract stating it is valid only if financing is obtained.

- When signing a contract, limit your first payment to not more than thirty percent of the contract price. The remaining payments should depend on the progress of the work. Ten percent of the contract amount should be held back until the job is complete, and all problems, if any, are corrected. Some states have home improvement laws that specify the amount of deposit and payment schedule. Check with your state and local consumer protection offices to see if there is such a law in your community.

- Thoroughly inspect the contractor's work before making final payment or signing a completion certificate.

Used Cars/Car Repair Checklist

The following guidelines will help you buy a used car or get your car repaired.

Used Cars

❏ Decide what kind of car you need and how much you can afford to spend. Talk to owners of similar cars.

❏ Decide whether you want to buy from a dealer or private owner. A car bought from a private owner usually has no warranty.

❏ In a private sale, check to be sure the seller is the registered owner of the car. Make sure you get the car's title and registration, bill of sale, and copies of all other financial transaction papers necessary to register the car in your name.

❏ If you're buying from a dealer, read the contract carefully before you sign, take the time to ask questions about unclear items, and keep a copy of the contract.

❏ Look for and read the buyer's guide, which must be displayed in the window of all used cars sold by dealers. The buyer's guide explains who must pay for repairs after purchase. It will tell you if there is a warranty on the car, what the warranty covers, and whether a service contract is available.

❏ Comparison shop for price, condition, warranty, and mileage for the model(s) you are interested in buying. Compare available interest rates and other terms of financial agreement.

❏ To estimate the total cost of the car, add the cost of interest for financing, the cost of a service contract (if any), and service or repair expenses you are likely to pay.

❏ Before buying the car, have a mechanic inspect it.

❏ Check the reliability of the dealer with your state or local consumer protection agency. Check the local Better Business Bureau to see if there are complaints against the dealer.

Car Repair

❏ Check the terms of your car's warranty. The warranty might require the dealer to perform routing maintenance and any needed repairs.

❏ Before having your car repaired, check the repair shop's complaint record with your state or local consumer protection office or local Better Business Bureau.

❏ Some repair shops have mechanics certified by the National Institute for Automotive Service Excellence (ASE) to perform one or more types of services. Be aware, however, that repair shops can display the ASE sign even if they have been tested for only one specialty.

❏ Do not tell the mechanic what you think needs to be fixed or replaced, unless it is obvious. Instead, describe the problem and its symptoms. Let the mechanic determine what needs fixing.

❏ For major repairs, think about getting a second opinion, even if the car must be towed to another shop.

❏ Before you leave the car, make sure you have a written estimate and that the work order reflects what you want done. Ask the mechanic to contact you before making repairs not covered in the work order.

❏ If additional work is done without your permission, you do not have to pay for the unapproved work and you have the right to have your bill adjusted.

❏ Ask to inspect and/or keep all replaced parts.

❏ Keep copies of all work orders and receipts and get all warranties in writing.

❏ Many states have "lemon" laws for new cars with recurring problems. Contact your local or state consumer office for more details.

Sources of Help for Consumers

There are many resources available to you to assist you with consumer problems and inquiries. These include your Better Business Bureaus, state and local consumer agencies, local newspapers, radio and television stations, state attorney general's office, and state department on aging. Also available are federal agencies, trade associations, and consumer groups. Look in your telephone directory or visit your local library for the complete names, addresses, and telephone numbers for these organizations.

You can write for a free copy of the *Consumer's Resource Handbook* by writing to the Consumer Information Center, Pueblo, Colorado 81009. This booklet provides a listing of federal, state, and local government agencies, as well as private businesses and organizations that can help you as a consumer. Some of these listings are included in the Appendix to this book.

For mail order and door-to-door sales inquiries, contact:

Federal Trade Commission
Correspondence Branch
Washington, D.C. 20580
(202) 326-2000

For mail order sales inquiries, contact:
U.S. Postal Service
Chief Postal Inspector
475 LaSalle Plaza, W.S.W.
Room 3517
Washington, D.C. 20260
(202) 268-2000

For complaints and information about mail order sales, write:
Director, Mail Order Action Line Service
Direct Marketing Association
1120 Avenue of the Americas
New York, N.Y. 10036-6700
(212) 768-7277

For complaints and information about door-to-door sales, write:
Code Administrator
Direct Selling Association
1666 K Street, Suite 1010
Washington, D.C. 20006
(202) 293-5760

You can also contact consumer groups such as:
Consumer Federation of America
1424 16th Street, N.W., Suite 604
Washington, D.C. 20036
(202) 387-6162

Other consumer groups are listed in guides at your local library. Directories of businesses and their addresses can be found there as well. Many directories give the address of top officers, public relations departments, and customer service sections.

19 *Maintaining Good Credit*

Why Good Credit Is Important

Your need to maintain a good credit rating is of paramount importance because typically you will not have the money yourself to purchase many of the big ticket items in your life, such as a car, house, or college education. Even your ability to obtain medication and medical treatment may very well depend on your credit rating. Thus, having access to credit is very important if you are to acquire and enjoy most major assets during your lifetime. Furthermore, changes in your life, such as divorce, loss of income, relocation, retirement, education for your children, and loss of a spouse, may all trigger a need for you to obtain credit or review your current credit history. Maintaining a good credit history and establishing sources of credit should always be a part of your financial planning.

Although lenders consider a variety of factors in deciding whether to give you credit, most of them rely heavily on your credit history. So, building a good credit history is essential if you want to be able to borrow money. If you do not have a credit history, you should begin to build one. If you have a steady income and have lived in the same area for at least a year, try applying for credit with a local business, such as a department store. Or you might borrow a small amount from your credit union or the bank where you have checking and savings accounts. A local bank or department store may approve your credit application even if you do not meet the standards of larger creditors. Before you apply for credit, ask whether the creditor reports credit history information to credit bureaus serving your area. Most creditors do, but some do not. If possible, you should try to get credit that will be reported. This builds your credit history.

If you do not have a credit file, you can visit or write your local credit bureau and request that a file be started on you. Most credit reporting agencies will require that you provide them with your identification, your address (last five years), Social Security number, place of employment, and verification of income. If you do not have employment income, take copies of Social Security, disability, pensions, annuities, alimony, and retirement checks. Remember that, under the law, employment income must be treated the same way as retirement or disability income in determining if credit is to be granted. If you have prior creditors, contact them to obtain copies of your last credit transactions. Also, if you have a bank account, attempt to get a letter of reference from your banker and submit these to the credit reporting agency.

Open checking and savings accounts at several financial institutions if you do not have any. These may be useful as credit references and as easier sources of credit because of your ongoing relationship. Most creditors will not extend you credit unless you have at least three good credit references. Apply for a major credit card. If you do not qualify, check to see if you can offer collateral or have someone cosign.

The Federal Trade Commission enforces a number of federal credit laws and provides free brochures and publications on many credit-related issues. The Federal Reserve System and the Federal Deposit Insurance Corporation also provide free consumer pamphlets and handbooks on a variety of credit topics. Much of the following information was provided by these sources.

How Credit Bureaus Work

Credit reporting agencies, often called credit bureaus, are companies that gather information on credit users and sell that information in the form of credit reports to credit grantors, such as banks, finance companies, and retailers. Credit bureaus keep records of consumers' debts and how regularly these debts are repaid. They gather information from creditors who send computer tapes or other payment data to credit bureaus, usually on a monthly basis, showing what each account-holder owes or has paid. The data show if payments are up-to-date or overdue, and if any action has been taken to collect overdue bills. The credit bureau adds this data to existing information in consumer files, creating a month-by-month history of activity on consumer accounts.

If you have been denied credit because of information that was supplied by a credit bureau, the Fair Credit Reporting Act requires the creditor to give you the name and address of the credit bureau that supplied the information. If you contact that bureau to learn what is in your file within thirty days of receiving a denial notice, the information is free. If not, the credit bureau may charge you a small fee ($8 for an individual and $16 for a husband and wife).

You always are entitled to learn what is in your credit file, but credit bureaus vary in how they disclose this information. Most will send you a printed copy of your credit report. Some, however, will ask you to visit the bureau to review your record or will give you information over the telephone once you have provided proper identification.

Once you have received your credit report, make sure that you understand the report. Often, credit reports are computer coded for record-keeping purposes and, thus difficult to understand. If you do not understand your report, the credit bureau is required by law to give you an explanation of what your report says. If you still do not understand, you can set up an appointment with a credit counselor to discuss your report.

If you request it, you have a right to receive a free copy of your credit report every 12 months from each of the nationwide credit reporting agencies (i.e., Equifax, Experian and TransUnion). To request your free copy, use the website: *www.annualcreditreport.com*; call 1-877-322-8228; or mail your request to: Annual Credit Report Request Service, P.O. Box 105281, Atlanta, GA 30348-5281.

How to Conduct Your Own Credit Check-up

Even if you have not been denied credit, you may wish to find out what information is in your credit file. Some financial advisors suggest that consumers review their credit reports every one or two years to check for inaccuracies or omissions. This could be especially important if you are considering making a major purchase such as buying a home. Checking in advance on the accuracy of information in your credit file could speed the credit-granting process.

To find which credit bureaus have your file, check the Yellow Pages under credit bureaus or credit reporting agencies for the phone numbers and addresses of the bureaus near you. The names and addresses of the three major credit reporting agencies are given at the end of this chapter. When you contact them, give all identifying information, such as your full name, Social Security number, current address, former address, and spouse's name (if applicable).

Ordinarily, a credit bureau will charge a small fee to give you your credit file information. To get a complete credit picture, ask all local credit bureaus if they maintain a file on you.

If you are married, you and your spouse probably have individual credit files. These files may contain identical or different information, depending on whether you and your spouse have shared or separate accounts. You and your spouse may find it helpful to review and compare your credit histories together.

Credit information on accounts opened before June 1, 1977, that are shared by a husband and wife often are reported only in the husband's name. However, creditors must report the credit history individually, in the name of each spouse, if you ask them to do so. Newer accounts should be reported on an individual basis automatically. If you find this is not the case, write to the creditor and request that the account be reported in both names. This will help both of you build a credit history. Married and formerly married women may encounter various credit-related problems. To address these common problems the Federal Trade Commission publishes a brochure entitled "Women and Credit Histories." To obtain this brochure, write to: Public Reference, Federal Trade Commission, Washington, DC 20580.

What a Credit Report Covers

Contrary to myth, a credit bureau neither tracks all aspects or your personal life nor evaluates credit applications. Credit bureaus are simply organizations that collect and transmit four principal types of information.

Identification and employment data: Your name, birth date, address, Social Security number, employer, and spouse's name are routinely noted. The bureau also may provide other information, such as your employment history, home ownership, income, and previous address, if a creditor requests it.

Payment history: Your account record with various creditors is listed, showing how much credit has been extended and how you have repaid it. Related events, such as referral of an overdue account to a collection agency, may be noted as well.

Inquiries: Credit bureaus are required to maintain a record of all creditors who have requested your credit history within the past six months. They normally include such creditor inquiries in your credit file for at least this long.

Public record information: Events that are a matter of public record and are related to your credit-worthiness, such as bankruptcies, foreclosures, or tax liens, may also appear in your report.

The information in your credit report is used to calculate a FICO credit score usually between 300 to 850. The higher your FICO score is, the better credit rating you would have, with scores above 700 generally representing good credit while scores below 600 indicate high-risk credit. A number of factors are evaluated in calculating your FICO score:

1) Your payment history represents about 35% of your FICO score.

2) How much you owe in relation to your available credit represents about 30% of your FICO score.

3) The length of your credit history (with longer credit histories being better) represents about 15% of your FICO score.

4) New credit that you opened accounts for about 10% of your FICO score.

5) Other factors such as the mix and types of credit represent about 10% of your FICO score.

You can obtain your FICO score from *www.myfico.com* or the major credit reporting agencies for a fee.

How to Correct Errors in Your Credit Report

Your credit file may contain errors that can affect your chances of obtaining credit in the future. Under the Fair Credit Reporting Act, you are entitled to have incomplete or inaccurate information corrected without charge.

If you dispute information in your report, the credit bureau must reinvestigate it within a "reasonable period of time," unless it believes the dispute is "frivolous or irrelevant." To check on the accuracy of a disputed item, the credit bureau will ask the creditor in question what its records show. If the disputed item is on the public record, the credit bureau will check there instead. If a disputed item cannot be verified, the credit bureau must delete it. If an item contains erroneous information, the credit bureau must correct the error. If the item is incomplete, the bureau must complete it. For example, if your file showed accounts that belong to another person, the credit bureau would have to delete them. If it showed that you were late in making payments but failed to show that you are no longer delinquent, the credit bureau would have to add information to show that your payments are now current. Also, at your request, the credit bureau must send a notice of the correction to any creditor who has checked your file in the past six months.

If the reinvestigation does not resolve your dispute, the Fair Credit Reporting Act permits you to file a statement of up to 100 words with the credit bureau explaining your side of the story. Employees of the credit bureau often are available to help you word your statement. The credit bureau must include this explanation in your report each time it sends it out.

Your credit file may not contain information on all of the accounts you have with creditors. Although most national department store and all-purpose bank credit card accounts will be included in your file, not all creditors supply information to credit bureaus. For example, some travel-and-entertainment and gasoline card companies, local retailers, and credit unions do not report to credit bureaus.

No one can legally do a credit check on you without your authorization. Moreover,

you want to avoid going from one creditor to another within a short period of time applying for credit. Each time that you complete a credit application, a credit report is usually run on you and reported to the credit bureau. Furthermore, sometimes credit checks are run on you without your knowledge, usually by places that offer instant credit, like used car lots and discount stores. If no credit account is opened as a result, then perspective creditors may view all the inquiries as rejections of your application for credit and feel uneasy in extending you credit. If you discover that there are unauthorized or numerous inquiries on your report, you should write a letter to the credit bureau and request that these inquiries be removed.

If you have been told that you were denied credit because of an "insufficient credit file" or "no credit file" and you have accounts with creditors that do not appear in your credit file, you can ask the credit bureau to add this information to future reports. Although they are not required to do so, for a fee many credit bureaus will add other accounts, if verifiable, to your credit file.

How Time Affects Your Credit Report
Under the Fair Credit Reporting Act, credit bureaus can report most negative information for no more than seven years. The seven-year period runs from the date of the last regularly scheduled payment that was made before the account became delinquent unless the creditor later took action on the account, such as charging it off or obtaining a judgment for the amount due. If a creditor took such an action, the seven years would run from the date of that event. For example, if a retailer turned over your past-due account to a collection agency in 1977, a credit bureau may report this event until 1984. You should be aware that if you made a payment after 1977 on this account, your action would not extend the permissible reporting period beyond 1984.

There are exceptions to the seven-year rule. Bankruptcies may be reported for ten years. Also, any negative credit-history information may be reported indefinitely in three circumstances:

- If you apply for $50,000 or more in credit;
- If you apply for a life insurance policy with a face amount of $50,000 or more;
- If you apply for a job paying $20,000 or more (and the employer requests a credit report in connection with the application).

You can contact the credit bureau if you believe negative information is being reported beyond the permitted period and ask that it be removed.

What You Can Do if You Have a Poor Credit History

Before creditors will give you credit, they look at how you have paid your bills in the past. Negative information in your credit file may lead creditors to deny you credit. Information that is considered negative includes late payments, repossessions, accounts turned over to a collection agency, charge-offs (accounts viewed as a "loss" by a creditor), judgments, liens, and bankruptcy.

A poor credit history that is accurate cannot be changed. There is nothing that you (or anyone else) can do to require a credit bureau to remove accurate information from your credit report until the reporting period has expired. However, this does not necessarily mean that you will be unable to obtain credit during the period. Because creditors set their own credit-granting standards, not all of them look at your credit history in the same way. Some creditors may look only at more recent years to evaluate you for credit, and they may grant you credit if your bill-paying history has improved. Before applying for credit, it may be useful to contact creditors informally to discuss their credit standards.

If you cannot obtain credit based on your own credit history, you may be able to do so if someone who has a good credit his-

tory cosigns a loan for you—this means the cosigner agrees to pay if you do not. Or you may be able to obtain a small loan or a credit card with a low dollar limit by using your savings account as collateral. If you pay promptly and your creditor reports to a credit bureau, this new information will improve your credit history picture.

How to Deal with Mounting Bills

A sudden illness or the loss of your job may make it impossible for you to pay your bills on time. Whatever your situation, if you find that you cannot make your payments, contact your creditors at once. Try to work out a modified payment plan with your creditors that reduces your payments to a more manageable level. If you have paid promptly in the past, they may be willing to work with you. Do not wait until your account is turned over to a debt collector. At that point, the creditor has given up on you. Most creditors do not want to spend time and money to collect delinquent accounts—all they want is their money! Therefore, in most cases, your creditors will be willing to work with you through your crisis. For example, you may want to offer your creditor interest payments on your debt and delay payments on your principal until your condition changes; also, check to see if your debt is covered by a payment protection plan or other insurance that would pay your debt. In some cases you may be able to get your creditor to accept a partial payment as satisfaction in full for your debt. In any event, you want to keep an open dialogue with your creditor keeping him abreast of your situation.

If you do work out a debt-repayment plan, ask your creditors to report your new, smaller payments to the credit bureau as timely. Otherwise, the credit bureau may report these payments as delinquent because you are paying less than the amount agreed to in your original credit agreement.

Automobile loans may present special problems. Most automobile financing agreements permit your creditor to repossess your car any time that you are in default on your payments. No advance notice is required. If your car is repossessed, you may have to pay the full balance due on the loan, as well as towing and storage costs, to get it back. If you cannot do this, the creditor may sell the car. Do not wait until you are in default. Try to solve the problem with your creditor when you realize you will not be able to meet your payments. It may be better to sell the car yourself and pay off your debt. This would avoid the added costs of repossession and a negative entry on your credit report.

Where to Find Low-Cost Help

If you cannot resolve your credit problems yourself or need additional assistance, you may want to contact the Consumer Credit Counseling Service (CCCS). This is a nonprofit organization with more than 200 offices located in forty-four states that counsels indebted consumers. CCCS counselors will try to arrange a repayment plan that is acceptable to you and your creditors. They also will help you set up a realistic budget and plan expenditures. These counseling offices, which are funded by contributions from credit-granting institutions, are offered at little or no cost to consumers. You can find the CCCS office nearest you by checking the white pages of your telephone directory or by sending a self-addressed stamped envelope to:

> National Foundation for
>   Consumer Credit
> 8611 Second Avenue, Suite 100
> Silver Spring, MD 20910
> (301) 589-5600

In addition, nonprofit counseling programs are sometimes operated by universities, military bases, credit unions, and housing authorities. They are likely to charge little or nothing for their assistance. Or, you can check with your local bank or consumer protection office to see if it has a listing of reputable, low-cost financial counseling services.

The Cost of Credit

If you are thinking of borrowing or opening a credit account, your first step should be to figure out how much it will cost you and whether you can afford it. Then you should shop around for the best terms.

Two laws help you compare costs:

- Truth in Lending requires creditors to give you certain basic information about the cost of buying on credit or taking out a loan. These "disclosures" can help you shop around for the best deal.
- Consumer Leasing disclosures can help you compare the cost and terms of one lease with another and with the cost and terms of buying for cash or on credit.

Credit costs vary. By remembering two terms, you can compare credit prices from different sources. Under Truth in Lending, the creditor must tell you (in writing and before you sign any agreement) the finance charge and the annual percentage rate.

The finance charge is the total dollar amount you pay to use credit. It includes interest costs, and other costs, such as service charges and some credit-related insurance premiums.

ADDRESSES OF THREE MAJOR CREDIT REPORTING AGENCIES

CRA NAME	ADDRESS/PHONE/E-MAIL
Transunion	P.O. Box 2000 Chester, PA 19022 1-800-916-8800 *www.transunion.com*
Experian	P.O. Box 9601 Allen, TX 75013 1-888-397-3742 *www.experian.com*
EQUIFAX	P.O. Box 740241 Atlanta, GA 30374 1-800-685-1111 (for credit reports) 1-888-766-0008 (for fraud) *www.equifax.com*

ADDITIONAL RESOURCES

For individuals with Internet access, there is an abundance of information on-line. For example, the full text of the Fair Credit Reporting Act can be found at: *www.eff.org/pub/Legislation/Newin/*

Another site of interest is: *www.consumer.com/consumer/CREDIT.html*

Form 28: Sample Letter to Correct Errors in Credit Report

To: _____

Name of Credit Report Agency

_____

Street Address

_____ _____ _____

City   State   Zip Code

From: _____   Social Security No.:

Name

_____   _____

Street Address

_____ _____ _____

City   State   Zip Code

Date: _____

Re: Correction of Errors in Credit Report

Dear Sir:

Please be advised that the following error(s) appear(s) in my credit report issued by your agency
on the date of _____.

(describe nature of error; be specific)

_____

_____

_____

Please correct my credit report as soon as possible to remove this incorrect information.
Contact me at the above address or by telephone at (telephone number and area code) if you have any
questions regarding this matter.

Sincerely,

(signature)

20 Copyrights to Your Writings and Artistic Works

Introducing You to Copyrights

Copyright is a right granted by federal law to the author or creator of literary or artistic works. It gives you as the author the sole privilege of reproducing and selling your work as well as the right to prevent others from copying or selling the work without your permission. This right covers works such as writings, paintings, photographs, sound recordings, motion pictures, music, and computer programs.

The Federal Copyright Act preempts copyright protection under state law for those works that are subject to federal copyright protection. This means that federal copyright protection is the only copyright protection available for these works.

The materials that follow will discuss the general law of copyright and the procedure for copyright registration for:

- a work of the performing arts,

- a nondramatic literary work,

- a work of the visual arts, and

- a sound recording.

The fee for applying for copyright registration at the time of this printing is $45. Typical legal fees for copyright registration range from about $100 to $500.

Scope of Copyright Protection

A copyright gives you the sole right to control the reproduction and distribution of your copyrighted work. You have the right to prevent others from reproducing the work without your permission.

Copyright does not prevent others from using the ideas or information revealed by your work. Copyright protects only the literary, musical, artistic, or graphic form in which you express your work. Anyone is free to use your concepts and may create his or her own expression of the same concepts as long as he or she does not copy your form of expression.

Under the Copyright Act, the owner of a copyright has the exclusive rights to do and to authorize any of the following:

- to reproduce the copyrighted work in copies or phonorecords;

- to prepare derivative works based upon the copyrighted work (examples of derivative works are translations, musical arrangements, dramatizations, motion picture versions, sound recording, abridgments, condensations, or any other forms in which a work may be recast, transformed, or adapted);

- to distribute copies or phonorecords of the copyrighted work to the public by sale or other transfer of ownership, or by rental, lease, or lending;

- to perform the copyrighted work publicly;

- to display the copyrighted work publicly.

Anyone who violates any of the exclusive rights of the copyright owner is an infringer of the copyright. The copyright owner may recover from the infringer statutory damages (which are an amount awarded in the discretion of the court) or actual damages plus any profits of the infringer. The copyright owner may also recover court costs and attorney's fees from the infringer if allowed by the court. The copyright owner may also obtain an injunction to prevent and restrain infringement of his or her copyright. Registration of the copyrighted work prior to the infringement is necessary to be eligible for statutory damages, court costs, and attorneys' fees. Copyright registration must also be obtained before any copyright infringement action can be brought. Copyright infringement actions must be brought within three years after the infringement takes place or should have been discovered.

Fair use of copyrighted works does not amount to copyright infringement. Fair use for purposes such as criticism, comment, news reporting, teaching (including multiple copies for classroom use), scholarship, or research is not an infringement of copyright.

Libraries may reproduce one copy of the copyrighted work if it is made without commercial advantage, the library is open to the public, and the reproduction includes a notice of copyright. This use by the libraries is not an infringement of copyright.

Copyright does not protect any idea, procedure, process, system, method of operation, concept, principle, or discovery. Copyright protects only the form of expression.

Generally, for works created after January 1, 1978, the duration of the copyright will be the life of the author plus 70 years after the author's death.

Works Protectable by Copyright

The Copyright Act permits copyright protection for original works of authorship. Seven types of works are listed that may be protected by copyright. These works include the following:

- literary works;

- musical works, including any accompanying words;

- dramatic works, including any accompanying music;

- pantomimes and choreographic works;

- pictoral, graphic, and sculptural works;

- motion pictures and other audiovisual works;

- sound recordings.

Other works not listed above may also be protected by copyright if they meet the definition of "original works of authorship."

Literary works are works, other than audiovisual works, that are expressed in words, numbers, or other verbal or numerical symbols, such as books, magazines, manuscripts, directories, catalogs, cards, and computer programs.

Musical works would include written musical arrangements, lyrics, and songs.

Dramatic works would include written plays and any written music that is a part thereof.

Pantomimes and choreographic works include physical expressions and dance.

Pictoral, graphic, and sculptural works include two and three-dimensional works of art, photographs, paintings, sketches, prints, maps, globes, charts, designs, technical drawings, diagrams, and models.

Motion picture and audiovisual works include films, movies, and video recordings.

Sound recordings are works that result from fixation of a series of musical, spoken, or other sounds, such as discs, tapes, and phonorecords, but do not include the sounds accompanying a motion picture or other audiovisual work.

Copyright protection is only available for original works of authorship. The originality requirement means that the work must be the independent creation of the person seeking copyright protection. The test for originality is met if the work owes its origin to the author and is independently created and not copied from other works. The mere fact that someone else has created something similar will not prevent you from obtaining copyright protection on your independent creation.

Copyright protection does not extend to names, titles, and slogans. These can be appropriately protected by trademark.

To qualify for federal copyright protection, the works of authorship must be fixed in a tangible form. This means that the work must be in a physical form such that it can be reproduced or otherwise communicated. Thus a mere idea or other abstract and imaginary creations cannot be copyrighted.

A work is given copyright when it is fixed in a copy or phonorecord for the first time. Publication is the distribution of copies or phonorecords of a work to the public by sale, rental, lease, or lending.

Copyright Notice
The copyright law requires a specific notice to enable the owner to obtain the strongest copyright protection for published works. If you plan to publish or publicly distribute your work, you can place a copyright notice on all such copies. Use of the copyright notice does not require the permission of the Copyright Office. The copyright notice may be used even if the work has not been registered with the U.S. Copyright Office. However, keep in mind that definitely since March 1989 and in some cases from 1978 to 1989 you will not lose your copyright if you fail to put copyright notice on your work. The benefit of a copyright notice is

that infringers cannot ask the court to lessen damages because they were unaware of your copyright.

The copyright notice consists of three parts: (1) the symbol "©" or the word "copyright" or the abbreviation "copr."; (2) the year of first publication; and (3) the name of the copyright owner. For example, the proper notice could follow these forms:

Copyright 1996 Carl W. Battle
© Carl W. Battle 1996
Copr. 1996 C. W. Battle

The notice should be affixed to the copies in such a manner and location as to give reasonable notice of the claim of copyright.

For phonograph records the notice can consist of (1) the symbol ℗; (2) the year of first publication; and (3) the name of the copyright owner.

Registering Your Copyright
You can register your copyright by filing an application with the U.S. Copyright Office. This involves filing the appropriate application form along with the required fee and deposit of your work. Detailed instructions for completing the copyright application are given at the end of this chapter along with a copy of Form TX (which is used for registering non-dramatic literary works). The instructions are also useful for Forms PA, SR, and VA, which are applicable for works of performing art, sound recording, and visual arts, respectively.

Use of Form PA for Work of the Performing Arts: Form PA is used for copyright registration covering works of the performing arts. This category includes works prepared for the purpose of being performed directly or indirectly before an audience.

Examples of works of the performing arts are:
- musical works, including any accompanying words;
- dramatic works, including any accompanying music;

- pantomimes and choreographic works;
- motion pictures and other audiovisual works.

Along with the application for copyright registration, submit two complete copies of the published work. Submit one complete copy if the work is unpublished. Be sure to sign the application form.

Use of Form SR for Sound Recording: Form SR is used for copyright registration covering a sound recording. This form should be used when the copyright claim is limited to the sound recording itself. Sound recordings are works that result from the creation of a series of musical, spoken, or other sounds. Sound recordings do not include the sounds that accompany a motion picture or other audiovisual work.

Along with the application for copyright registration, submit two complete phonorecords or recordings of the published work along with any printed material. Submit one phonorecord or recording if the work is unpublished. Be sure to sign the application form.

Use of Form TX for Nondramatic Literary Work: Form TX is used for copyright registration covering nondramatic literary works. A sample Form TX is provided at the end of this chapter. This category includes all types of works written in words or other symbols, except dramatic works and audiovisual works. Examples of nondramatic literary works are books, poetry, magazines, directories, catalogs, advertising copy, and compilations of information.

Along with the application for copyright registration, submit two complete copies of the published work. Submit one complete copy if the work is unpublished. Be sure to sign the application form.

Use of Form VA for Work of the Visual Arts: Form VA is used for copyright registration covering works of the visual arts. This category includes pictoral, graphic, and sculptural works such as

paintings, photographs, prints, art reproductions, maps, charts, diagrams, technical drawings, labels, and advertisements.

Along with the application for copyright registration, submit two complete copies of the published work. Submit one copy if the work is unpublished. If the work is unique or a limited edition, you can submit photos, photocopies, or other identifying materials instead of an original copy. Be sure to sign the application form.

Checklist for Registering a Copyright

❑ Fill out appropriate application form. (Use a typewriter or print in dark ink.)

❑ Use one of the following forms:

- Form PA—Works of the Performing Arts
- Form SR—Sound Recordings
- Form TX—Nondramatic Literary Work
- Form VA—Work of the Visual Arts

❑ Sign the form in the space provided for certification.

❑ Enclose with the application a check or money order for the $45 application fee payable to: Register of Copyrights.

❑ Mail completed application and the necessary copies of the work to:

Register of Copyrights
Library of Congress
101 Independence Ave., SE
Washington, DC 20559-6000

❑ Consult an attorney if your copyright involves difficult or complex issues.

Form 29:

 # Form TX

Detach and read these instructions before completing this form.
Make sure all applicable spaces have been filled in before you return this form.

When to Use This Form: Use Form TX for registration of published or unpublished nondramatic literary works, excluding periodicals or serial issues. This class includes a wide variety of works: fiction, nonfiction, poetry, textbooks, reference works, directories, catalogs, advertising copy, compilations of information, and computer programs. For periodicals and serials, use Form SE.

Deposit to Accompany Application: An application for copyright registration must be accompanied by a deposit consisting of copies or phonorecords representing the entire work for which registration is to be made. The following are the general deposit requirements as set forth in the statute:

Unpublished Work: Deposit one complete copy (or phonorecord)

Published Work: Deposit two complete copies (or one phonorecord) of the best edition.

Work First Published Outside the United States: Deposit one complete copy (or phonorecord) of the first foreign edition.

Contribution to a Collective Work: Deposit one complete copy (or phonorecord) of the best edition of the collective work.

The Copyright Notice: Before March 1, 1989, the use of copyright notice was mandatory on all published works, and any work first published before that date should have carried a notice. For works first published on and after March 1, 1989, use of the copyright notice is optional. For more information about copyright notice, see Circular 3, *Copyright Notices.*

For Further Information: To speak to a Copyright Office staff member, call (202) 707-3000 (TTY: (202) 707-6737). Recorded information is available 24 hours a day. Order forms and other publications from the address in space 9 or call the Forms and Publications Hotline at (202) 707-9100. Access and download circulars, forms, and other information from the Copyright Office website at *www.copyright.gov.*

Please type or print using black ink. The form is used to produce the certificate.

1 SPACE 1: Title

Title of This Work: Every work submitted for copyright registration must be given a title to identify that particular work. If the copies or phonorecords of the work bear a title or an identifying phrase that could serve as a title, transcribe that wording *completely* and *exactly* on the application. Indexing of the registration and future identification of the work will depend on the information you give here.

Previous or Alternative Titles: Complete this space if there are any additional titles for the work under which someone searching for the registration might be likely to look or under which a document pertaining to the work might be recorded.

Publication as a Contribution: If the work being registered is a contribution to a periodical, serial, or collection, give the title of the contribution in the "Title of This Work" space. Then, in the line headed "Publication as a Contribution," give information about the collective work in which the contribution appeared.

2 SPACE 2: Author(s)

General Instructions: After reading these instructions, decide who are the "authors" of this work for copyright purposes. Then, unless the work is a "collective work," give the requested information about every "author" who contributed any appreciable amount of copyrightable matter to this version of the work. If you need further space, request Continuation Sheets. In the case of a collective work, such as an anthology, collection of essays, or encyclopedia, give information about the author of the collective work as a whole.

Name of Author: The fullest form of the author's name should be given. Unless the work was "made for hire," the individual who actually created the work is its "author." In the case of a work made for hire, the statute provides that "the employer or other person for whom the work was prepared is considered the author."

What Is a "Work Made for Hire"? A "work made for hire" is defined as (1) "a work prepared by an employee within the scope of his or her employment"; or (2) "a work specially ordered or commissioned for use as a contribution to a collective work, as a part of a motion picture or other audiovisual work, as a translation, as a supplementary work, as a compilation, as an instructional text, as a test, as answer material for a test, or as an atlas, if the parties expressly agree in a written instrument signed by them that the works shall be considered a work made for hire." If you have checked "Yes" to indicate that the work was "made for hire," you must give the full legal name of the employer (or other person for whom the work was prepared). You may also include the name of the employee along with the name of the employer (for example: "Elster Publishing Co., employer for hire of John Ferguson").

"Anonymous" or "Pseudonymous" Work: An author's contribution to a work is "anonymous" if that author is not identified on the copies or phonorecords of the work. An author's contribution to a work is "pseudonymous" if that author is identified on the copies or phonorecords under a fictitious name. If the work is "anonymous" you may: (1) leave the line blank; or (2) state "anonymous" on the line; or (3) reveal the author's identity. If the work is "pseudonymous" you may: (1) leave the line blank; or (2) give the pseudonym and identify it as such (for example: "Huntley Haverstock, pseudonym"); or (3) reveal the author's name, making clear which is the real name and which is the pseudonym (for example, "Judith Barton, whose pseudonym is Madeline Elster"). However, the citizenship or domicile of the author *must* be given in all cases.

Dates of Birth and Death: If the author is dead, the statute requires that the year of death be included in the application unless the work is anonymous or pseudonymous. The author's birth date is optional but is useful as a form of identification. Leave this space blank if the author's contribution was a "work made for hire."

Author's Nationality or Domicile: Give the country of which the author is a citizen or the country in which the author is domiciled. Nationality or domicile *must* be given in all cases.

Nature of Authorship: After the words "Nature of Authorship," give a brief general statement of the nature of this particular author's contribution to the work. Examples: "Entire text"; "Coauthor of entire text"; "Computer program"; "Editorial revisions"; "Compilation and English translation"; "New text."

SPACE 3: Creation and Publication

General Instructions: Do not confuse "creation" with "publication." Every application for copyright registration must state "the year in which creation of the work was completed." Give the date and nation of first publication only if the work has been published.

Creation: Under the statute, a work is "created" when it is fixed in a copy or phonorecord for the first time. Where a work has been prepared over a period of time, the part of the work existing in fixed form on a particular date constitutes the created work on that date. The date you give here should be the year in which the author completed the particular version for which registration is now being sought, even if other versions exist or if further changes or additions are planned.

Publication: The statute defines "publication" as "the distribution of copies or phonorecords of a work to the public by sale or other transfer of ownership, or by rental, lease, or lending." A work is also "published" if there has been an "offering to distribute copies or phonorecords to a group of persons for purposes of further distribution, public performance, or public display." Give the full date (month, day, year) when, and the country where, publication first occurred. If first publication took place simultaneously in the United States and other countries, it is sufficient to state "U.S.A."

SPACE 4: Claimant(s)

Name(s) and Address(es) of Copyright Claimant(s): Give the name(s) and address(es) of the copyright claimant(s) in this work even if the claimant is the same as the author. Copyright in a work belongs initially to the author of the work (including, in the case of a work made for hire, the employer or other person for whom the work was prepared). The copyright claimant is either the author of the work or a person or organization to whom the copyright initially belonging to the author has been transferred.

Transfer: The statute provides that, if the copyright claimant is not the author, the application for registration must contain "a brief statement of how the claimant obtained ownership of the copyright." If any copyright claimant named in space 4 is not an author named in space 2, give a brief statement explaining how the claimant(s) obtained ownership of the copyright. Examples: "By written contract"; "Transfer of all rights by author"; "Assignment"; "By will." Do not attach transfer documents or other attachments or riders.

SPACE 5: Previous Registration

General Instructions: The questions in space 5 are intended to show whether an earlier registration has been made for this work and, if so, whether there is any basis for a new registration. As a general rule, only one basic copyright registration can be made for the same version of a particular work.

Same Version: If this version is substantially the same as the work covered by a previous registration, a second registration is not generally possible unless: (1) the work has been registered in unpublished form and a second registration is now being sought to cover this first published edition; or (2) someone other than the author is identified as copyright claimant in the earlier registration, and the author is now seeking registration in his or her own name. If either of these two exceptions applies, check the appropriate box and give the earlier registration number and date. Otherwise, do not submit Form TX. Instead, write the Copyright Office for information about supplementary registration or recordation of transfers of copyright ownership.

Changed Version: If the work has been changed and you are now seeking registration to cover the additions or revisions, check the last box in space 5, give the earlier registration number and date, and complete both parts of space 6 in accordance with the instructions below.

Previous Registration Number and Date: If more than one previous registration has been made for the work, give the number and date of the latest registration.

SPACE 6: Derivative Work or Compilation

General Instructions: Complete space 6 if this work is a "changed version," "compilation," or "derivative work" and if it incorporates one or more earlier works that have already been published or registered for copyright or that have fallen into the public domain. A "compilation" is defined as "a work formed by the collection and assembling of preexisting materials or of data that are selected, coordinated, or arranged in such a way that the resulting work as a whole constitutes an original work of authorship." A "derivative work" is "a work based on one or more preexisting works." Examples of derivative works include translations, fictionalizations, abridgments, condensations, or "any other form in which a work may be recast, transformed, or adapted." Derivative works also include works "consisting of editorial revisions, annotations, or other modifications" if these changes, as a whole, represent an original work of authorship.

Preexisting Material (space 6a): For derivative works, complete this space *and* space 6b. In space 6a identify the preexisting work that has been recast, transformed, or adapted. The preexisting work may be material that has been previously published, previously registered, or that is in the public domain. An example of preexisting material might be: "Russian version of Goncharov's 'Oblomov.'"

Material Added to This Work (space 6b): Give a brief, general statement of the new material covered by the copyright claim for which registration is sought. *Derivative work* examples include: "Foreword, editing, critical annotations"; "Translation"; "Chapters 11–17." If the work is a *compilation*, describe both the compilation itself and the material that has been compiled. Example: "Compilation of certain 1917 speeches by Woodrow Wilson." A work may be both a derivative work and compilation, in which case a sample statement might be: "Compilation and additional new material."

SPACE 7, 8, 9: Fee, Correspondence, Certification, Return Address

Deposit Account: If you maintain a Deposit Account in the Copyright Office, identify it in space 7a. Otherwise leave the space blank and send the fee with your application and deposit.

Correspondence (space 7b): Give the name, address, area code, telephone number, fax number, and email address (if available) of the person to be consulted if correspondence about this application becomes necessary.

Certification (space 8): The application cannot be accepted unless it bears the date and the *handwritten signature* of the author or other copyright claimant, or of the owner of exclusive right(s), or of the duly authorized agent of author, claimant, or owner of exclusive right(s).

Address for Return of Certificate (space 9): The address box must be completed legibly since the certificate will be returned in a window envelope.

Form TX
For a Nondramatic Literary Work
UNITED STATES COPYRIGHT OFFICE

REGISTRATION NUMBER

TX   TXU

EFFECTIVE DATE OF REGISTRATION

Month   Day   Year

DO NOT WRITE ABOVE THIS LINE. IF YOU NEED MORE SPACE, USE A SEPARATE CONTINUATION SHEET.

1

TITLE OF THIS WORK ▼

PREVIOUS OR ALTERNATIVE TITLES ▼

PUBLICATION AS A CONTRIBUTION If this work was published as a contribution to a periodical, serial, or collection, give information about the collective work in which the contribution appeared.   **Title of Collective Work ▼**

If published in a periodical or serial give: Volume ▼   Number ▼   Issue Date ▼   On Pages ▼

2

a

NAME OF AUTHOR ▼

DATES OF BIRTH AND DEATH
Year Born ▼   Year Died ▼

Was this contribution to the work a "work made for hire"?
☐ Yes
☐ No

AUTHOR'S NATIONALITY OR DOMICILE
Name of Country
OR { Citizen of ▶_____
Domiciled in▶_____

WAS THIS AUTHOR'S CONTRIBUTION TO THE WORK
Anonymous?   ☐ Yes ☐ No
Pseudonymous?   ☐ Yes ☐ No

If the answer to either of these questions is "Yes," see detailed instructions.

NATURE OF AUTHORSHIP Briefly describe nature of material created by this author in which copyright is claimed. ▼

NOTE

Under the law, the "author" of a "work made for hire" is generally the employer, not the employee (see instructions). For any part of this work that was "made for hire" check "Yes" in the space provided, give the employer (or other person for whom the work was prepared) as "Author" of that part, and leave the space for dates of birth and death blank.

b

NAME OF AUTHOR ▼

DATES OF BIRTH AND DEATH
Year Born ▼   Year Died ▼

Was this contribution to the work a "work made for hire"?
☐ Yes
☐ No

AUTHOR'S NATIONALITY OR DOMICILE
Name of Country
OR { Citizen of ▶_____
Domiciled in▶_____

WAS THIS AUTHOR'S CONTRIBUTION TO THE WORK
Anonymous?   ☐ Yes ☐ No
Pseudonymous?   ☐ Yes ☐ No

If the answer to either of these questions is "Yes," see detailed instructions.

NATURE OF AUTHORSHIP Briefly describe nature of material created by this author in which copyright is claimed. ▼

c

NAME OF AUTHOR ▼

DATES OF BIRTH AND DEATH
Year Born ▼   Year Died ▼

Was this contribution to the work a "work made for hire"?
☐ Yes
☐ No

AUTHOR'S NATIONALITY OR DOMICILE
Name of Country
OR { Citizen of ▶_____
Domiciled in▶_____

WAS THIS AUTHOR'S CONTRIBUTION TO THE WORK
Anonymous?   ☐ Yes ☐ No
Pseudonymous?   ☐ Yes ☐ No

If the answer to either of these questions is "Yes," see detailed instructions.

NATURE OF AUTHORSHIP Briefly describe nature of material created by this author in which copyright is claimed. ▼

3

a

YEAR IN WHICH CREATION OF THIS WORK WAS COMPLETED
This information must be given
◀ Year in all cases.

b

DATE AND NATION OF FIRST PUBLICATION OF THIS PARTICULAR WORK
Complete this information ONLY if this work has been published.
Month ▶_____ Day ▶_____ Year ▶_____
◀ Nation

4

See instructions before completing this space.

COPYRIGHT CLAIMANT(S) Name and address must be given even if the claimant is the same as the author given in space 2. ▼

TRANSFER If the claimant(s) named here in space 4 is (are) different from the author(s) named in space 2, give a brief statement of how the claimant(s) obtained ownership of the copyright. ▼

**DO NOT WRITE HERE
OFFICE USE ONLY**

APPLICATION RECEIVED

ONE DEPOSIT RECEIVED

TWO DEPOSITS RECEIVED

FUNDS RECEIVED

MORE ON BACK ▶ • Complete all applicable spaces (numbers 5-9) on the reverse side of this page.
• See detailed instructions.   • Sign the form at line 8.

DO NOT WRITE HERE

Page 1 of _____ pages

EXAMINED BY

CHECKED BY

☐ CORRESPONDENCE
Yes

FOR
COPYRIGHT
OFFICE
USE
ONLY

DO NOT WRITE ABOVE THIS LINE. IF YOU NEED MORE SPACE, USE A SEPARATE CONTINUATION SHEET.

PREVIOUS REGISTRATION Has registration for this work, or for an earlier version of this work, already been made in the Copyright Office?

☐ Yes   ☐ No   If your answer is "Yes," why is another registration being sought? (Check appropriate box.) ▼

a. ☐ This is the first published edition of a work previously registered in unpublished form.

b. ☐ This is the first application submitted by this author as copyright claimant.

c. ☐ This is a changed version of the work, as shown by space 6 on this application.

If your answer is "Yes," give: **Previous Registration Number** ▶   **Year of Registration** ▶

5

DERIVATIVE WORK OR COMPILATION
Preexisting Material Identify any preexisting work or works that this work is based on or incorporates. ▼

a

6

Material Added to This Work Give a brief, general statement of the material that has been added to this work and in which copyright is claimed. ▼

b

See instructions
before completing
this space.

DEPOSIT ACCOUNT If the registration fee is to be charged to a Deposit Account established in the Copyright Office, give name and number of Account.
Name ▼   **Account Number** ▼

a

7

CORRESPONDENCE Give name and address to which correspondence about this application should be sent.   Name/Address/Apt/City/State/Zip ▼

b

Area code and daytime telephone number ▶   Fax number ▶

Email ▶

CERTIFICATION* I, the undersigned, hereby certify that I am the

Check only one ▶ {
☐ author
☐ other copyright claimant
☐ owner of exclusive right(s)
☐ authorized agent of _____

of the work identified in this application and that the statements made
by me in this application are correct to the best of my knowledge.

Name of author or other copyright claimant, or owner of exclusive right(s) ▲

8

Typed or printed name and date ▼ If this application gives a date of publication in space 3, do not sign and submit it before that date.

_____ Date ▶ _____

Handwritten signature (X) ▼

X _____

Certificate
will be
mailed in
window
envelope
to this
address:

Name ▼

Number/Street/Apt ▼

City/State/ZIP ▼

YOU MUST:
· Complete all necessary spaces
· Sign your application in space 8

**SEND ALL 3 ELEMENTS
IN THE SAME PACKAGE:**
1. Application form
2. Nonrefundable filing fee in check or money
order payable to *Register of Copyrights*
3. Deposit material

MAIL TO:
Library of Congress
Copyright Office
101 Independence Avenue SE
Washington, DC 20559-6222

9

*17 USC § 506(e): Any person who knowingly makes a false representation of a material fact in the application for copyright registration provided for by section 409, or in any written statement filed in connection with the application, shall be fined not more than $2,500.

Form TX – Full   Rev: 07/2006   Print: 07/2006 – 30,000   Printed on recycled paper   U.S. Government Printing Office: 2004-320-958/60,122

21 *Registering Your Trademarks*

The Function of Trademarks

The main function of a trademark is to indicate the origin or source of goods or services. A trademark is any word, name, symbol, device, or any combination thereof adopted and used by a manufacturer or merchant to identify his goods and to distinguish them from those manufactured or sold by others. A trademark may also function to symbolize or guarantee the quality of goods which bear the trademark. Rights in a trademark are acquired only by use of the trademark on particular goods. This right to use a trademark is a property interest that the trademark owner can assert to prevent others from using the mark or one which is confusingly similar.

Trademark rights are governed by both federal and state laws. This text will review only those rights granted by federal law and the means of acquiring such federal rights.

Federal registration of a trademark is not mandatory, but this registration does provide some major benefits to the trademark owner. To be eligible for federal registration, a trademark must actually be used in commerce, or the owner must have a bona fide intent to use the trademark in commerce. The intent to use a trademark can be extended for periods of six months up to a maximum of two years and is a good way for reserving a trademark with the U.S. Patent and Trademark Office. A trademark is deemed to be used in commerce when it is placed in any manner on goods or their containers or on tags or labels affixed thereto and the goods are sold or transported in interstate commerce.

Federal registration of a trademark protects the exclusive right of the trademark owner to use the trademark nationwide. Federal registration gives the trademark owner the right to use the registration symbol ®, which may deter others from using the trademark. If the trademark has not been registered, you should use the symbol TM to protect your trademark rights under state law. Federal law also gives the trademark owner the right to sue unauthorized users of the trademark for an injunction, damages, or recovery of profits.

What Trademarks Can Be Registered

Federal law provides for the registration of trademarks on two types of registers, designated as the Principal Register and the Supplemental Register. Trademarks that are created, arbitrary, or fanciful may (if otherwise qualified) be registered on the Principal Register. A trademark that does not qualify for registration on the Principal Register may be registered on the Supplemental Register if it is capable of distinguishing applicant's goods and normally has been used in commerce for at least one year.

If all other requirements are satisfied, a trademark may be registered on the Principal Register unless it consists of a mark which: (1) when applied to the goods or services of the applicant is merely descriptive or deceptively misdescriptive of them; or (2) when applied to the goods or services of the applicant is primarily geographically descriptive or deceptively misdescriptive; or (3) is primarily a surname. As an exception to the general rules, marks may be registered on the Principal Register if they have become distinctive as applied to the applicant's goods in commerce. This usually requires proof of exclusive and continuous use of the mark by the applicant in commerce for the prior five years.

A trademark cannot be registered on either the Principal Register or the Supplemental Register if it:

(a) Consists of or comprises immoral, deceptive, or scandalous matter;

(b) Consists of or comprises the flag or coat of arms or other insignia of any country or state;

(c) Consists of or comprises a name, portrait, or signature identifying a particular living individual, except by his or her written consent; or

(d) Consists of or comprises a mark which so resembles a mark registered in the Patent and Trademark Office, or a mark or trade name previously used in the United States by another and not abandoned, as to be likely when applied to the goods of another person to cause confusion or to cause mistake or to deceive.

Filing a Trademark Application

The owner of a trademark used or intended to be used in commerce may register the trademark by filing an application for registration in the U.S. Patent and Trademark Office. The application must be filed in the name of the trademark owner and comprises **1)** a written application (a sample Trademark/Service Mark Application form is provided at the end of this chapter); **2)** a drawing of the mark; **3)** three specimens or facsimiles of the mark; and **4)** the filing fee (for a paper filing $375.00 and for an electronic filing $325.00 for registration in each class at the time of this printing).

The application must be in the English language and must specify: the name, citizenship, domicile, and post office address of the applicant.

The application must indicate that the applicant has adopted and is actually using the mark shown in the drawing which accompanies the application, or that the applicant has a bona fide intention to use the mark in interstate commerce. It must specify the particular goods on or in connection with which the mark is used or is intended to be used and the class, according to the official classification, in which the goods or services fall, if known to the applicant (an International Classification list is provided later in this chapter). Also include the date of applicant's first use of the mark and the date of the applicant's first use of the mark in interstate commerce, if any; and the mode or manner in which the mark is or will be used.

The application must be signed and verified (sworn to) or include a declaration by the applicant or by a member of the firm or an officer of the corporation or association that is applying for registration of the trademark. The application for registration of a trademark may be made by the owner or by an attorney or other person authorized to practice before the Trademark Office.

The drawing must be a substantially exact representation of the mark as actually used or to be used in connection with the goods or services. The drawing of a mark may be dispensed with if the mark is not capable of representation by a drawing, but in such case the written application must contain an adequate description of the mark. If the application is for registration of only a word, letter, or numeral, or any combination thereof, not depicted in special form, the drawing may be the mark typed in capital letters on paper.

The drawing must be made upon pure white durable paper that has a smooth surface. The size of the sheet on which a drawing is made must be 8 to 8½ inches wide and 11 inches long. The size of the mark must be such as to leave a margin of at least 1 inch on the sides and bottom of the paper and at least 1 inch between it and the heading. The drawing can not be more than 4 inches high and 4 inches wide. Across the top of the drawing, beginning one inch from the top edge and not exceeding one third of the sheet, there must be a heading and, listed on separate lines, applicant's complete name, applicant's address, the dates of first use of the mark and first use of the mark in interstate commerce (if applicable), and the goods or services for which the mark is used.

A trademark may be placed in any manner on the goods, their containers or displays, or on tags or labels attached to the goods. The three specimens shall be duplicates of the actually used labels, tags, containers, or displays and shall be capable of being arranged flat and be of a size not larger than 8 1/2 by 11 inches. When, due to the manner of affixing or using the mark, specimens as stated above cannot be furnished, three copies of a suitable photograph or other acceptable reproduction within the above size requirements can be furnished.

It is recommended that a trademark search be carried out before a mark is used or an application for registration is filed. The Trademark Register of the United States, published yearly by Patent Searching Service, National Press Building, Suite 1297, Washington, DC 20045, provides a list of active registered U.S. trademarks.

If you are the owner of a trademark, you can file the trademark application yourself with the U.S. Patent and Trademark Office, Washington, DC 20231. Consult an attorney if your trademark registration involves complex or difficult issues. Typical attorneys' fees for filing a trademark registration range from about $300 to $1,000.

After your application has been examined, the U.S. Patent and Trademark Office will allow your registration if all requirements have been met and your mark is not confusingly similar to other marks. If your application has indicated a bona fide intent to use the mark, you must normally file a statement of actual use (along with dates of actual use, three specimens, and the required fee) within six months after receiving a notice of allowance from the Patent and Trademark Office. After allowance, the mark is published for opposition and, if no opposition is filed, the mark is registered. Additional information on trademarks can be obtained from the U.S. Patent and Trademark Office Web site at: *www.uspto.gov*.

After registering your trademark, you will have to file a statement of use after 5 years and a renewal every 10 years to maintain the registration.

International Classification of Goods and Services

The following is a list of the classes of goods and services which you should designate in the application for registration of a trademark:

Goods

Class 1. Chemical products
Class 2. Paints, coatings, preservatives, and dyestuffs
Class 3. Substances for laundry use, cleaning, polishing, and scouring; soaps and cosmetics
Class 4. Industrial oils, lubricants, fuels, and candles
Class 5. Pharmaceutical, veterinary, and sanitary substances; infants' foods; disinfectants; fungicides and herbicides
Class 6. Common metals and their alloys; cables and wires (nonelectric); metallic pipes and tubes; nails and screws
Class 7. Machines and machine tools
Class 8. Hand tools and instruments; cutlery, forks, and spoons; side arms; razors
Class 9. Scientific, nautical, photographic, surveying, and electrical apparatus and instruments
Class 10. Surgical, medical, dental, and veterinary instruments and apparatus

Class 11. Apparatus for lighting, heating, refrigerating, drying, ventilating, water supply, and sanitary purposes

Class 12. Vehicles; apparatus for locomotion by land, air, or water

Class 13. Firearms; ammunition and projectiles; explosive substances; fireworks

Class 14. Precious metals, jewelry, precious stones, chronometric instruments.

Class 15. Musical instruments (other than talking machines and wireless apparatus)

Class 16. Paper, cardboard, articles of paper or cardboard, printed matter, photographs, typewriters, and office requisites

Class 17. Rubber, plastics; materials for packing, stopping, or insulating; hose and pipes (nonmetallic)

Class 18. Leather articles, skins, hides, traveling bags, and umbrellas

Class 19. Building materials, stone, cement, lime, mortar, plaster, and gravel

Class 20. Furniture, mirrors, picture frames, and articles

Class 21. Small domestic utensils and containers of non-precious metals, glassware

Class 22. Ropes, nets, tents, sails, sacks; padding and stuffing materials; raw fibrous textile materials

Class 23. Yarns, threads

Class 24. Tissues; bed and table covers; textile articles other classes

Class 25. Clothing, including boots, shoes, slippers, and headgear

Class 26. Lace and embroidery, ribbons, buttons, pins, and needles; artificial flowers

Class 27. Carpets, rugs, mats, and matting; linoleums and other materials for covering existing floors; wall hangings (nontextile)

Class 28. Games and playthings; gymnastic and sporting articles (except clothing); ornaments and decorations for Christmas trees

Class 29. Meats, dried and cooked fruits and vegetables, dairy products, edible oils, and salad dressings

Class 30. Coffee, tea, cocoa, sugar, rice, flour, cereals, bread, confectionery, and spices

Class 31. Agricultural, horticultural, and forestry products

Class 32. Beer, ale, and mineral waters and other nonalcoholic drinks

Class 33. Wines, spirits, and liqueurs, alcoholic beverages (excluding beers)

Class 34. Tobacco, smokers' articles; matches

Services

Class 35. Advertising and business

Class 36. Insurance and financial

Class 37. Construction and repair

Class 38. Communication

Class 39. Transportation and storage

Class 40. Material treatment

Class 41. Education and entertainment

Class 42. Miscellaneous (includes services which do not fit in other classes)

Form 30: Trademark/Service Mark Application, Principal Register, with Declaration

Mark (Identify the mark) _____   Class No. (If known) _____

To the Assistant Secretary and Commissioner of Patents and Trademarks:

Applicant Name:

Applicant Address:

Applicant Entity: (Check one and supply requested information)

❏ Individual—Citizenship (Country): _____

❏ Partnership—Partnership Domicile (State and Country): _____

  Names and Citizenship (Country) of General Partners: _____

  _____

❏ Corporation—State (Country, if appropriate) of Incorporation: _____

❏ Other (Specify Nature of Entity and Domicile): _____

Goods and/or Services:

  Applicant requests registration of the above-identified trademark/service mark shown in the accompanying drawing in the United States Patent and Trademark Office on the Principal Register established by the Act of July 5, 1946. (15 U.S.C. 1051 et. seq., as amended.) for the following goods/services:_____

  _____

Basis for Application: (Check one or more, but not both the first and second boxes, and supply requested information)

❏ Applicant is using the mark in commerce on or in connection with the above identified goods/services. (15 U.S.C. 105(a), as amended.) Three specimens showing the mark as used in commerce are submitted with this application.

• Date of first use of the mark anywhere _____

• Date of first use of the mark in commerce which the U.S. Congress may regulate:_____

• Specify the type of commerce _____
      (e.g., interstate, between the U.S. and a specified foreign country)

• Specify manner or mode of use of mark on or in connection with the goods/services _____

      (e.g., trademark is applied to labels, service mark is used in advertisements)

❏ Applicant has a bona fide intention to use the mark in commerce on or in connection with the above identified goods/services. (15 U.S.C. 1051(b), as amended.)

• Specify intended manner or mode of use of mark on or in connection with the goods or services
      _____
      (e.g., trademark will be applied to labels, service mark will be used in advertisements)

❏ Applicant has a bona fide intention to use the mark in commerce on or in connection with the above identified goods/services, and asserts a claim of priority based upon a foreign application in accordance with 15 U.S.C. 1126(d), as amended.

  Country of foreign filing: _____   Date of foreign filing:_____

❏ Applicant has a bona fide intention to use the mark in commerce on or in connection with the above identified goods/services and, accompanying this application, submits a certification or certified copy of a foreign registration in accordance with 15 U.S.C. 1126(e), as amended.

Country of registration:_____   Registration number: _____

Declaration

The undersigned being hereby warned that willful false statements and the like so made are punishable by fine or imprisonment, or both, under 18 U.S.C. 1001, and that such willful false statements may jeopardize the validity of the application or any resulting registration, declares that he/she is properly authorized to execute this application on behalf of the applicant; he/she believes the applicant to be the owner of the trademark/service mark sought to be registered, or, if the application is being filed under 15 U.S.C. 105(b), he/she believes applicant to be entitled to use such mark in commerce; to the best of his/her knowledge and belief no other person, firm, corporation, or association has the right to use the above

_____   _____
Signature   Date

_____   _____
Print or Type Name and Posotion   Telephone

22 Protecting Your Inventions with Patents

An Introduction to Patents

After you have created a new idea or invention, you should consider how to protect it under the patent laws. There are two basic types of patents, which typically can be useful in providing protection for most inventions: a utility patent and a design patent. This chapter will initially focus on utility patents, which cover the functional or operational features of an invention. Discussed later in the chapter are design patents, which can be used to protect the artistic or ornamental features of any article manufactured by man.

Whether a utility patent or a design patent will be pursued, you should take early steps to document the invention. To document an invention, you should get a close friend or associate (who understands the invention, but who is not an inventor thereof) to sign his or her name on a dated diagram or written description of the invention, which has also been dated and signed by you. You can also file a "disclosure document" with the U.S. Patent Office or a provisional patent application. Taking one of these measures will provide evidence of the time that you came up with the invention, in case of a dispute with other inventors over who conceived it first. Filing a disclosure document with the U.S. Patent Office does not give the inventor any patent protection—it only provides evidence of the invention. A provisional patent application is an informal application filed at the U.S.

Patent Office to prove an early filing date for the invention. This can be converted to a regular patent application within one year of filing.

You should make a patent search to see whether or not the invention has already been patented. You can make a search on a computerized patent database, such as LEXIS/NEXIS or the U.S. Patent Office Web site (*www.uspto.gov*), or at the U.S. Patent and Trademark Office in Alexandria, Virginia. The staff at the Patent Office will give you some help in conducting patent searches and using Patent Office facilities. If the invention is complex or it involves complicated issues, you may need the help of a patent agent or patent attorney.

If the invention has not already been patented, you can prepare a patent application and file it with the U.S. Patent and Trademark Office. Specific information on preparing and filing a simple U.S. utility patent application is presented later in this chapter.

A U.S. utility patent can be obtained on a new, useful, and unobvious process, machine, article of manufacture, or composition of matter or a new and useful improvement of any of these. In order for an invention to be patentable in the United States, the invention must be: (1) new, (2) useful, and (3) unobvious.

If the invention has been described in a printed publication anywhere in the world or if it has been in public use or on sale in this country before the date that the inventor made the invention, a patent cannot be obtained. In this connection, it is immaterial when the invention was made or whether the printed publication or public use was by the inventor or by someone else. If the inventor or anyone described the invention in a printed publication or used the invention publicly or placed it on sale, the inventor must apply for a patent before one year has gone by; otherwise, any right to a patent will be lost.

The usefulness test is easily met if the inventor can show that the invention operates to perform some function. An invention may be useful, even if it is destructive. For example, a gun may be patentable subject matter, although its primary purpose is to kill or destroy.

Typically the most difficult hurdle to overcome in establishing patentability is whether the invention is obvious. A patent can not be obtained even though the invention is not identically disclosed or described in the "prior art" if the differences between the invention and the "prior art" are such that the subject matter "as a whole" would have been "obvious" at the time the invention was made to a person having "ordinary skill in the art" to which the subject matter pertains.

Even if the subject matter sought to be patented is not exactly shown by the prior art and involves one or more differences over the most similar thing already known, a patent may still be refused if the differences would be obvious. The subject matter sought to be patented must be sufficiently different from what has been used or described before so that it may be said to amount to invention over the prior art. Small advances that would be obvious to a person having ordinary skill in the art are not considered inventions capable of being patented. For example, the substitution of one material for another, or changes in size, is ordinarily not patentable.

If you are merely utilizing the teachings or suggestions of the published liter- ature or prior art to solve a problem and no unexpected results are obtained, it is doubtful that the invention overcomes the obviousness test. The invention must be evaluated on the basis of how it relates to the problem faced, the need for a solution, how the invention differs from the prior art, and its prospects of commercial success.

Certain inventions are held not to be patentable because of policy reasons. For example, printed matter cannot be patented, but must be protected by copyright. Inventions useful solely in the utilization of special nuclear material or atomic energy for atomic weapons are excluded from patent protection by the Atomic Energy Act. Remember also that a patent cannot be obtained upon a mere idea or suggestion—rather, a complete description and reduction to practice of the invention are required.

While you will probably have to invest time, money, and effort into the invention to make it a success, you can get help from a number of sources. Patent attorneys and agents can help you make a patent search and file and prosecute a patent application. Invention Promoters are firms that offer (for a fee) to take on the whole job of protecting and promoting the idea. Invention brokers typically work for a portion of the profits from an invention. They may help inventors raise capital and form companies to produce and market the invention. They often provide sophisticated management advice.

Other sources include University Invention/Entrepreneurial Centers, some funded by the National Science Foundation, which provide help for inventors and innovators. The Small Business Administration's Small Business Institutes (SBIs) are located at several hundred colleges and universities around the country and they may be able to provide the market research, feasibility analysis, and business planning assistance necessary to make an invention successful.

The Office of Energy-Related Inventions in the U.S. Department of Commerce's National Bureau of Standards sometimes evaluates non-nuclear energy-related inventions and ideas for devices, materials, and procedures without charge. Inventor's clubs, associations, and societies are useful sources for networking and gathering information. Talking with other inventors is probably the most helpful thing that an inventor can do.

The patent laws and court decisions provide a set of rules and guidelines for determining what inventions are entitled to patent protection. You must evaluate the invention against the required criteria, and if these criteria are met, there is a strong likelihood patent protection of some degree will be available.

Keep in mind that before you can have a patentable invention, there must first be conception and reduction to practice. "Conception" means the mental formulation of the invention in sufficient detail that someone familiar with the subject matter to which the invention relates could make and use the invention. Reduction to practice generally involves making or constructing the invention (i.e., preparing a model, diagram, or written description) and testing it to demonstrate its usefulness for its conceived purpose.

Articles of manufacture and machines are the most common types of inventions involving industrial designs. Articles of manufacture include nearly every man-made object from a paper clip to a skyscraper. Machines include any mechanical or electrical apparatus or devise (for example, a camera, a bicycle, a computer, an airplane, or the like).

To qualify as new under U.S. law, an invention must:

1. Not have been known, published, or used publicly anywhere by others before the invention was made by the patent applicant; or

2. Not have been patented or described by anyone in a printed publication any-where, or on sale in the U.S., more than one year prior to the U.S. filing date of the patent application; or

3. Not have been abandoned by the patent applicant; or

4. Not have been first patented in a foreign country, prior to the date of the patent application, based on an application filed more than 12 months before the filing of the U.S. application; or

5. Not have been described in a patent granted to another where the other patent application was filed in the U.S. before the invention by the patent applicant; or

6. Not have been made in the U.S. by another, before the invention by the patent applicant.

The failure of the invention to meet any one of the above criteria means the invention is not novel, but anticipated by the prior art, and bars the right to a U.S. patent.

The disclosure or sale of the invention which will result in a bar to patentability can happen in a number of ways. This may consist of the sale or mere offer of sale of the invention to others, advertising the invention, or any other written publication thereof; audio and video disclosure of the invention, and any disclosure of the invention in a speech, journal article, promotional literature, and the like. Any of these acts by the inventor or others whereby the invention is disclosed to the public more than one year before filing an appropriate patent application constitutes a bar to a U.S. patent for that invention.

Preparing and Filing a U.S. Utility Patent Application

After reviewing the prior art and determining that the invention is patentable, you should file for patent protection for the invention. For a U.S. inventor, the easiest process is to file a regular or provisional patent application with the U.S. Patent Office. You can begin this process by hiring a good patent attorney or agent, or you might be able to prepare and file the patent application yourself if you have a good understanding of how to draft a sufficient patent application and get it filed at the U.S. Patent Office.

A complete U.S. utility patent application has several components, some or which are mandatory and others are optional. The mandatory components of a U.S. utility patent application are:

1. A specification with one or more claims
2. Drawings, if necessary to describe or "disclose" the invention
3. The names of the inventors
4. The required declaration
5. The requisite filing fee ($300 at the time of this printing/fee is reduced to half for small entity)

The specification, claims, and drawings in a patent application become a part of the granted and published patent and normally follow a specific format. The specification should consist of the following parts:

a. Title
b. Reference to any related patent applications, if any
c. Background of the invention
d. Summary of the invention
e. Brief description of the drawings, if any
f. Detailed description of the invention
g. One or more claims
h. Abstract

A specification with claims, as well as necessary drawings and names of all inventors, must be included in the patent application in order for it to be given a filing date. A declaration and filing fee are also mandatory for an application to be complete, but these can be submitted within two months of filing the application without losing the original filing date.

In addition to the above mandatory items, the following optional items should also accompany a completed application: an application transmittal letter, an infor-

mation disclosure statement listing relevant prior art, a Small Entity Statement (if applicable), and a self-addressed return postcard to acknowledge receipt by the U.S. Patent Office.

The specification is the core of a completed patent application. Before you begin to draft the specification, it is a good idea to do the following preliminary work to prepare to write the specification:

Become familiar with the patent regulations. There are two primary sets of statutes or regulations that govern all patent matters. These are the Patent Statute, 35 United States Code ("35 U.S.C."); and The Patent Rules, 37 Code of Federal Regulations, which is a more detailed set of regulations based on the Patent Statute. All of the requirements for drafting an application can be found in *The Patent Statute* and *The Patent Rules*. Copies are available from The Government Printing Office (call 202-512-1800 to order them or access the GPO's Web site at *http://www.access.gpo.gov*).

- Write a brief (one to three paragraphs) description of the invention. Be sure to include all the unique elements of the invention in this description. If there are several variations of the invention, describe all of them.

- List all the advantages and benefits of the invention, particularly those which are surprising and unexpected.

- If the invention requires drawings in order to fully describe or disclose it, make preliminary sketches, numbering all relevant parts in the drawings. Use as many views as necessary to fully describe and disclose the invention. These sketches are important since they are the basis for the formal drawings that will become part of the application and granted patent.

- Review all relevant prior art that you have located. You can use this art to help come up with terminology and see how similar inventions are described and drawn. Finally, this prior art should be submitted to the Patent Office with an Information Disclosure Statement.

- Try drafting a sample claim. A claim is a formalized, precise description of the invention. See the discussion on "Drafting Claims" later in this chapter for further explanation. This claim should be one sentence that broadly describes the invention and includes all of the necessary elements of the invention.

- Review other U.S. patents in the field of the invention to help decide how best to organize the patent application. Sections of text from these patents can be copied and included in your patent application.

It is very important that the patent specification meet the requirements of the patent laws, which basically are that:

1. The specification must adequately describe the invention.

2. The specification must teach, or "enable," someone else who has skill in the technical area of the invention to make and use the invention.

3. The specification must present the best way known by the inventor for practicing the invention.

There are a number of reasons why it is imperative that your application meets the requirements of the Patent Statute when you file. Firstly, failure to meet these requirements can result in a rejection of your application by the Patent Office or in a subsequent finding of patent invalidity should the granted patent ever be litigated. Secondly, after the patent application has been filed, you are not allowed to add new information (called "new matter") without re-filing the application. Thirdly, everything you will "claim" as your invention must be in the specification.

Other requirements for the specification are that it be typed on letter-sized paper (8.5" × ll"), legal-sized paper (8.5" × 13" or 14"), or A4-sized paper (21 cm × 29.7 cm). Spacing should be one-and-a-half lines or double-spaced. The specification, claims, and abstract should each begin on a new page. Use the following margins for letter- and legal-sized paper: at least 1.5" at the top and bottom and at least 1" on the right and left. Number each page of the specification, preferably at the bottom.

Here is a summary of the different parts of the utility patent application specification:

Title Page

The title page should have the title of the invention as well as the names and, if possible, the addresses of all the inventors. It is very important that all inventors be identified. Failure to include the correct inventor(s) could result in a patent being held unenforceable. The title should be descriptive and state in just a few words what is the essence of the invention.

References to Related Applications, if Any

If the applicant has previously filed any applications for the same or one or more related inventions, those applications should be referenced at the beginning of the patent specification. For example, the applicant should use language such as: "This application is a [continuation/continuation-in-part/divisional] of application Serial No. _____, filed on _____, entitled "_____".

Omit this part if there are no related applications.

Background of the Invention

This part serves the purposes of providing information about the field of the invention and describing the current state of the art. It typically includes a discussion of the prior art and how the invention is distinguishable over it.

Summary of the Invention

Include a brief synopsis of the invention and its benefits. It can begin by summarizing the objectives identified earlier. Then the subject matter of the invention should be set out in one or more clear, concise sentences or paragraphs. In many cases, the summary of the invention can simply be a recitation of the main claim in the application and a brief explanation of the elements of the invention.

Brief Description of the Drawings

If the application includes drawings, the applicant must provide a brief description of them in the specification. This part of the application typically begins with a sentence such as: "The accompanying drawings further describe the invention." After that introduction, in separate paragraphs, write only one or two sentences describing the drawings such as, for example: "Figure 1 is a perspective view of the machine constructed in accordance with the invention."

Detailed Description of the Invention

This is the most comprehensive part of the specification. In this section of the specification the applicant must fully, clearly, concisely, and exactly describe the invention to enable a technically skilled person to make and use the invention without extensive experimentation. Additionally, the applicant must disclose the "best mode" known by him for practicing the invention. Further, the applicant must disclose every element of the invention that the applicant plans to claim.

Abstract

The abstract is presented on a separate sheet of paper at the end of the specification—after the claims. When the patent is published it will appear on the first page. The abstract should be no more than about a 250-word summary of the invention. The purpose of the abstract is to disclose the novel elements of the invention and to help the examiner and the public quickly determine the nature of the technical disclosure. For simplicity, the abstract could be a summary of the main patent claim.

The Claims

The last part of the specification is the claims, which are numbered sentences that define the patentable invention. The claims are perhaps the most important part of the patent application. The claims must describe the invention clearly enough so that anyone reading them knows what is the scope, or the "metes and bounds," of the invention.

Following are rules of thumb that should be followed when drafting patent claims:

1. Make sure all claims are supported by the specification. All claimed elements should be described in the specification exactly the same way they appear in the claims.

2. Use only one sentence per claim. Use commas, semi-colons, and colons, but make sure the only period in the claim comes at the very end.

3. Make sure an element has been named once in the claim before modifying or qualifying it. Failure to follow this rule will result in the rejection of the claim for "lack of antecedent basis." More specifically, when naming an element for the first time say: " . . . a rod," or ". . . an insignia." After this first use, the applicant should say ". . . said rod," or " . . . the insignia."

4. Make sure the elements of the claimed invention logically interrelate. A claim must recite an operative combination of elements, not a mere aggregation of elements. The interrelationship between the parts may be structural or it may be functional. Structural relationships between elements are described by words, such as, "connected to," "secured to," "near," "adjacent to," "attached to," or "mixed with."

An example includes: ". . . wherein A is connected to B, D is adjacent to C, or E is mixed with F." Functional relationships between elements are described by words such as: "to support"; "in order to"; "so that it moves." An example is: ". . . wherein A is positioned to support B . . ."

5. Avoid overly precise numbers, where possible. If appropriate, use the word "about." The word "about" is acceptable in claims to indicate that a specific number is not absolutely specific. Examples of the use of "about" in claims include: "comprising about 2% water"; "heating said liquid for about 25 minutes"; or "a circumference of no more than about 3 feet." The term "about" helps in obtaining a broader interpretation of the claim.

6. Use functional language if appropriate. Sometimes an element in a claim can best be broadly defined by what it does (i.e., its function). For example, a "means for attaching" could include screws, nails, and adhesives.

7. Be consistent in the use of terms. Once the applicant has used a term in a claim to identify a particular element, he should use that same term consistently throughout the claims. However, define the term as broadly as possible in the description.

8. Avoid unnecessary wordiness. Do not recite in the claims any element unless it is critical to practicing the invention.

9. The applicant should be sure to claim what he plans to sell or license. The claims should encompass all possible marketable versions of the invention, including the version that the applicant plans to commercialize.

Drawings

The patent applicant should prepare or have a draftsman prepare sketches of the invention. These sketches can be submitted as part of the original filing to meet the drawings requirement. The U.S. Patent Office has many formalities that must be met for formal drawings. Formal drawings must be on a certain size and type of paper, margins must be a certain width, shading and hatching must be used in certain ways, and there are rules for the use of symbols, legends, and arrows. All of these rules can be found in 37 C.F.R. §§ 1.81-1.85, which is provided on the U.S. Patent Office website (*www.uspto.gov*).

Declaration

The application must be accompanied by a Declaration signed by all the inventors. In this document the inventor(s) declare(s) he/they is/are the sole or joint inventors of the subject matter claimed in the invention. They are also acknowledging a duty to disclose information of which they are aware that is material to the examination of the application. This includes: 1) all prior art of which they are aware at the time the application is filed or that they become aware of during the prosecution of the application, and 2) any other information believed to be relevant to a thorough review of the application by the Examiner. A sample Declaration form is provided at the end of this chapter.

It is important that the declaration not be executed until the application is completed and reviewed by the inventor(s). This rule is strictly maintained by the Patent Office. Therefore, sign the Declaration only after the final changes have been made and you have read the final draft of the application.

Filing Fee

There is a basic fee for filing an application with up to three independent claims and a total of twenty claims. If the number of independent and/or dependent claims exceeds this, then the fee increases accordingly. Because the fee schedule for patent applications is regularly updated, the applicant should contact the Patent Office before the patent application is to be filed to determine the latest fees. Make the check for the total amount payable to Commissioner of

Patents and Trademarks. Fees are reduced by 50 percent for applicants who qualify as "small entities." At the time of this printing, the regular filing fee for a utility application was $300 and $150 for a small entity. Generally, a small entity is an independent inventor, a business with fewer than 500 employees, or a nonprofit organization. If you are filing as a small entity, you must also submit a Verified Statement of Small Entity status. A sample Verified Statement of Small Entity Status Form can be found on the U.S. Patent Office Web site.

Filing the patent specification, Declaration, and Filing Fee meets the statutory requirements for a patent application. However, there are additional documents that the applicant should complete, if appropriate, and file as part of the application with the U.S. Patent Office.

Application Transmittal Letter

The application should include an Application Transmittal Letter addressed to the Commissioner of Patents and Trademarks. This is a cover letter that lists the contents of the package you are sending to the PTO and includes information such as the names of the inventors, the total number of pages of specification and claims, and the number of sheets of drawings. It is also used to calculate the filing fees. See the U.S. Patent Office Web site for a sample Application Transmittal Letter.

Information Disclosure Statement

An applicant for a patent has a legal obligation to disclose to the Patent Office any information that is material to the patentability of the invention. To meet this full disclosure requirement, you should file an Information Disclosure Statement (available from the U.S. Patent Office Web site) at the time of filing the application. If you uncover a piece of prior art after the patent application has been filed or if you discover that one embodiment of the invention does not work, you must advise the Patent Office

before the patent issues. Otherwise, if the patent is granted and it is determined that the applicant withheld material information from the Patent Office, a court could rule that the patent is unenforceable.

Certificate of Express Mailing

At the beginning or at the end of the Application Transmittal Letter, you should prepare a Certificate of Express Mailing. This is a signed statement indicating the date that the application was sent by U.S. Express Mail to the U.S. Patent Office. If the patent application is sent to the U.S. Patent Office by Express Mail and it includes a Certificate of Express Mailing, then the application will receive the filing date that the application was deposited with the U.S. Postal Service. If you hand-deliver the patent application to the U.S. Patent Office, a Certificate of Express mailing is not necessary. See the sample Certificate of Express Mailing form presented later in this chapter.

If you have followed all of the above steps, the patent application should be ready for filing with the U.S. Patent Office. Make sure all signatures are in place, no pages or drawings are missing, and all documents are in proper form and ready for submission. The specification and all related papers and the filing fee should be placed unfolded in a large envelope addressed to: Box Patent Application, Commissioner for Patents, Washington, DC 20231. Alternatively to mailing, the application can be hand-carried to the U.S. Patent Office. Remember, if you are going to mail the application, you should only use U.S. Express Mail Service. In that way the filing date will be the date the application is mailed. Furthermore, if you send the application via U.S. Express Mail, you will have proof of the date it was sent in the form of the Express Mail receipt. Otherwise, the filing date will be the date it is received by the PTO. This is true even if you use an overnight delivery service such as FedEx.

Instead of a regular utility patent application, you can file a less formal provisional application to save initial costs and obtain the earliest filing date. The filing fee for a provisional patent application is $200, and this fee is reduced to $100 for a small entity. Like a regular application, a provisional application must adequately and completely describe the invention. But the description does not require all the formalities and sections discussed above for a regular patent application. Before twelve months have passed after filing a provisional application, you can convert it to a regular application.

The review and examination process at the U.S. Patent Office, from filing the application to the grant of a patent, takes two to three years. When a patent application arrives at the U.S. Patent Office, the Applications Branch examines the papers to make sure the required parts of the application have been submitted. The application is then assigned a filing date and a serial number. A Patent Examiner reviews the application for compliance with U.S. Patent Office formalities and the Patent Statute and Patent Regulations. This review includes a prior art search of earlier patents and publications to determine whether the claims are novel and unobvious. The Examiner will then prepare and mail a report called an "Office Action" setting forth his/her opinion of the application. The Office Action identifies which claims, if any, are acceptable or "allowed" and which are unacceptable or "rejected," and it gives all the reasons for the rejections. The Office Action also indicates if there are any other problems with the application. The first Office Action is usually received about nine to twelve months after the application is filed. The applicant is typically given three months to respond to the Office Action and this time period can be extended to six months by paying the required fee. Further information on the patent examination process for utility and design patent applications is presented later in this chapter.

If the Examiner finds that the patent claims are patentable and acceptable, the Examiner will issue a Notice of Allowance. After the applicant receives a Notice of Allowance, all that remains is to take care of any formal matters and to pay the issue fee. At the time of this printing, the regular issue fee for a utility patent is $1,400, which is reduced to one half for a small entity.

Filling In The Utility Patent Application Form

On a separate title page, fill in the title of the invention in item 1 and the complete names of all the inventors in item 2.

In item 3, complete any references to related patent applications, including serial numbers and filing dates.

In item 4, write a background of the invention, including discussion of the prior art and the problems solved by the invention.

In item 5, prepare a brief summary of the invention.

Prepare a brief description of the drawings, if any, in item 6.

In item 7, write a detailed description of the invention.

Starting on a separate page, in item 8, draft the claims covering the invention, with each claim being a separate numbered sentence.

Starting on a separate page, write a brief and descriptive abstract of the invention in item 9.

Filling in the Combined Declaration and Power of Attorney Form

In item 1, indicate whether the inventor is sole or joint. Write in a title of the invention. Check the appropriate box(es) to indicate whether the patent application specification is attached, was filed on the specified date and having the identified serial number, or amended on the specified date.

In item 4, indicate any prior foreign patent applications on which the inventor is claiming priority benefits. Include application serial numbers, countries, filing dates, and an indication of whether or not priority benefits are being claimed.

In item 5, indicate any prior United States patent applications on which the inventor is claiming priority benefits. Include application serial numbers, filing dates, and status.

In item 6, indicate the attorney or agent whom the inventor has appointed to prosecute the application. Include the telephone number and address to which calls and correspondence should be sent.

At the end of the form, fill in the full names of all of the inventors, along with their residences, citizenships, and post office addresses. Have each inventor sign and date the form.

Checklist for Filing a Utility Patent Application

❏ Take steps to maximize the patentability of the invention. Before creating the invention, the inventor should define the problem that he or she is faced with or the objective you are trying to reach and record this information and his ideas. The inventor will also need to review prior art to help generate potential solutions and to determine what is new and patentable. After the analysis of the prior art is complete, formulate a research strategy to make the invention. As soon as an idea is conceived of how to solve the problems, write a concise statement of the idea in a notebook. This statement should include all the parameters that are believed to be nec-essary for solving the problem and as many individual features, elements, compounds, compositions, or process steps that are necessary for the idea to work. Then describe the plan to proceed to prove whether the idea actually is the answer to solving the problems defined earlier.

❏ Explore all the variables of the invention (i.e., materials of construction, physical parameters, ranges for each component, temperatures, pressures, etc.). In order to obtain the broadest patent coverage, the designer should explore the outer limits of his invention. An invention is not completely defined until the inventor knows how to change each of the variables to determine when the invention works and when it does not.

❏ Prepare the patent specification complete with the following components:

  ❏ Title Page, including names of all inventors
  ❏ References to related applications, if any
  ❏ Background of the Invention
  ❏ Summary of the Invention
  ❏ Brief Description of the Drawings, if applicable
  ❏ Detailed Description of the Invention
  ❏ Claims, starting on a separate page
  ❏ Abstract, starting on a separate page

❏ All drawings are present, and each drawing sheet is given a figure number. The inventor's name and address are on the top back of each sheet of formal drawings.

❏ The Declaration is completed, signed, and dated in ink by all inventors after having reviewed the patent application specification.

- ❏ A check or money order payable to the Commissioner of Patents and Trademarks for the correct filing fee is enclosed.

- ❏ If applicable, the Verified Statement of Small Entity Status form is completed, signed, and dated in ink.

- ❏ An Information Disclosure Statement (Form PTO-1449) is completed. Copies of all cited references are attached.

- ❏ A properly completed and signed Transmittal Letter is enclosed which identifies every document that is being sent to the U.S. Patent Office. A Certificate of Express Mail is included with the Transmittal Letter.

- ❏ A self-addressed return receipt postcard, with the mailing date and all papers listed on the back.

- ❏ Place the complete patent application in a large envelope and send via Express Mail to:

  Box Patent Application
  Commissioner for Patents
  Washington, DC 20231

- ❏ Respond to any Office Actions from the U.S. Patent Office within the time prescribed or after requesting an extension of time.

- ❏ Pay the issue fee if a Notice of Allowance and Issue Fee Due is received from the U.S. Patent Office.

- ❏ Pay the required maintenance fees to the U.S. Patent Office every 3½ years if you want to maintain the patent.

Form 31: Utility Patent Application Form

(Put title of the invention and names of the inventors together on a separate page)

1) _____(Title of the Invention)

2) _____(Names of the Inventors)

3) Reference to related patent applications:

_____

_____

_____

4) Background of the Invention:

_____

_____

_____

_____

_____

5) Summary of the Invention:

_____

_____

_____

_____

_____

6) Brief Description of the Drawings:

_____

_____

_____

_____

_____

7) Detailed Description of the Invention:

_____

_____

_____

_____

_____

8) Claims: (Start on a separate page)

Claim 1. _____

_____

Claim 2. _____

_____

Claim 3. _____

_____

9) Abstract: (Start on a separate page)

CERTIFICATE OF EXPRESS MAILING PURSUANT TO 37 C.F.R.§1.10

I hereby certify that this New Application Transmittal and the documents referred to as enclosed herein are being deposited with the United States Postal Service on this date _____ in an envelope bearing "Express Mail Post Office to Addressee" Mailing Number _____ addressed to the Commissioner for Patents, Washington, DC 20231.

_____

(Typed or printed name of person mailing)

_____

(Signature of person mailing papers, Date)

Form 32: COMBINED DECLARATION AND POWER OF ATTORNEY

1. As a below named inventor, I hereby declare that:

(i) my residence, post office address and citizenship are stated below next to my name; and that

(ii) I verily believe I am an original, first and __ sole __ joint inventor of the improvement in:
   [Title of Invention]

described and claimed in the attached specification which
___ is attached hereto.
___ was filed on_____as Application Serial No._____
___ and was amended on_____.   .

2. I hereby state that I have reviewed and understand the contents of the above-identified specification, including the claims, as amended by any amendment referred to above.

3. I acknowledge the duty to disclose information which is material to patentability as defined in 37 C.F.R. § 1.56.

4. I hereby claim foreign priority benefits pursuant to 35 U.S.C. § 119 from any foreign application(s) listed below and have also identified below any foreign application(s) for patent or inventor's certificate which have a filing date prior to that of the application from which priority is claimed.

Prior Foreign Application(s) (if any):

Number	Country	Filing Date	Priority Claimed
_____	_____	_____	_____
_____	_____	_____	_____

5. I hereby claim the benefit under 35 U.S.C. § 120 from any United States application(s) listed below and, insofar as the subject matter of each of the claims of this application is not disclosed in the prior United States application in the manner provided by the first paragraph of 35 U.S.C. § 112, I acknowledge the duty to disclose material information as defined in 37 C.F.R. § 1.56 which occurred between the filing date of the prior application and the national or PCT international filing date of this application:

Application Serial No.	Filing Date	Status (Patented Pending, Abandoned)
_____	_____	_____
_____	_____	_____

6. I hereby appoint the following attorney(s) and or agent(s) to prosecute this application and to transact all business in the Patent and Trademark Office connected therewith:

Address all telephone calls to _____ at telephone number: _____

Address all correspondence to: _____
_____

7. I hereby declare that all statements made herein of my own knowledge are true and that all statements made on information and belief are believed to be true, and further, that these statements were made with knowledge that willful false statements and the like are punishable by fine or imprisonment, or both, pursuant to 18 U.S.C. § 1001 and that such willful false statements may jeopardize the validity of the application or any patent issued thereon.

FULL NAME OF INVENTOR: _____

     Signature of Inventor: _____ Date: _____
     Residence: _____
     Citizenship: _____

Preparing and Filing a U.S. Design Patent Application

In addition to utility patents, design patents can be very useful in protecting ornamental inventions. In general terms, a "utility patent" protects the way an article is used and works, while a "design patent" protects the way an article looks. A design patent protects the new shape or ornamental or artistic features of an article. Unlike a utility patent, a design patent does not protect the functional elements of an invention. If a design has any functionality, then it cannot be protected with a design patent at all, even if the design is also ornamental. Some examples of designs which can be patented are unique bottle shapes, a computer screen display, an artistic lamp, an ornamental pin, a watch design, the grill of an automobile, and the like. Ornamental designs are an important feature of practically every product on the market.

You can file for a design patent and a utility patent on the same article. The design patent would be directed to the exterior appearance of the article, whereas the utility patent would be directed to its function. Keep in mind that you may also be able to copyright your unique design in addition to obtaining a patent on it. Because one form of patent or intellectual property coverage does not preclude another, you should consider all the available options for protecting the invention.

A design patent has a 14-year term from the date of grant, and it protects against any design that is substantially similar to the patented design. A design patent is relatively easy to obtain if the design is new and nonfunctional. A design patent application is also simple to prepare and should include a preamble, a specification that explains the design, a single claim, one or more drawings, a formal inventor's declaration, and the filing fee. A sample design patent application form is presented at the end of this chapter.

A design patent covers the visual ornamental features that are embodied in, or applied to, an article of manufacture. Because a design patent is based upon appearance, the subject matter of a design patent application may relate to the configuration or shape of an article, to the surface ornamentation applied to an article, or to the combination of these.

The U.S. patent laws provide for the granting of a design patent to any person who has invented any new, original, and ornamental design for an article of manufacture. An ornamental design may be embodied in a portion of or in the entire article. Keep in mind that a design patent protects only the appearance of the article and not structural or utilitarian features.

A design for a product, which is required by the function of the product, cannot be covered by a design patent because the design is not ornamental. This means that to obtain a design patent the appearance of the product must not be dictated by the function that the product performs. It is also required that for a design to be patentable, the design must be original. Thus, a design that simulates a known or naturally occurring object or person is not original.

A design patent application must include the following:

Preamble, stating name of the applicant, title of the design, and a brief description of the nature and intended use of the article in which the design is embodied.

Description of the figure(s) of the drawing:

1. A single claim
2. Drawings or photographs
3. Executed oath or declaration; and
4. The required filing fee ($200 at the time of this printing). If applicant is a small entity, (an independent inventor, a small business concern, or a nonprofit organization), the filing fee and other fees are reduced by half.

A design must be shown in the drawing as applied to an article of manufacture if the design is directed solely to surface ornamentation. The article of manufacture itself forms no part of the design, and the article must be shown in broken lines in the drawings.

The preamble should state the name of the design patent applicant, the title of the design, and a brief description of the nature and intended use of the article in which the design is embodied. This information will be printed on the design patent if the patent is issued.

The title of the design patent application should be specific and descriptive. The title must identify the article in which the design is embodied by the name publicly known and used. The title should not contain trademarks or other marketing designations.

Only one patent claim covering the respective design may be included in a design patent application. This is because each ornamental design is a distinct invention and must be filed in a separate design patent application. The claim is important because it defines the design which applicant wishes to patent, in terms of the article in which it is embodied or applied. The claim has to be presented in the formal language: "The ornamental design for (name of the article which embodies the design or to which it is applied) as shown and described." The design patent applicant should use consistent terminology in the title, preamble, drawings, and patent claim.

The descriptions of the figures indicate what each view of the drawings represents (e.g., front view, top view, side view, rear view, perspective view, etc.). Because the drawings themselves are the best depiction of the design, the brief descriptions of the drawings are the only written explanation of the design that is required in the specification of a design patent application. However, statements or feature descriptions may be included in the design patent application for clarification, such as the following:

i) a description which disclaims parts of the article that form no part of the claimed design;

ii) a description of parts of the claimed design which are not shown in the drawings, such as views which are the same or mirror images of each other;

iii) a description which states the nature and use of the claimed design, particularly if this is not included in the preamble; and

iv) a statement indicating that any broken-line illustration of the background structure in the drawing is not part of the claimed design.

The drawings are one of the most important parts of a design patent application. A drawing or a black-and-white photograph of the claimed design must be included in every design patent application. These drawings or photographs of the claimed design should be a clear and complete depiction of the design that is to be patented. The design drawing or photograph must include sufficient views of the design to constitute a complete disclosure of the appearance of the design claimed.

The U.S. Patent Office has specific and detailed requirements for the proper drawings and/or photographs that are included in design patent applications. These requirements are published in Chapter 37 of the Code of Federal Regulations Sections 1.84(b)(1) and 1.152 (available from the Superintendent of Documents, United States Government Printing Office, Washington, DC 20402. Telephone: 202.512.1800) and at the U.S. Patent Office Web site (*www.uspto.gov*).

The design patent applicant is required to execute an oath or declaration in compliance with the U.S. Patent Office requirements. A sample Combined Declaration and Power of Attorney Form which is useful for design patent applications is provided and discussed earlier in this chapter on utility patents.

The Patent Examination Process
Helpful information on the patent examination process and other matters relating to

design patents can be found in "A Guide to Filing a Design Patent Application" at the U.S. Patent Office Web site. Useful information from the U.S. Patent Office Web site on the design patent application process (also applicable to utility patents) is presented here:

Filing An Application

When a complete design patent application, along with the appropriate filing fee, is received by the Office, it is assigned an Application Number and a Filing Date. A "Filing Receipt" containing this information is sent to the applicant. The application is then assigned to an examiner. Applications are examined in order of their filing date.

Examination

The actual "examination" entails checking for compliance with formalities, ensuring completeness of the drawing disclosure, and a comparison of the claimed subject matter with the "prior art." "Prior art" consists of issued patents and published materials. If the claimed subject matter is found to be patentable, the application will be "allowed," and instructions will be provided to the applicant for completing the process to permit issuance as a patent. The examiner may reject the claim in the application if the disclosure cannot be understood or is incomplete, or if a reference or combination of references found in the prior art shows the claimed design to be unpatentable. The examiner will then issue an Office Action detailing the rejection and addressing the substantive matters which affect patentability.

Response

If, after receiving an Office action, applicant elects to continue prose-cution of the application, a timely reply to the action must be submitted. This reply should include a request for reconsideration or further examination of the claim, along with any amendments desired by the applicant, and must be in writing. The reply must distinctly and specifically point out the supposed errors in the Office action and must address every objection and/or rejection in the action. If the examiner has rejected the claim over prior art, a general statement by the applicant that the claim is patentable, without specifically pointing out how the design is patentable over the prior art, does not comply with the rules. In all cases where the examiner has said that a reply to a requirement is necessary, or where the examiner has indicated patentable subject matter, the reply must comply with the requirements set forth by the examiner or specifically argue each requirement as to why compliance should not be required. In any communication with the Office, applicant should include the following items:

1. Application number (checked for accuracy).
2. Group art unit number (copied from filing receipt or the most recent Office action).
3. Filing date.
4. Name of the examiner who prepared the most recent Office action.
5. Title of invention

It is the applicant's responsibility to make sure that the reply is received by the Office prior to the expiration of the designated time period set for reply. This time period is set to run from the "Date Mailed," which is indicated on the first page of the Office action. If the reply is not received within the designated time period, the application will be considered abandoned. In the event that applicant is unable to reply within the time period set in the Office action, abandonment may be prevented if a reply is filed within six months from the mail date of the Office action provided a petition for extension of time and the fee set forth in 37 CFR § 1.17(a) are filed. The fee is determined by the amount of time requested and increases as the length of time increases. These fees are set by Rule and could change at any time. An "Extension of Time" does not have to be obtained prior to the submission of a reply to an Office action; it may be mailed along with the reply. Note: an extension of time cannot be obtained when responding to a "Notice of Allowance."

To ensure that a time period set for reply to an Office action is not missed, a Certificate of Mailing should be attached to the reply. This Certificate establishes that the reply is being mailed on a given date. It also establishes that the reply is timely, if it was mailed before the period for reply had expired, and if it is mailed with the United States Postal Service. A Certificate of Mailing is not the same as Certified Mail. A suggested format for a Certificate of Mailing is as follows:

"I hereby certify that this correspondence is being deposited with the United States Postal Service as first class mail in an envelope addressed to: Box Design, Commissioner for Patents, Washington, DC 20231,

on (DATE MAILED)"

(Name—Typed or Printed)

_____

Signature_____

Date_____

If a receipt for any paper filed in the USPTO is desired, applicant should include a stamped, self-addressed postcard that lists on the message side, applicant's name and address, the application number, and filing date, the types of papers submitted with the reply (i.e., 1 sheet of drawings, 2 pages of amendments, 1 page of an oath/declaration, etc.). This postcard will be stamped with the date of receipt by the mailroom and returned to applicant. This postcard will be applicant's evidence that the reply was received by the Office on that date. If applicant changes his or her mailing address after filing an application, the Office must be notified in writing of the new address.

Applicant's failure to receive and properly reply to these Office communications will result in the application being held abandoned. Notification of change of address should be made by separate letter, and a separate notification should be filed for each application.

Reconsideration
Upon submission of a reply to an Office action, the application will be reconsidered and further examined in view of applicant's remarks and any amendments included with the reply. The examiner will then either withdraw the rejection and allow the application or, if not persuaded by the remarks and/or amendments submitted, repeat the rejection and

make it Final. Applicant may file an appeal with the Board of Patent Appeals and Interferences after given a final rejection or after the claim has been rejected twice. Applicant may also file a new application prior to the abandonment of the original application, claiming benefit of the earlier filing date. This will allow continued prosecution of the claim.

The preparation, filing, and prosecution of a design patent application with the U.S. Patent Office requires a basic knowledge and understanding of the patent laws, rules, and procedures. Although a knowledgeable applicant can handle the design patent application, the assistance of a patent attorney or patent agent may be needed to obtain the greatest patent protection to which the applicant is entitled.

Filling in the Design Patent Application Form

- In item 1, include the complete names of all of the inventors. Also include a title of the invention.

- Include in item 2 a cross-reference to any related patent applications, along with application serial numbers and filing dates.

- In item 3, include a brief description indicating the type of view (e.g., front, side, rear, top, etc.) shown for each of the figures of drawings. For Figure 1, which shows a perspective view, fill in the name of the article which incorporates the design.

- In item 4, include any additional feature description, such as the nature and use of the claimed design, particularly if this is not included in the preamble.

- In the patent claim under item 5, fill in the name of the article which incorporates the design.

Checklist for Filing a Design Patent Application

❏ Prepare the complete design patent application arranged with the following components:

❏ Design application transmittal form (available from the U.S. Patent Office Web site)

❏ Specification. The specification should include the following sections in order:

  ❏ Preamble, stating the name of the applicant, title of the design, and a brief description of the nature and intended use of the article in which the design is embodied
  ❏ Cross-reference to related applications
  ❏ Description of the figures of the drawing
  ❏ Feature description
  ❏ A single claim

❏ Drawings or photographs (each drawing sheet is given a figure number and the inventor's name and address are on the top back of each sheet of formal drawings)

❏ Executed oath or declaration

❏ A check or money order payable to the Commissioner of Patents and Trademarks for the correct filing fee is enclosed.

❏ If applicable, the Verified Statement of Small Entity Status form is completed, signed, and dated in ink.

❏ An Information Disclosure Statement (Form PTO-1449) is completed. Copies of all cited references are attached.

❏ A Certificate of Express Mail is included with the Transmittal Form.

❏ A self-addressed return receipt post-card, with the mailing date and all papers listed on the back

❏ Place the complete patent application in a large envelope and send via Express Mail to:

Box Design Patent Application
Commissioner for Patents
Washington, DC 20231

❏ Respond to any Office Actions from the U.S. Patent Office within the time prescribed or after requesting an extension of time.

❏ Pay the issue fee ($800 at the time of this printing) if a Notice of Allowance and Issue Fee Due is received from the U.S. Patent Office.

Form 33: Design Patent Application Form

1.   PREAMBLE

I, [Name(s) of the Inventor(s)]_____

have invented a new design for a

(Title of the Invention)_____ as set forth in the

following specification:

2.   CROSS-REFERENCE TO RELATED APPLICATIONS

3.   BRIEF DESCRIPTION OF THE DRAWINGS

Figure 1 is a perspective view of a (Name of Article)_____ showing

my new design;

Figure 2 is a _____ view thereof;

Figure 3 is a _____ view thereof;

Figure 4 is a _____ view thereof;

and

Figure 5 is a _____ view thereof.

4.   FEATURE DESCRIPTION

5.   CLAIM

I claim: The ornamental design for

(Name of Article)_____ as shown and described.

23 *Obtaining Debt Relief Through Bankruptcy*

Deciding to File for Bankruptcy

The decision to file for bankruptcy is a serious one and should be given much consideration. The purpose of the bankruptcy laws is to provide a means for a debtor to obtain some relief from his or her debts. Because bankruptcy can show on your credit rating for many years, and because it can be time consuming and involve some legal expenses, you should only consider bankruptcy if no other financial solutions are available. Before filing for bankruptcy, consider all other options. Do a comprehensive financial analysis to see if filing for bankruptcy is in your best interest. Seek the advice of a professional financial advisor if necessary. You might even consider joining Debtors Anonymous, a helpful twelve-step program which may give you insights as to how your financial difficulties can be faced without bankruptcy. Enrollment in credit counseling is now required before you can file for bankruptcy after October 17, 2005.

Bankruptcy procedures in any state are governed by the Federal Bankruptcy Code. As a debtor prior to October 17, 2005, you normally had the choice as to the type of bankruptcy you filed, identified by the governing chapter of the Bankruptcy Code. For cases involving the liquidation of personal or business debts, you would file under Chapter 7 of the Bankruptcy Code, (i.e., a "Chapter 7" bankruptcy). Chapter 13 is used to restructure or adjust debt. It is available only to individuals. Chapter 11 is primarily used by businesses to provide some time for temporary relief from creditors. During this time you can formulate a plan to restructure your business debt. Although an individual can file under Chapter 11, this is not commonly done. For Chapter 11 proceedings, it is strongly recommended you engage the services of an attorney.

Liquidation under Chapter 7 may be called "straight bankruptcy." It involves the collection and distribution to creditors of all of your nonexempt property. You do keep certain exempt property. You will generally receive a discharge as to most prior debts after liquidation.

Under Chapter 13, you look for a reorganization of your debts. In a Chapter 13 case, you generally pay off your creditors through a three- to five-year plan that is approved by the Bankruptcy Court. After payments according to the plan, you are discharged as to most prior debts and you typically retain all your property.

Major changes to the U.S. bankruptcy laws took effect October 17, 2005, which made it less attractive for consumers to seek bankruptcy protection. The relevant changes will be reviewed later in this chapter, but they generally will require that a debtors: i) go to credit counseling before filing bankruptcy; ii) meet a means test before filing for a Chapter 7 bankruptcy; and iii) seek bankruptcy via Chapter 13 if the debtor's annual household income is above the median income for the state where the debtor resides.

This chapter will only deal with simple, voluntary cases filed after October 17, 2005, by you as an individual or jointly by you and your spouse under Chapter 7 or Chapter 13. Although bankruptcy cases can be complex and require legal counsel, some are simple and can be handled without an attorney. Legal fees for a simple bankruptcy case range from about $800 to $2,000, depending on location and complexity. In addition, there is a filing fee at the time of this printing of $274 for Chapter 7 or $189 for Chapter 13 filings. You should be aware that involuntary cases may be filed against you by a creditor. Also, bankruptcy cases may be filed by or against a corporation or a partnership.

All voluntary bankruptcy proceedings begin with the filing of a petition with the proper Bankruptcy Court. You must generally file your bankruptcy petition in the Bankruptcy Court or Federal District Court in the judicial district where you live.

You can file for bankruptcy individually, without involving your spouse in the bankruptcy case, or you and your spouse can file jointly. It is common for one spouse to transfer his or her assets to the other spouse before filing for individual bankruptcy. It is important, however, that you do not make such transfers to defraud creditors. Therefore, they should be made more than one year before filing for bankruptcy and without intent to defraud creditors. Otherwise, they will be considered fraudulent transfers and the assets will be considered part of the property to be distributed to creditors.

Filing under Chapter 7—Liquidation

The goal in filing for bankruptcy under Chapter 7 is to: 1) give you a "fresh start," and; 2) liquidate your assets and distribute them to legitimate creditors. There are two benefits to you in filing for bankruptcy under Chapter 7:

1) When you file a bankruptcy petition you get immediate, but temporary, protection from collection efforts of your creditors. The filing of the bankruptcy petition automatically stops creditors from trying to collect payment from you, whether by harassing letters, telephone calls, or lawsuits to collect debts. This relief is called a "stay." The stay usually lasts until the bankruptcy proceeding is closed. However, for proper cause, a creditor may ask the Bankruptcy Court to terminate the stay.

2) A bankruptcy discharge gives you permanent relief from most, but not all, of your debts. Bear in mind, however, that in exchange for the discharge of debts, you will have to give up all your nonexempt property and may have an unfavorable credit rating for several years.

Keep in mind that your annual household income must be at or below the median income for your state to satisfy the means test for a Chapter 7 filing.

The Chapter 7 Bankruptcy Petition

Your case for bankruptcy under Chapter 7 is commenced by filing a bankruptcy petition with the Clerk of the Bankruptcy Court. If filing as an individual you should use Form No. 1—Debtor's Petition, provided at the end of this chapter. Form No. 1A—Debtor's Joint Petition should be used when filing a joint petition with your spouse. The petition should indicate that it is being filed under Chapter 7. A joint bankruptcy case is not always certain but may be allowed by the Court for ease of administration where a husband and wife are jointly liable on their debts and jointly hold most of their property.

There is no requirement that you be insolvent to file for bankruptcy under Chapter 7. The bankruptcy petition must be filed in good faith and fraudulent transfers are not permitted. The Bankruptcy Court may dismiss your case if it is an abuse of the law. There is no limit to the total amount of your debt to file a Chapter 7 case. If your financial condition indicates that you have more than enough income for necessities, you may be prohibited by the Court from using Chapter 7, but may use Chapter 13 instead.

The bankruptcy petition can only be filed by a person who resides in the United States or has property, a domicile, or a place of business in the United States. The petition must be signed by you as the debtor. In the case of a joint petition, it must be signed by both you and your spouse.

The bankruptcy petition must be accompanied by a number of forms and schedules detailing your current financial situation. These include schedules of assets and liabilities, schedules of current income and expenditures, a schedule of property that you believe should be exempt from liquidation under local or federal bankruptcy rules, and a statement of financial affairs. Sample forms and schedules are appended at the end of this chapter.

Form No. 3 contains Schedules of Liabilities and Assets. Schedules A-1 to A-3 of Form No. 3 can be used to identify all of your creditors and the amount owed to each—your liabilities. The list of creditors must include their names, addresses and zip codes. Creditors are divided into the following three groups: 1) those holding security; 2) those not holding security but having priority, such as employees to whom you owe wages and taxes; and, 3) unsecured creditors without priority. The bankruptcy court may require that this list of creditors be formatted according to certain specifications. Check with the Clerk's office in the court where you are filing your bankruptcy petition to make sure your list of creditors is properly formatted. Schedules B-1 and B-2 of Form No. 3 is used to list all real and personal property you own—your assets. In addition to all your tangible assets such as real property, cash on hand, and household goods, you must also list all intangible property in which you have an interest, such as interests in companies, liq-

uidated debts owed to you, and general intangibles such as patents and copyrights. If you have any questions about what to include in your list of assets, you may want to check with a bankruptcy attorney.

Other information related to detailing your assets and liabilities is included in attached Form No. 4: Statement of Financial Affairs and Form No. 5: Statement of Current Income and Current Expenditures. You may also be required to file a Statement of Intentions if your schedule of assets and liabilities includes consumer debts that are secured by property that you own as collateral (such as a car, furniture, or other household items). This statement indicates the property you plan to retain and the property you plan to surrender for your secured consumer debts.

Filing Fee

The filing fee for a voluntary petition under Chapter 7 is currently $274. The fee is the same whether the petition is for you individually or jointly with your spouse.

The bankruptcy petition must be accompanied by the required filing fee. Checks or money orders should be made payable to "Clerk, U.S. Bankruptcy Court," or "Clerk, U.S. District Court," where applicable.

The filing fee may be paid in installments if an application for such installments is made to the Bankruptcy Court. The application for installment payment should be filed with the bankruptcy petition. The application is filed in duplicate and must be signed by you and also by your spouse if a joint petition is filed. The application should state that you are unable to pay the filing fee, except in the form of installments. The Bankruptcy Court may the permit the payment of the fee in no more than four installments. The last installment shall be paid no later than 120 days after filing. A sample Application to Pay Filing Fee in Installments (Official Form No. 2) is provided at the end of this chapter.

Exempt Property

Certain property and assets of yours are exempt and not involved in the bankruptcy proceeding. The kinds of property that are exempt are provided for by either state or federal law. Remember that you do not lose exempt property to the Bankruptcy Trustee. You normally have a choice of whether you would like the federal or state exemptions. Some states, however, will only allow you to claim the state exemptions. Generally, you can use the state exemptions for the state you lived in for the 730 days (2 years) before filing for bankruptcy.

The following table indicates whether the state or federal exemptions are allowed in each of the respective states:

State	Exemptions Allowed
Alabama	State
Alaska	State
Arizona	State
Arkansas	State or Federal
California	State
Colorado	State
Connecticut	State or Federal
Delaware	State
Florida	State
Georgia	State
Hawaii	State or Federal
Idaho	State
Illinois	State
Indiana	State
Iowa	State
Kansas	State
Kentucky	State
Louisiana	State
Maine	State
Maryland	State
Massachusetts	State or Federal
Michigan	State or Federal
Minnesota	State or Federal
Mississippi	State
Missouri	State
Montana	State
Nebraska	State
Nevada	State
New Hampshire	State
New Jersey	State or Federal
New Mexico	State or Federal
New York	State
North Carolina	State
North Dakota	State
Ohio	State
Oklahoma	State
Oregon	State
Pennsylvania	State or Federal
Rhode Island	State or Federal
South Carolina	State
South Dakota	State
Tennessee	State
Texas	State or Federal
Utah	State
Vermont	State or Federal
Virginia	State
Washington	State or Federal
Washington, DC	Local or Federal
West Virginia	State
Wisconsin	State or Federal
Wyoming	State

Be sure to check the exemptions and requirements for your particular state.

The federal law will allow you to claim (to the extent of any interest or equity you may have) the following as exempt property (the amounts double for married couples):

- Up to $18,450 in real estate or personal property used by you or a dependent as a residence (homestead exemption), or in a burial plot for you or a dependent.

- Up to $475 per item for household furnishings, household goods, appliances, clothing, boats, animals, crops, or musical instruments held for personal family, or household use, provided that the total amount of exemptions under this class can not exceed $9,850.

- Up to $1,225 total in jewelry held for personal, family, or household use.

- A general exemption of $925 plus up to $9,250 of any unused portion of the homestead exemption above. Thus, if you have no homestead exemption, you are allowed a general exemption of $10,175.

- Up to $1,850 in any books or tools of your trade or the trade of your dependent .

- Up to $2,950 in one automobile.

- Social security, unemployment, public assistance, veterans, crime victims' compensation, or disability benefits.

- Payment of a pension, stock bonus, annuity, or profit sharing or other similar plan, to the extent necessary for your support or the support of any dependent.

- Personal injury compensation payments up to $18,450.

- Life insurance policy with a value up to $9,850.

- Health aids.

- Other miscellaneous exemptions, such as alimony, support, and certain wrongful death and insurance payments.

- Any property that you are claiming as exempt should be listed in Schedule B-4 of Form No. 3.

Under the new bankruptcy law, the homestead exemption under the state exemptions generally cannot exceed $125,000 if the property was acquired within 1,215 days (3.3 years) before filing for bankruptcy. Additionally, the value of the state homestead exemption is reduced by the amount of any value added to the homestead property by the disposition of non-exempt property with the intent to defraud creditors within 10 years prior to the bankruptcy filing.

Administration of the Chapter 7 Bankruptcy

The bankruptcy petition, along with the required attached forms and schedules must be filed in the Bankruptcy Court for the district of your domicile, place of business, or where principal assets were located during the 180-day period prior to your filing for bankruptcy. Check the specific filing requirements for your jurisdiction to determine how many copies must be filed and whether there are other required formalities. Make sure you retain a copy of all papers for your records. If you are filing a bankruptcy petition without the aid of a lawyer, you must file the petition in person with the Clerk of the proper Bankruptcy Court. The day-to-day administration of bankruptcy cases is supervised by United States Trustees, who are appointed by the U.S. Justice Department.

Once the bankruptcy petition has been filed, creditors will be notified of the commencement of the case. This notice provides basic information about the bankruptcy proceeding and also states the date of the first meeting of creditors. This meeting, conducted pursuant to Section 341 of the Bankruptcy Code, is commonly called "the 341 meeting." As the debtor, you are required to attend this meeting. The Trustee assigned to your case will question you under oath, and the creditors will have the right to ask you questions concerning assets, liabilities, and general financial affairs.

The Trustee's principal duty in a Chapter 7 case is to collect and reduce to money the property of your estate. In a Chapter 7 case, you will normally have to give up all of the nonexempt property that you own at the time of filing the bankruptcy petition to be able to receive a discharge from your debts. In addition, the Trustee will also be able to collect certain property acquired by you within 180 days after filing for bankruptcy. This after-acquired property may include such things as inheritances, marital property settlements, and life insurance proceeds. The Trustee generally collects your nonexempt property, sells it, and, after taking a certain amount for compensation, distributes the cash to your creditors.

Filing under Chapter 13— Adjustment of Debts

In filing for bankruptcy under Chapter 13, you are seeking an adjustment of your debts for a period of time according to a court-approved plan. After the required payments are made according to the plan, you will receive a discharge. Unlike Chapter 7, you keep your property and assets in a Chapter 13 bankruptcy case. There is a stay of collection efforts by creditors against you and cosigners on your debts.

There are a number of reasons you should consider filing under Chapter 13 instead of Chapter 7. If you own real estate and the mortgage is in arrears, Chapter 7 may not help if you wish to retain the real estate. Under Chapter 13, you may propose a plan to cure the arrears over 36 months (or more in some cases). If you have unsecured debt that is nondischargeable under Chapter 7, they may be dischargeable under Chapter 13. However, alimony, child support, and student loans are not dischargeable under Chapter 13.

As mentioned earlier, you may be required to file for bankruptcy under Chapter 13 (instead of Chapter 7) if you meet the means test by having an annual household income above the median income for your state.

Filing Requirements under Chapter 13

Only certain individuals are allowed to file for bankruptcy under Chapter 13. Each individual must have an income, such as wages, a pension, social security, public assistance, or other regular payments. The individual (and his or her spouse if filing jointly) must have fixed, unsecured debts of less than $307,675 and fixed, secured debts of less than $922,975. An unsecured debt has no collateral—that is, no specific prop-

erty has been set aside for the creditor to use in satisfaction of the debt if it is not paid. A secured debt does have collateral. The individual must reside in the United States or have property, a domicile, or a place of business in the United States.

The filing fee for a Chapter 13 case is currently $189.

The Chapter 13 Bankruptcy Petition

A Chapter 13 case is commenced by the filing of a bankruptcy petition with the proper Bankruptcy Court. You should use Form No. 1 for individual cases and Form No. 1A for joint cases. The petition should indicate that it is being filed under Chapter 13.

The procedures for filing the Chapter 13 petition are basically the same as for a Chapter 7 case discussed earlier. You should file Schedules of Liabilities and Assets (Form No. 3), a Chapter 13 Statement (Form No. 6), including list of creditors with addresses, and a Chapter 13 Plan (Form No. 7).

You must file a plan in a Chapter 13 case representing your best effort to make payments to creditors. The plan may not provide for payments exceeding three years, unless the court, for good cause, approves a longer period, which can be no longer than five years. Under this plan, you will typically pay your income to the Bankruptcy Trustee, after you have deducted a reasonable amount for living expenses. The Trustee will then make payments to your creditors according to the plan.

The plan must provide for full payment of all priority claims such as taxes, wages, or certain undelivered or unprovided goods and services that you owe. The plan should also provide for any secured debts, such as your mortgages. However, regular future payments on your secured debts should not be provided for under the plan, but should be paid outside of the plan as they are part of your regular living expenses. This is because your secured creditors are not generally affected by your Chapter 13 filing, since they can attach the collateral securing their debts if they are not paid. For example, if you have a home mortgage payment of $1,000 a month, you should treat this as part of your regular living expenses and not as a debt payment under your Chapter 13 plan. Any back payments, however, should be included in your plan to keep your secured creditors from taking foreclosure actions due to these arrearages.

In preparing your Chapter 13 plan, you should also do a separate analysis to see how your creditors would do under a Chapter 7 filing. Your Chapter 13 plan should at least provide as much satisfaction to your creditors as they would receive under a Chapter 7 case. Otherwise, your creditors may object to your plan and may be able to force you into a Chapter 7 bankruptcy.

You should start making payments under your plan within 30 days after filing. The court may dismiss your case if you do not make the required payments.

Fraudulent Transfers

If you plan to file for bankruptcy, you are not permitted to transfer your property to friends and relatives or anyone else for little or no payment. Such a transfer is a fraud and will not be allowed by the Bankruptcy Court. To be fraudulent, the transfer must be done with the intent on your part to defraud your creditors or the Bankruptcy Court. If a transfer is held to be a fraudulent transfer, the creditors will be allowed to go after and recover the property that has been transferred. This usually covers all fraudulent transfers made within one year before you file for bankruptcy. Also, if the Bankruptcy Court finds that you have made a fraudulent transfer, the Court may refuse to grant a discharge to you. You are not allowed to conceal any of your property or assets.

Receiving a Discharge from Your Debts

If you receive a discharge, you are generally relieved from paying most debts that arose before your filing for bankruptcy.

A discharge from your debts is not guaranteed in a bankruptcy proceeding. However, the Bankruptcy Court will usually grant you a discharge unless the discharge is contested by your creditors or the bankruptcy trustee.

A discharge may be contested and denied to you for the following reasons:

- You have committed a fraudulent conveyance or have concealed property;

- You have falsified records, withheld records, made false claims, or attempted a bribe during the bankruptcy proceeding;

- You have refused to obey an order of the Bankruptcy Court;

- You have filed and received a bankruptcy discharge within the past eight years if you are filing for Chapter 7 bankruptcy. You may not receive a discharge in a Chapter 13 bankruptcy if you have filed and received a discharge in i) Chapter 7 within the previous four years or ii) Chapter 13 within the previous two years.

In a Chapter 13 case, you usually receive a discharge after completion of the payments required under your Chapter 13 plan. In both Chapter 7 and Chapter 13 cases, the Bankruptcy Court will conduct a discharge hearing.

Non-Dischargeable Debts

Even if you are granted a discharge, the discharge will not apply to certain nondischargeable debts. You will still have to pay the debts that can not be discharged. The following debts will generally not be discharged through bankruptcy:

- Taxes;

- Money obtained by fraud;

- Debts from willful or malicious injury to another person or property

- Credit purchases of $500 or more for luxury goods or services made within 90 days of bankruptcy filing

- Loans or cash advances of $750 or more taken within 70 days of bankruptcy filing

- Debts not listed on Schedule (Form No. 6);

- Embezzlement or theft;

- Support and alimony;

- Fines;

- Student loans for a period of five years (discharge from a student loan may be requested after you have made payments on the loan for five years or more); and

- Debts that arise after the filing for bankruptcy.

These debts may be discharged in a Chapter 13 bankruptcy if they are included in and paid under the Chapter 13 plan.

Checklist for Filing for Bankruptcy

Chapter 7—Voluntary Individual Liquidation

❏ Undergo credit counseling with an approved, nonprofit budget and credit counseling agency at least 180 days before filing for bankruptcy. Contact your local Bankruptcy Court for the approved credit counseling agencies near you.

❏ Determine if you satisfy the means test for a Chapter 7 filing. Annual household income must be at or below the median income for your state.

❏ Check with the Court Clerk of your local Bankruptcy Court for specific filing format, forms, documents, and other requirements. Complete these documents as required by your local Bankruptcy Court.

❏ Prepare Petition (Form No. 1 or Form No. 1A).

❏ Prepare an Application to Pay Filling Fee in Installments (Form No.2) if necessary.

❏ Prepare Schedules of Liabilities and Assets, including List of Creditors with addresses (Form No. 3).

❏ Prepare Statement of Financial Affairs (Form No. 4).

❏ Prepare Schedule of Current Income and Current Exenditures (Form No. 5).

❏ Prepare Statement of Intentions indicating property that you plan to keep or surrender if you have consumer debts which are secured by property that you own.

❏ File petition, along with schedules, statements, lists, and $274 filing fee with the proper Bankruptcy Court. Obtain case number and filing date from Court Clerk.

❏ Attend meeting of creditors and any other hearings as required by the Court.

❏ Turn over all nonexempt assets to Trustee.

Chapter 13—Adjustment of Debts

❏ Undergo credit counseling with an approved, nonprofit budget and credit counseling agency at least 180 days before filing for bankruptcy.

❏ Determine if you meet the requirements for a Chapter 13 filing. You must have regular income; fixed, unsecured debts of less than $307,675; and fixed, secured debts of less than $922,975.

❏ Check with the Court Clerk of your local Bankruptcy Court for specific filing format, forms, documents, and other requirements. Complete these documents as required by your local Bankruptcy Court.

❏ Prepare Petition (Form No. 1 or Form No. 1A).

❏ Prepare Schedule of Liabilities and Assets (Form No. 3).

❏ Prepare Chapter 13 Statement (Form No. 6).

❏ Prepare List of Creditors with addresses.

❏ Prepare Chapter 13 Plan (Form No. 7).

❏ File petition, along with schedules, statements, lists, and $189 filing fee with the proper Bankruptcy Court.

Obtain case number and filing date from Court Clerk.

❏ Make payments to the Bankruptcy Trustee according to the Chapter 13 plan.

❏ Attend hearings as required by the court.

Using an Attorney

❏ Consult an attorney if your Chapter 7 or Chapter 13 bankruptcy case involves difficult or complex issues. If you check any of the items below, your case may involve complicated issues that may require legal counsel.

❏ Are you operating a business?

❏ Have you given property or assets to friends or relatives for little or no payment within the past year?

❏ Are you involved as a partner in a partnership?

❏ Have you received a bankruptcy discharge under Chapter 7 within the past four years or under Chapter 13 within the past two years?

❏ Are you a stockbroker?

❏ Are you filing for reorganization of your debts under Chapter 11?

Voluntary Bankruptcy Case: Debtor's Petition

United States Bankruptcy Court for the _____ District of _____

Case No._____

Debtor's Name_____
(Include all names used within last six years)

Social Security No._____   Telephone No._____

1. Petitioner's address is:_____

2. Petitioner has resided (or has been domiciled) in this district for the preceding 180 days (or for a longer portion of such period than in any other district).

3. Petitioner is an individual and is qualified to file this petition and is entitled to the benefits of Title 11 of the United States Code as a voluntary debtor.

4. Petitioner is aware of and understands the relief available under Chapters 7, 11, 12, or 13 of Title 11, United States Code, and chooses to proceed under Chapter _____.

5. Other Declarations:

Wherefore, the petitioner respectfully requests relief in accordance with Chapter _____ of Title 11, United States Code.

I, _____, the petitioner named in the foregoing petition, declare under penalty of perjury that the foregoing is true and correct.

Date_____   Petitioner's Signature_____

Address _____

_____

Form No. 34A

Voluntary Bankruptcy Case: Debtor's Joint Petition

United States Bankruptcy Court for the _____ District of _____

Case No._____

❑ Debtor's Name_____
(Include all names used by debtor and spouse within last six years)

❑ Debtor's Spouse's Name_____

Debtor's Social Security No._____   Telephone No._____

Spouse's Social Security No._____

1. Petitioner's address is:_____

_____

2. Petitioners have resided (or have been domiciled) in this district for the preceding 180 days (or for a longer portion of such period than in any other district).

3. Petitioners are qualified to file this petition and are entitled to the benefits of Title 11 of the United States Code as a voluntary debtor.

4. Petitioners are aware of and understand the relief available under Chapters 7, 11, 12, or 13 of Title 11, United States Code, and choose to proceed under Chapter _____.

5. Other Declarations:

Wherefore, the petitioners respectfully requests relief in accordance with Chapter _____ of Title 11, United States Code.

We, _____, the petitioners

named in the foregoing petition, declare under penalty of perjury that the foregoing is true and correct.

Date _____   Petitioner's Signature_____

Petitioner's Signature_____

Address _____

_____

Form No. 35

Application to Pay Filing Fee in Installments

United States Bankruptcy Court for the _____ District of _____

Case No._____

Debtor's Name_____

(Include all names used within last six years)

Social Security No._____   Telephone No._____

(Include name and Social Security No. of Debtor's spouse if a joint petition is filed.)

Applicant is filing herewith a voluntary petition under Chapter _____.

Applicant is unable to pay the filing fee except in installments.

Applicant seeks permission to pay such fees to the Clerk of the Bankruptcy Court as follows:

                                    Amount   Date

1. _____

2. _____

3. _____

4. _____

Applicant has paid no money and transferred no property to his/her attorney or any other person for services relative to this case or any pending bankruptcy case. Applicant will make no such payment or transfer until the filing fee is paid. Applicant declares under penalty of perjury that the foregoing is true and correct.

Wherefore, applicant requests that he/she be permitted to pay the filing fee in installments.

Date_____   Applicant _____

                                      Applicant _____

                                      (Both Debtor and Spouse must sign if a joint petition is filed.)

                                      Address _____

Form No. 36		

Schedules of Liabilities and Assets

United States Bankruptcy Court for the _____ District of _____

Case No._____

Debtor's Name_____

(If a joint petition, prepare separate schedules for debtor's spouse)

Debtor's Social Security No. _____   Telephone No._____

Spouse's Social Security No. _____

These schedules are prepared for ❑ Debtor ❑ Debtor's Spouse_____(name)

Schedule A.—Statement of All Liabilities of Debtor

(Schedules A-1, A-2, and A-3 must include all the claims against the debtor, or debtor's spouse where applicable, or his/her property as of the date of the filing of the petition by or against him or her. Attach additional sheets properly identified and made a part hereof if necessary.)

Schedule A-1. - Unsecured Creditors Having Priority

Nature of claim	Name of creditor, account number, and complete mailing address with zip code	Specify when claim was incurred and the consideration therefor; specify name of any partner or any joint contractor on any debt	Indicate if claim is contingent, unliquidated, or disputed	Amount of claim
a Wages, salary, and commissions, vacation, severance and sick leave pay owing to workmen, servants, clerks, or traveling or city salesmen on salary or commission basis, whole or part time, whether or not selling exclusively for the debtor, not exceeding $10,000 to each, earned within 180 days before filing of petition or cessation of business if earlier (specify date)				
b Contribution to employee benefit plans for services rendered within 180 days before filing of petition or cessation of business, if earlier (specify date)				
c Claims of farmers, not exceeding $4,925 per individual				
d Claims of U.S. fishermen, not exceeding $4,925 per individual				
e Deposits by individuals, not exceeding $2,225 for each for purchase, lease, or rental of property or services for personal, family, or household use that were not delivered or provided				
f Claims of a spouse or child for alimony, maintenance, or support				
Taxes owing (itemize) 1. To the United States 2. To any state 3. To any other taxing authority				
			TOTAL	

Schedules of Liabilities and Assets (Continued)

Schedule A-2.—Creditors holding secured claims

Name of Creditor and complete mailing address including zip code (if unknown, so state)	Description of security and date when obtained by creditor	Specify when claim was incurred and the consideration therefor; when claim is contingent, unliquidated, disputed, or subject to setoff, evidenced by a judgment, negotiable instrument, or other writing, or incurred as partner or joint contractor, so indicate; specify name of any partner or joint contractor on any debt	Indicate if claim is contingent, unliquidated, or disputed	Market Value	Amount of claim without deduction of value of security
			TOTAL		

Schedule A-3.—Creditors Having Unsecured Claims Without Priority

Name of creditor (including last known holder of any negotiable instrument) and complete mailing address including zip code (if unknown, so state)	Specify when claim was incurred and the consideration therefor; when claim is contingent, unliquidated, disputed, subject to setoff, evidenced by a judgment, negotiable instrument, or other writing, or incurred as partner or joint contractor, so indicate; specify name of any partner or joint contractor on any debt	Indicate if claim is contingent, unliquidated, or disputed	Amount of claim
		TOTAL	

Schedules of Liabilities and Assets (Continued)

Schedule B.—Statement of All Property of Debtor

(Schedules B-1, B-2, B-3, and B-4 must include all property of the debtor as of the date of the filing of the petition by or against him/her. Attach additional sheets properly identified and made a part hereof, if necessary.)

Schedule B-1.—Real Property

Description and location of all real property in which debtor has an interest (including equitable and future interests, interests in estates by the entirety, community property, life estates, leaseholds, and rights and powers exercisable for his/her own behalf)	Nature of interest (specify all deeds and written instruments relating thereto)	Market value of debtor's interest without deduction for secured claims listed in Schedule A-2 or exemptions claimed in Schedule B-4
	TOTAL	

Schedules of Liabilities and Assets (Continued)

Schedule B-2.— Personal Property

Type of Property	Description and Location	Market value of debtor's interest without deduction for secured claims listed on Schedule A-2 or exemptions claimed in Schedule B-4
a. Cash on hand		
b. Deposits on money with banking institutions, savings and loan associations, credit unions, public utility companies, landlords, and others		
c. Household goods, supplies, and furnishings		
d. Books, pictures, and other art objects; stamp, coin, and other collections		
e. Wearing apparel, jewelry, firearms, sports equipment, and other personal possessions		
f. Automobiles, trucks, trailers, and other vehicles		
g. Boats, motors, and their accessories		
h. Livestock, poultry, and other animals		
i. Farming equipment, supplies, and implements		
j. Office equipment, furnishings, and supplies		
k. Machinery, fixtures, equipment, and supplies (other than those listed in Items j and i) used in business		
l. Inventory		
m. Tangible personal property of any other description		
n. Patents, copyrights, franchises, and other general intangibles (specify all documents and writings relating thereto)		
o. Government and corporate bonds and other negotiable and nonnegotiable instruments		
p. Other liquidated debts owing debtor		
q. Contingent and unliquidated claims of every nature, including counterclaims of the debtor (give estimated value of each)		
r. Interests in insurance policies (itemize surrender or refund values of each)		
s. Annuities		
t. Stock and interests in incorporated and unincorporated companies (itemize separately)		
u. Interests in partnerships		
v. Equitable and future interests, life estates, and rights or powers exercisable for the benefit of the debtor (other than those listed in Schedule B-1) (specify all written instruments relating thereto)		
w. Other personal property (itemize)		
	TOTAL	

Schedule B-3.—Property not otherwise scheduled

Type of Property	Description and Location	Market value of debtor's interest without deduction for secured claims listed in Schedule A-2 or exemption claimed in Schedule B-4
a. Property transferred under assignment for benefit of creditors, within 120 days prior to filing of petition (specify date of assignment, name and address of assignee, amount realized there-from by the assignee, and disposition of proceeds so far as known to debtor)		
b. Property of any kind not otherwise scheduled		
	TOTAL	

Debtor selects the following property as exempt pursuant to 11 U.S.C. 522(b) and (d) [or the laws of the State of _____]

Schedule B-4. —Property Claimed as Exempt

Type of Property	Location, description, and, so far as relevant to the claim of exemption, present use of property	Specify statute creating the exemption	Value claimed exempt
		TOTAL	

Schedules of Liabilities and Assets (Continued)

Summary of debts and property. (From the statement of the debtor in Schedules A and B)

Schedule	Debts	Totals
A-1/a,b,c,d	Wages, etc. having priority	
A-1(e)	Deposits of money	
A-1/f(1)	Taxes owing United States	
A-1/f(2)	Taxes owing states	
A-1/f(3)	Taxes owing other taxing authorities	
A-2	Creditors holding secured claims	
A-3	Unsecured claims without priority	
	Schedule A total	

Schedule	Property	Totals
B-1	Real Property (total value)	
B-2/a	Cash on hand	
B-2/b	Deposits	
B-2/c	Household goods	
B-2/d	Books, pictures, and collections	
B-2/e	Wearing apparel and personal possessions	
B-2/f	Automobiles and other vehicles	
B-2/g	Boats, motors, and accessories	
B-2/h	Livestock and other animals	
B-2/i	Farming supplies and implements	
B-2/j	Office equipment and supplies	
B-2/k	Machinery, equipment, and supplies used in business	
B-2/l	Inventory	
B-2/m	Other tangible personal property	
B-2/n	Patents and other general intangibles	
B-2/o	Bonds and other instruments	
B-2/p	Other liquidated debts	
B-2/q	Contingent and unliquidated claims	
B-2/r	Interest in insurance policies	
B-2/s	Annuities	
B-2/t	Interests in corporations and unincorporated companies	
B-2/u	Interests in partnerships	
B-2/v	Equitable and future interests, rights, and powers	
B-2/w	Other personal property	
B-3/a	Property assigned for benefit of creditors	
B-3/b	Property not otherwise scheduled	
B-4	Property claimed as exempt **Totals**	
	Schedule B total	

Total Assets: _____ Total Liabilities: _____

Unsworn Declaration under Penalty of Perjury of Individual to Schedules A and B

I, _____, declare under penalty of perjury that I have read the foregoing schedules,

consisting of _____ sheets, and that they are true and correct to the best of my knowledge, information, and belief.

Date _____   Signature _____

Form No. 36A

Chapter 7 Individual Debtor's Statement of Intention

United States Bankruptcy Court for the _____ District of _____

Case No._____

In re:

Debtor's Name _____

Debtor's Social Security No._____

1. I have filed a schedule of assets and liabilities which includes consumer debts secured by property of the estate.

2. I intend to do the following with respect to the property of the estate which secures those consumer debts:

    a. Property to Be Surrendered.

Description of Property	**Creditor's Name**
1.	
2.	
3.	
4.	

    b. Property to Be Retained

[--------------------Check any applicable statement.-------------------]

Description of Property	Creditor's Name	Property is claimed as exempt	Property will be redeemed pursuant to 11 U.S.C. Sec. 722	Property will be reaffirmed pursuant to 11 U.S.C. Sec. 524(c)
1.				
2.				
3.				
4.				

Date: _____

Signature of Debtor:_____

Unsworn Declaration under Penalty of Perjury of Individual to Schedules A and B

I, _____, declare under penalty of perjury that I have read the foregoing schedules, consisting of _____ sheets, and that they are true and correct to the best of my knowledge, information, and belief.

Date _____ Signature _____

Form No. 37:

Statement of Financial Affairs

United States Bankruptcy Court for the _____ District of _____

Case No._____

Debtor's Name_____

(Include all names used within past six years)

Debtor's Social Security No._____   Telephone No._____

Spouse's Social Security No._____

[Each question should be answered or the failure to answer explained. If the answer is "none," or "not applicable" this should be stated. If additional space is needed for the answer to any question, a separate sheet, properly identified and made a part hereof, should be used and attached. If a joint petition, prepare a separate statement for debtor's spouse.

The term, "original petition," as used in the following questions, shall mean the petition filed under Rule 1002 or 1004.]

This statement is prepared for: ❑ Debtor   ❑ Debtor's Spouse_____(name)

1. Name and residence

    a. What is your full name and social security number?

    b. Have you used, or been known by, any other names within the six years immediately preceding the filing of the original petition herein? (If so, give particulars.)

    c. Where do you now reside?

    d. Where else have you resided during the six years immediately preceding the filing of the original petition herein?

2. Occupation and income

    a. What is your occupation?

    b. Where are you now employed? (Give the name and address of your employer, or the address at which you carry on your trade or profession, and the length of time you have been so employed or engaged.)

    c. Have you been in a partnership with anyone, or engaged in any business during the six years immediately preceding the filing of the original petition herein? (If so, give particulars, including names, dates, and places.)

    d. What amount of income have you received from your trade or profession during each of the two calendar years immediately preceding the filing of the original petition herein?

    e. What amount of income have you received from other sources during each of these two years? (Give particulars, including each source and the amount received therefrom.)

3. Tax returns and refunds

    a. Where did you file your federal and state income tax returns for the two years immediately preceding the filing of the original petition herein?

    b. What tax refunds (income and other) have you received during the year immediately preceding the filing of the original petition?

    c. To what tax refunds (income or other), if any, are you, or may you be, entitled? (Give particulars, including information as to any refund payable jointly to you and your spouse or any other person.)

4. Bank Accounts and safe deposit boxes

a. What bank accounts have you maintained, alone or together with any other person, and in your own or any other name within the two years immediately preceding the filing of the original petition herein? (Give the name and address of each bank, the name in which the deposit is maintained, and the name and address of every other person authorized to make withdrawals from such account.)

b. What safe deposit box or boxes or other depository or depositories have you kept or used for your securities, cash, or other valuables within the two years immediately preceding the filing of the original petition herein? (Give the name and address of the bank or other depository, the name in which each box or other depository was kept, the name and address of every other person who had the right of access thereto, a brief description of the contents thereof, and, if the box has been surrendered, state when surrendered, or, if transferred, when transferred, and the name and address of the transferee.)

5. Books and records

a. Have you kept books of account or records relating to your affairs within the two years immediately preceding the filing of the original petition herein?

b. In whose possession are these books or records? (Give names and addresses.)

c. If any of these books or records are not available, explain.

d. Have any books of account or records relating to your affairs been destroyed, lost, or otherwise disposed of within the two years immediately preceding the filing of the original petition herein? (If so, give particulars, including date of destruction, loss, or disposition, and reason therefor.)

6. Property held for another person

What property do you hold for any other person? (Give name and address of each person, and describe the property, or value thereof, and all writings relating thereto.)

7. Prior bankruptcy

What cases under the Bankruptcy Act or Title 11, United States Code have previously been brought by or against you? (State the location of the bankruptcy court, the nature and number of each case, the date when it was filed, and whether a discharge was granted or refused, the case was dismissed, or a composition, arrangement, or plan was confirmed.)

8. Receiverships, general assignments, and other modes of liquidation

a. Was any of your property, at the time of the filing of the original petition herein, in the hands of a receiver, trustee, or other liquidating agent? (If so, give a brief description of the property, the name and address of the receiver, trustee, or other agent, and, if the agent was appointed in a court proceeding, the name and location of the court, the title and number of the case, and the nature thereof.)

b. Have you made any assignment of your property for the benefit of your creditors, or any general settlement with your creditors, within one year immediately preceding the filing of the original petition herein? (If so, give dates, the name and address of the assignee, and a brief statement of the terms of assignment or settlement.)

9. Property in hands of third person

   a. Is any other person holding anything of value in which you have an interest? (Give name and address, location and description of the property, and circumstances of the holding.)

10. Suits, executions, and attachments

   a. Were you a party to any suit pending at the time of the filing of the original petition? (If so, give the name and location of the court and the title case number, status, and nature of the proceeding.)

   b. Were you a party to any suit terminated within the year immediately preceding the filing of the original petition herein? (If so, give the name and location of the court, the title and nature of the proceeding, and the result.)

   c. Has any of your property been attached, garnished, or seized under any legal or equitable process within the year immediately preceding the filing of the original petition herein? (If so, describe the property seized or person garnished, and at whose suit.)

11. Loans repaid

What repayments on loans in whole or in part have you made during the year immediately preceding the filing of the original petition herein? (Give the name and address of the lender, the amount of the loan and when received, the amounts and dates of payments and, if the lender is a relative or insider, the relationship.)

12. Transfers of property

   a. Have you made any gifts, other than ordinary and usual presents to family members and charitable donations, during the year immediately preceding the filing of the original petition herein? (If so, give names and addresses of donees and dates, description, and value of gifts.)

   b. Have you made any other transfer, absolute or for the purpose of security, or any other disposition of real or tangible personal property during the year immediately preceding the filing of the original petition herein? (Give a description of the property, the date of the transfer or disposition, to whom transferred, or how disposed of, and, if the transferee is a relative or insider, the relationship, the consideration, if any, received therefor, and the disposition of such consideration.)

13. Repossessions, foreclosures, and returns

Has any property been returned to, or repossessed or sold via foreclosure, or transferred in lieu of foreclosure by, the seller or by a secured party during the year immediately preceding the filing of the original petition herein? (If so, give particulars including the name and address of the party getting the property and its description and value.)

14. Losses

   a. Have you suffered any losses from fire, thefts, or gambling during the year immediately preceding or since the filing of the original petition herein? (If so, give particulars, including dates, names, and places, and the amounts of money or value and general description of property lost.)

b. Was the loss covered in whole or part by insurance? (If so, give particulars.)

15. Payments or transfers to attorneys

   a. Have you consulted an attorney during the year immediately preceding or since the filing of the original petition herein? (Give dates, name, and address.)

   b. Have you during the year immediately preceding or since the filing of the original petition herein paid any money or transferred any property to the attorney or to any other person on his behalf? (If so, give particulars, including amount paid or value of property transferred and date of payment or transfer.)

   c. Have you, either during the year immediately preceding or since the filing of the original petition herein, agreed to pay any money or transfer any property to an attorney at law, or to any other person on his behalf? (If so, give particulars, including amount and terms of obligation.)

16. Other

I, _____, declare under penalty of perjury that I have read the answers contained in the foregoing statement of financial affairs and they are true and correct to the best of my knowledge, information, and belief.

Date_____   Debtor's Signature _____

                                                    (or spouse's signature, if applicable)

Schedule of Current Income and Current Expenditures

United States Bankruptcy Court for the _____ District of _____

Case No._____

Debtor's Name_____

(Include all names used within past six years)

Debtor's Social Security No._____ Telephone No._____

Spouse's Social Security No._____

[Complete this form by answering each question. If your answer to a question is "none" or "not applicable," so state.]

A. Family Status

1. The debtor is: [check one of the following] ❑ Married ❑ Single ❑ Separated ❑ Divorced

2. The name of the debtor's spouse is _____

3. The debtor supports the following dependents [other than the debtor's spouse]:

Name	**Age**	**Relationship to Debtor**

B. Employment and Occupation

1. The debtor is employed by _____(name of employer)

as _____(nature of position).

2. The debtor is self-employed as _____ (nature of business or profession)

at the following principal place of business _____ (address).

3. The debtor's spouse is employed by _____(name of employer)

as _____ (nature of position).

4. The debtor's spouse is self-employed as _____ (nature of business or profession)

at the following principal place of business _____ (address).

Schedule of Current Income and Current Expenditures (continued)

C. Current Income

Give estimated average current monthly income of debtor and spouse, consisting of:

	Debtor	Spouse
1. Gross pay (wages, salary, or commissions)	$_____	$_____
2. Take home pay (gross pay less all deductions)	$_____	$_____
3. Regular income available from the operation of a business or profession	$_____	$_____
4. Other income:		
Interest and dividends	$_____	$_____
From real estate or personal property	$_____	$_____
Social Security	$_____	$_____
Pension or other retirement income	$_____	$_____
Other (specify) _____	$_____	$_____
5. Alimony, maintenance, or support payments:		
Payable to the debtor for the debtor's use	$_____	$_____
Payable to the debtor for the support of another (attach additional sheet listing the name, age, and relationship to the debtor of persons for whose benefit payments are made)	$_____	$_____
Total estimated current monthly income	$_____	$_____

If you anticipate receiving additional income on other than a monthly basis in the next six months (such as an income tax refund), attach additional sheet of paper and describe.

If you anticipate a substantial change in your income in the immediate future, attach additional sheet of paper and describe.

Schedule of Current Income and Current Expenditures (continued)

D. Schedule of Current Expenditures: (give estimated average current monthly expenditures of debtor and spouse)

1. Home expenses:

    a. Rent or home loan payment (including any assessment or maintenance fee) $_____

    b. Real estate taxes $_____

    c. Utilities:

        Electricity $_____

        Gas $_____

        Water $_____

        Telephone $_____

        Other (specify)_____ $_____

                        Total Utilities $_____

    d. Home maintenance (repairs and upkeep) $_____

                   Total, all home expenses $_____

2. Other expenses:

    a. Taxes (not deducted from wages or included in home loan payment or included in real estate taxes) $_____

    b. Alimony, maintenance, or support payments

        (attach additional sheet listing name, age, and relationship of beneficiaries) $_____

    c. Insurance (not deducted from wages)

        Life $_____

        Health $_____

        Auto $_____

        Homeowner's or Renter's $_____

        Other (specify) _____ $_____

                 Total insurance expenses $_____

    d. Installment payments:

        Auto $_____

        Other (specify) _____ $_____

    e. Transportation (not including auto payments) $_____

    f. Education (including tuition and school books) $_____

    g. Food $_____

    h. Clothing $_____

    i Medical, dental, and medicines $_____

    j. Laundry and cleaning $_____

    k. Newspapers, periodicals, and books $_____

    l. Recreation, clubs, and entertainment $_____

    m. Charitable contributions $_____

    n. Other expenses (specify) _____ $_____

             Total estimated current monthly expenses $_____

Schedule of Current Income and Current Expenditures (continued)

If you anticipate a substantial change in your expenses in the immediate future, attach additional sheet of paper and describe.

Unsworn Declaration under Penalty of Perjury

I/ We, _____ , declare under penalty of perjury that I/We have read the foregoing schedule and any attachment, consisting of _____ sheets in all, and that they are true and correct to the best of my/our knowledge, information, and belief.

Signature of Debtor _____   Date _____

Signature of Spouse_____   Date _____

(If joint petition, both debtors must sign.)

Form No. 39

Chapter 13 Statement

United States Bankruptcy Court for the _____ District of _____

In re: Case No._____

Debtor's Name_____

(Include all names used within past six years)

Social Security No._____   Telephone No._____

[Each question shall be answered or the failure to answer explained. If the answer is "none" or "not applicable" so state. If additional space is needed for the answer to any question, a separate sheet, properly identified and made a part hereof, should be used and attached.

The term "original petition," used in the following questions, shall mean the original petition filed under 301 of the Code or, if the Chapter 13 case was converted from another chapter of the Code, shall mean the petition by or against you which originated the first case.

This form must be completed in full whether a single or a joint petition is filed. When information is requested for "each" or "either spouse filing a petition" it should be supplied for both when a joint petition is filed. For a single petition, supply information relating only to the debtor filing the petition.]

1. Name and residence.

    a. Give full name.

        Husband (or if single, Debtor) _____

        Wife_____

    b. Where does debtor, if single, or each spouse filing a petition now reside?

        (1) Mailing address of husband [or Debtor] _____

                                  _____

        (2) Mailing address of wife _____

                                  _____

        (3) Telephone number including area code: Husband [or, if single, Debtor] _____

                                          Wife   _____

    c. What does debtor, if single, or each spouse filing a petition consider his or her residence, if different from that listed in b, above?

        Husband [or Debtor]_____

        Wife_____

2. Occupation and income.

a. Give present occupation of debtor, if single, or each spouse filing a petition. (If more than one, list all for debtor or each spouse filing a petition.)

Husband (or Debtor) _____

Wife _____

b. What is the name, address, and telephone number of present employer (or employers) of debtor, if single, or each spouse filing a petition? (Include also any identifying badge or card number with employer.)

Husband (or Debtor) _____

_____

Wife _____

_____

c. How long has debtor, if single, or each spouse filing a petition been employed by present employer?

Husband (or Debtor) _____

Wife _____

d. If debtor or either spouse filing a petition has not been employed by present employer for a period of one year, state the name of prior employer(s) and nature of employment during that period.

Husband (or Debtor) _____

_____

Wife _____

_____

e. Has debtor or either spouse filing a petition operated a business, in partnership or otherwise, during the past three years? (If so, give the particulars, including names, dates, and places.)

Husband (or Debtor) _____

_____

Wife _____

_____

f. Answer the following questions for debtor, if single, or each spouse whether single or joint petition is filed unless spouses are separated and a single petition is filed:

(1)   What are your gross wages, salary, or commissions per pay period?

	Husband (or Debtor)	Wife
(a) Weekly	_____	_____
(b) Semi-monthly	_____	_____
(c) Monthly	_____	_____
(d) Other (specify)	_____	_____

(2)   What are your payroll deductions per pay period for:

	Husband	Wife
(a) Payroll taxes (including social security)	_____	_____
(b) Insurance	_____	_____
(c) Credit union	_____	_____
(d) Union dues	_____	_____
(e) Other (specify)	_____	_____

(3)   What is your take-home pay per pay period? _____   _____

(4)   What was the amount of your gross income
        for the last calendar year?   _____   _____

(5)   Is your employment subject to seasonal or other change?   _____   _____

(6)   Has either of you made any wage assignments or allotments? [If so, indicate which spouse's wages were assigned or allotted, the name and address of the person to whom assigned or allotted, and the amount owing, if any, to such person. If allotment or assignment is to a creditor, the claim should also be listed in Item 11a.]

3.   Dependents. (To be answered by debtor if unmarried, otherwise for each spouse whether single or joint petition is filed unless spouses are separated and a single petition is filed.)

   a.   Does either of you pay (or receive) alimony, maintenance, or support? (Yes or no) _____.
            If so, how much per month?_____ For whose support? (Give name, age, and relationship to you.)
            Husband (or Debtor) _____

            _____
            Wife _____

            _____

   b.   List all other dependents, other than present spouse, not listed in (a) above. (Give name, age and relationship to you.)
            Husband (or Debtor) _____

            _____
            Wife _____

            _____

4. Budget.

  a. Give your estimated average future monthly income, if unmarried,

   otherwise for each spouse whether single or joint petition is filed,

   unless spouses are separated and a single petition is filed.

   (1) Husband's [or Debtor's] monthly take-home pay _____

   (2) Wife's monthly take-home pay _____

   (3) Other monthly income [specify] _____

   Total _____

  b. Give estimated average future monthly expenses of family (not including

   debts to be paid under plan), consisting of:

   (1) Rent or home mortgage payment (include lot rental for trailer) _____

   (2) Utilities:

     Electricity _____

     Heat _____

     Water _____

     Telephone _____

   Total Utilities _____

   (3) Food _____

   (4) Clothing _____

   (5) Laundry and cleaning _____

   (6) Newspapers, periodicals, and books (including school books) _____

   (7) Medical and drug expenses _____

   (8) Insurance (not deducted from wages)

     (a) Auto _____

     (b) Other _____

   (9) Transportation (not including auto payments to be paid under plan) _____

   (10) Recreation _____

   (11) Dues, union, professional, social or otherwise (not deducted from wages) _____

   (12) Taxes (not deducted from wages) _____

   (13) Alimony, maintenance, or support payments _____

   (14) Other payments for support of dependents not living at home _____

   (15) Religious and other charitable contributions _____

   (16) Other (specify) _____ _____

   Total _____

  c. Excess of estimated future monthly income over estimated future expenses

   (Total from Item 4a above minus total from Item 4b above.) **_____**

  d. Total amount to be paid each month under plan **_____**

5. Payment of attorney.

  a. How much have you agreed to pay or what property have you agreed to transfer to your attorney in connection with this case?

  b. How much have you paid or what have you transferred to the attorney?

  _____

6. Tax refunds. [To be answered by debtor, if unmarried, otherwise for each spouse whether single or joint petition is filed, unless spouses are separated and a single petition is filed.]

  To what tax refunds (income or other), if any, is either of you, or may either of you, be entitled? [Give particulars, including information as to any refunds payable jointly to you or any other person. All such refunds should also be listed in Item 13b.]

7. Financial accounts, certificates of deposit, and safe deposit boxes. [To be answered by debtor, if unmarried, otherwise for each spouse whether single or joint petition is filed unless spouses are separated and a single petition is filed.]

  a. Does either of you currently have any accounts or certificates of deposit or shares in banks, savings and loan, thrift, building and loan and homestead associations, credit unions, brokerage houses, pension funds and the like? [If so, give name and address of each institution, number and nature of account, current balance, and name and address of every other person authorized to make withdrawals from the account. Such accounts should also be listed in Item 13b.]

  b. Does either of you currently keep any safe deposit boxes or other depositories? [If so, give name and address of bank or other depository, name and address of every other person who has a right of access thereto, and a brief description of the contents thereof, which should also be listed in Item 13b.]

8. Prior Bankruptcy.

  What cases under the Bankruptcy Act or Bankruptcy Code have previously been brought by or against you or either spouse filing a petition? (State the location of the bankruptcy court, the nature and number of each case, the date when it was filed, and whether a discharge was granted or denied, the case was dismissed, or a composition, arrangement, or plan was confirmed.)

9. Foreclosures, executions, and attachments. (To be answered by debtor, if unmarried, otherwise for each spouse whether single or joint petition is filed unless spouses are separated and a single petition is filed.)

  a. Is any of the property of either of you, including real estate, involved in a foreclosure proceeding, in or out of court? (If so, identify the property and the person foreclosing.)

  b. Has any property or income of either of you been attached, garnished, or seized under any legal or equitable process within the 90 days immediately preceding the filing of the original petition herein? (If so, describe the property seized, or person garnished, and at whose suit.)

10. Repossessions and returns.

(To be answered by debtor, if unmarried, otherwise for each spouse whether single or joint petition is filed unless spouses are separated and a single petition is filed.)

Has any property of either of you been returned to, repossessed, or seized by the seller or by any other party, including a landlord, during the 90 days immediately preceding the filing of the original petition herein? (If so, give particulars, including the name and address of the party taking the property and its description and value.)

11. Transfers of Property.

(To be answered by debtor, if unmarried, otherwise for each spouse whether single or joint petition is filed unless spouses are separated and a single petition is filed.)

a. Has either of you made any gifts, other than ordinary and usual presents to family members and charitable donations, during the year immediately preceding the filing of the original petition herein? (If so, give names and addresses of donees and dates, description and value of gifts.)

b. Has either of you made any other transfer, absolute or for the purpose of security, or any other disposition of real or personal property during the year immediately preceding the filing of the original petition herein? (Give a description of the property, the date of the transfer or disposition, to whom transferred or how disposed of, and, if the transferee is a relative or insider, the relationship, the consideration, if any, received therefor, and the disposition of such consideration.)

12. Debts.

(To be answered by debtor, if unmarried, otherwise for each spouse whether single or joint petition is filed.)

a. Debts Having Priority.

(1) Nature of Claim	(2) Name of creditor, account number, and complete mailing address including zip code	(3) Specify when claim was incurred and the consideration there- for; when claim is is subject to setoff, evidenced by a judgment, negotiable instrument, or other writing	(4) Indicate if claim is contingent, unliquidated, or disputed	(5) Amount of claim
1. Wages, salary, and commissions, including vacation, severance and sick leave pay owing to employees not exceeding $10,000 to each, earned within 180 days before filing of petition or cessation of business (if earlier specify date.)				$_____
2. Contributions to employee benefit plans for services rendered within 180 days before filing of petition or cessation of business (if earlier, specify date.)				$_____
3. Deposits by individuals, not exceeding $2,225 for each, for purchase, lease, or rental of property or services for personal, family, or household use that were not delivered or provided.				
4. Claims of a spouse or child for alimony, maintence, or support				$_____
5. Taxes owing (itemize by type of tax and taxing authority) (A) To the United States (B) To any state (C) To any other taxing authority				$_____ $_____ $_____
			Total	_____

b. Secured Debts. List all debts which are or may be secured by real or personal property. (Indicate in sixth column, if debt is payable in installments, the amount of each installment, the installment period [monthly, weekly, otherwise], and number of installments in arrears, if any. Indicate in last column whether husband or wife is solely liable, or whether you are jointly liable.)

Creditor's name, account number and complete mailing address, including zip code	Consideration or basis for debt	Amount claimed by creditor	If disputed, amount admitted by debtor	Description of collateral (include year and make of automobile)	Installment amount, period and number of installments in arrears	Husband or wife, solely liable or jointly liable

Total secured debts _____

c. Unsecured Debts. List all other debts, liquidated and unliquidated, including taxes, attorney's fees, and tort claims.

Creditor's name, account number, and complete mailing address, including zip code	Consideration or basis for debt	Amount claimed by Creditor	If disputed, amount admitted by Debtor	Husband or wife, solely liable or jointly liable

Total unsecured debts $_____

13. Codebtors. (to be answered by debtor, if unmarried, otherwise for each spouse whether single or joint petition is filed.)

   a. Are any other persons liable, as cosigners, guarantors, or in any other manner, on any of the debts of either of you or is either of you so liable on the debts of others? (If so, give particulars, indicating which spouse is liable and including names of creditors, nature of debt, names and addresses of codebtors, and their relationship, if any, to you.)

   b. If so, have the codebtors made any payments on the debts? (Give name of each codebtor and amount paid by codebtor.)

   c. Has either of you made any payments on the debts? (If so, specify total amount paid to each creditor, whether paid by husband or wife, and name of codebtor.)

14. Property and Exemptions.

   (To be answered by debtor, if unmarried, otherwise for each spouse whether single or joint petition is filed.)

   a. Real Property. List all real property owned by either of you at date of filing of original petition herein.

   (Indicate in last column whether owned solely by husband or wife, or jointly.)

Description and location of property	Name of any coowner other than spouse	Present market value (without deduction for mortgage or other security interest)	Amount of mortgage or other security interest on this property	Name of mortgagee or other secured creditor	Value claimed exempt (specify federal or state statute creating the exemption)	Owned solely by husband or wife or jointly

b. Personal Property. List all other property, owned by either of you at date of filing of original petition herein.

Description	Location of property if not at debtor's residence	Name of coowner other than spouse	Present market value (without deduction for mortgage or other security interest)	Amount of mortgage or other security interest on this property	Name of mortgagee or other secured creditor	Value claimed exempt (specify federal or state statute creating the exemption)	Owned solely by husband or wife or jointly
Autos [give year and make]							
Household goods							
Personal effects							
Cash or financial account							
other (specify) _____							

(To be signed by both spouses when joint petition is filed.)

I, _____, (if joint petition is filed and I, _____,) declare under penalty of perjury that I have read the answers contained in the foregoing statement, consisting of _____ sheets, and that they are true and complete to the best of my knowledge, information, and belief.

Husband (or Debtor) _____

Wife _____

Date _____

Chapter 13 Plan

United States Bankruptcy Court for the _____ District of _____

Debtor's Name _____ Case No _____

Spouse's Name _____

Debtor's Social Security No._____

Spouse's Social Security No. _____

1. Amount of each payment to be made by the debtor to the Bankruptcy Trustee. $_____

2. Frequency of payments. (Check one)
❑ Weekly ❑ Bi-Weekly ❑ Semi-Monthly ❑ Monthly ❑ Other_____

3. Amount to be paid on priority claims:

Name	Payment per Month under Plan	Total Amount to be Paid
_____	_____	_____
_____	_____	_____
_____	_____	_____

4. For secured creditors, provide the following data:

Name	Description of Collateral (Value)	Payment per Month under Plan	Total Amount to be Paid
_____	_____	_____	_____
_____	_____	_____	_____
_____	_____	_____	_____
_____	_____	_____	_____
_____	_____	_____	_____
_____	_____	_____	_____
_____	_____	_____	_____
_____	_____	_____	_____

(Attach additional sheets properly identified and made a part hereof, if necessary to complete Item 4 or 5.)

5. Amount to be paid to unsecured creditors:

Name	Payment per Month under Plan	Total Amount to be Paid
_____	_____	_____
_____	_____	_____
_____	_____	_____
_____	_____	_____
_____	_____	_____
_____	_____	_____
_____	_____	_____
_____	_____	_____

6. Bankruptcy Trustee's Compensation: $_____ per _____

7. The Plan will be completed in _____ months.

8. Other information:

Living expenses $_____ per month

Earnings and income $_____ per month

Date_____   Debtor's Signature_____

Spouse's Signature_____

(if joint petition is filed)

List of Creditors

Name: Address:	Name: Address:	Name: Address:
Name: Address:	Name: Address:	Name: Address:
Name: Address:	Name: Address:	Name: Address:
Name: Address:	Name: Address:	Name: Address:
Name: Address:	Name: Address:	Name: Address:
Name: Address:	Name: Address:	Name: Address:
Name: Address:	Name: Address:	Name: Address:
Name: Address:	Name: Address:	Name: Address:
Name: Address:	Name: Address:	Name: Address:
Name: Address:	Name: Address:	Name: Address:

24 *How to Handle an IRS Audit*

Dealing with the IRS

The assessment and collection of tax revenues by the federal government is an enormous undertaking and the federal government has devoted substantial resources and personnel to this task. The primary financial arm of the federal government is the Department of the Treasury. The Internal Revenue Service (IRS) is a part of the Department of the Treasury. The IRS is the agency with the responsibility of assessing and collecting federal taxes.

It is relatively easy for a taxpayer who is involved in this process to become overwhelmed by the massiveness of the United States government. However, if you are undergoing a tax audit or examination, you should approach it with calmness, sincerity, and an understanding of the assessment and collection process. This chapter will review the law and administrative procedures involved in federal tax assessment and collection and help you in dealing with the IRS.

You are entitled to courteous and considerate treatment from IRS employees at all times. If you ever feel that you are not being treated with fairness, courtesy, and consideration by an IRS employee, you should tell the employee's supervisor. However, because the primary objective of every taxpayer is to make the audit quick and painless, it is best to avoid creating a hostile or confrontational atmosphere until all efforts at diplomacy have failed.

You also have the right to have your tax returns kept confidential. However, if a lien or a lawsuit if filed, certain aspects of your tax case will become public records.

Most tax returns are accepted by the IRS as filed. But if your tax return is selected for audit by the IRS, it does not necessarily suggest that you are dishonest. The audit may or may not result in more taxes. Your case may be closed without change or you may receive a refund.

The Audit Process

(1) Selection of Returns

After your tax return is filed with the IRS, it is checked at the regional service center for completeness and mathematical accuracy. If a mathematical error is found, it is corrected at the service center and you are sent a correction notice of the error. If the error results in an increase in tax liability, either the refund due will be reduced accordingly or a notice and demand for payment will be sent to you. If the error results in a decrease in tax liability, you will receive a refund of that amount.

The above process should not be confused with an audit of your tax return. Any changes made to your return at this point in processing are based solely on the information contained in the tax forms and schedules. This procedure does not involve the verification of any information contained in the tax return.

Selection of most returns for audit is done through a computer program called Discriminant Function System (DFS). The "content" of this program is highly classified and only a select few individuals have access to it. Under this program, tax returns are evaluated and given a score based on historical data. The scored returns are checked by IRS personnel who are called "classifiers." Classifiers select those returns with the highest probability of error and then identify certain items on the selected returns for audit. For example, the classifier might select rental income and expenses, medical and interest deductions, and child care credits for examination. Other items on the selected return will not be examined unless the examining agent decides during the audit that additional items should be reviewed also.

Some returns are selected for audit under the Taxpayer Compliance Measurement Program (TCMP). This program is a random selection process to determine correct tax liability. Approximately every four years the program is usually conducted to measure and evaluate taxpayer compliance characteristics. The information obtained from these special audits is also used to update and improve the DFS system.

A TCMP audit should be distinguished from a regular audit in that the examination is not limited to a few selected items on the tax return. The audit is in depth and every item on the return is examined. Each and every income item, including exclusions of income, all exemptions and filing status, deductions, expenses, and credits are fully verified. The TCMP audits are used to generate statistical information and IRS generally does not want to drop even one audit from the sample.

Tax returns are also selected for audit through a variety of other systems. These audits may be based on information reports received by IRS from outside sources, examination of claims for refund, and through a matching of information documents. The latter system is called the Information Returns Program (IRP) in which Forms W-2, 1099, etc., are matched with the tax return to determine if all the income received has been reported on the tax return for that tax year.

A new tool in the IRS arsenal to monitor tax fraud is the Market Segment Specialization Program (MSSP). Prior to the MSSP, auditors were responsible for conducting audits on a wide variety of taxpayers, ranging from international conglomerates to sole proprietors. The MSSP, however, is designed to train auditors in specific industry segments. Ideally, this specialized training will increase efficiency and allow auditors to more accurately identify fraudulent claims. Unlike the guidelines to the DFS computer program, the guidelines for the MSSP are available to the public. Currently, the IRS has completed approximately 24 industry segments. To receive a copy, call 202-622-5164 or write to IRS FOI Reading Room, P.O. Box 388, Ben Franklin Station, Washington, DC 20044.

(2) Audit of Your Tax Return

The audit or examination of your tax return may be conducted by correspondence, office interview, or field interview. The place and method of examination is determined by the IRS. The IRS will conduct correspondence audits only when the items shown on the tax return are very simple. Interest expenses, medical expenses, and charitable contributions are items that are commonly audited by correspondence. If your return is selected for a correspondence audit, but you would like to discuss the matter personally with an examiner, you may request a transfer of the case to the district office nearest you.

Office interviews are usually conducted by tax auditors. Tax auditors typically examine individual income tax returns which include itemized deductions, business expenses, rental income, and expenses, Schedules C and F, most tax credits, and all income items. Tax auditors may also examine employment tax returns. Most of these audits are held in a local IRS office.

Field examinations are usually conducted by revenue agents and held at the taxpayer's place of business. Revenue agents typically examine individual income tax returns, partnership and corporate returns, and employment tax returns.

During a tax audit you may act on your own behalf or may be represented by an attorney, certified public accountant, by a person enrolled to practice before the IRS, or by the person who prepared the tax return and signed it as the preparer. If you filed a joint return, either you or your spouse may be present for the audit.

(3) Notification of an Audit

Notification of an audit is usually done by letter. The letter should inform you of the method of examination and, depending on the method, identify the time and place of examination, the appointment clerk or examiner's name, supervisor's name, and the office telephone number. The letter should identify those items which have been selected for audit and describe the kind of information and records needed to verify the items. Only provide the auditor with the information and records specifically requested. Providing excess information will only complicate the auditor's task and possibly lead to further points of inquiry. The letter will also include information regarding your appeal rights and repetitive audits, both of which are discussed later.

In office examinations you are usually requested to phone the IRS office for an appointment within ten days of receipt of the notification letter. If you do not respond to the notice, the IRS may take one or more of the following actions:

- Issue a report of proposed adjustments to taxes in which all deductions for the selected items are disallowed, resulting in an increase in tax liability.

- Send you another notice by registered or certified mail.

- Issue a summons to require your presence, along with the appropriate books and records, before the examiner.

(4) What Happens during an IRS Audit?

IRS examiners are authorized to examine any books, papers, records, or memoranda bearing upon matters required to be included in your federal tax returns, to take testimony relative thereto, and to administer oaths. The examiner will generally ask pertinent questions regarding the selected items on your tax return to determine if they are allowable. If the item is allowable, the examiner will verify the amount claimed on the return. If you are unable to verify the amount claimed or if you have claimed an unallowable item, an adjustment will be made to that item. See IRS Publication 552 for record-keeping requirements.

For example, suppose that you have claimed $100 that you gave to a neighbor whose home was destroyed by fire as a charitable contribution. Although you may be able to verify this donation through appropriate receipts, the examiner will explain that this is not an allowable deduction. To be an allowable charitable deduction the donation must be given to charitable organizations recognized by the IRS as tax-exempt organizations. Contributions to individuals, even for charitable purposes, are not deductible.

After a review of each selected item on your return, the examiner will give you the audit results and fully explain all adjustments.

Some audits may require more than one interview to close. If your records are incomplete, you may be given another opportunity to secure the necessary information. Some examinations are delayed because they require research by the examiner before a conclusion can be reached. About half of the audits conducted in office interviews by tax auditors are concluded on the first interview. However, field examinations usually take more than one interview.

Once the issues for audit have been examined, the examiner will review them with you and explain all adjustments. You should discuss each item until you are sure that you understand the reason for the adjustment. If you disagree with any adjustment you should inform the examiner of the reasons for disagreement. You may request a discussion of the issue with the examiner's group supervisor. After the discussion of the issues, the examiner will prepare a report of the audit adjustments and compute any increase or decrease in tax liability. If you agree with the adjustments, you should sign the report. If you disagree with the adjustments, you may exercise your appeal rights.

At the close of the audit, the examiner will normally request payment of any additional taxes plus interest and any applicable penalties. Interest is computed from the due date of the tax return until the date that the tax is paid, and it fluctuates with current national interest rates. If you are unable to pay at the close of the audit, you will be billed and payment will usually be demanded within 10 days of billing. If you are due a refund as the result of the audit, you will be refunded that amount with interest. Some audits do not result in any changes to the return and the return will be accepted as filed. These audits are called "no-change" cases and you will be notified by letter when the case is closed by the examining office. Remember that an examination or audit of your tax return does not necessarily indicate that you are suspected of any dishonesty or fraud. To facilitate the entire process, you should have your records in order, request a full explanation of the audit results, and speak with the group supervisor whenever you feel this is needed.

(5) Repetitive Audits

The repetitive audit process was implemented to relieve taxpayers from repetitive audits, and the process serves both taxpayers and the Internal Revenue Service. You may qualify for repetitive audit procedures if you meet both of the following requirements:

- Your tax return was examined for the same items in either of the two previous years before the year currently under examination; and

- The previous examination resulted in no change to your tax liability or only a small change.

If you think that you meet the above requirements you should contact the person shown on the notification letter. The audit will normally be suspended pending a repetitive audit determination. If it is determined that you fall within the requirements of the repetitive audit procedures, the audit will be discontinued, unless the return was selected for audit under the Taxpayer Compliance Measurement Program.

If you have any problems that you have been unable to resolve after contacting the appropriate office, you may call or write the local IRS Problem Resolution Office. This office cannot change the tax laws or any technical decisions made by examination personnel, but it can take responsibility for other problems that arise and ensure that they receive prompt and proper attention.

Appealing an IRS Audit

If you do not agree with all or any one of the audit adjustments, you may appeal. The first step in this process is to discuss the disputed issues with the group supervisor. If the audit cannot be closed by agreement at the examination level, you may appeal within the IRS system or to the appropriate federal courts.

When you request to exercise your appeal rights, the examiner will give you a report of audit adjustments, an explanation of audit adjustments, a letter notifying you of your right to appeal within thirty days from the date of the letter (thirty-day letter), and IRS Publication 5, which explains your appeal rights. If a protest letter is required in response to the thirty-day letter, it should be prepared and sent to the examiner within the thirty-day period. Protest letter requirements are discussed later. Otherwise, an oral request for an appeal normally suffices as a response to the thirty-day letter.

If you do not sign the audit agreement form or request an appeal within thirty days of the thirty-day letter, a Notice of Deficiency (ninety-day letter) will be issued. Once the ninety-day letter is issued, you generally cannot appeal within the IRS system. Rather, you must petition the United States Tax Court. If you do not petition the Tax Court within the ninety-day period, the tax will be assessed at the end of that period, and you will be billed for the tax due plus interest and any applicable penalties. If you pay the disputed tax in full and file a claim for refund of it that is disallowed or if no action is taken by IRS within six months, then you may take your case to the U.S. District Court or the Court of Appeals for the Federal Circuit. In summary, you may elect any one of the following procedures if you have requested an appeal within the *thirty-day* period:

- Appeal to the Regional Appeals Office within the IRS. If you do not agree with the determination at this level, you may still take your case to the appropriate federal courts.

- Appeal to the U.S. Tax Court if the disputed issue involves income tax or certain excise taxes. You must first request that a ninety-day letter be issued to you by IRS. You have ninety days from the date of the ninety-day letter to petition the Tax Court. If you file your appeal during this time, you are not required to pay the disputed tax before proceeding with the appeal. You may also elect to have your case heard under procedures for Small Tax Cases if the dispute does not involve more than $10,000 for any one tax year. The decisions rendered under Small Tax Case procedures are final.

- Appeal to the U.S. District Court or the U.S. Claims Court. These courts will hear cases only after the tax has been paid and a claim for refund filed. If your claim for refund is rejected by the IRS, you will receive a notice of claim disallowance. You must file suit in either federal court within two years after (a) refund claim disallowance or (b) the passage of six months after filing your claim for a refund if the IRS fails to take action on it. Decisions of the Tax Court and the Claims Court, as well as District Courts, are appealable to the appropriate Federal Court of Appeals and ultimately to the Supreme Court.

Protest Letter Requirements

A formal protest letter may be required in some situations to exercise your appeal rights from an IRS audit. If a written protest letter is required, you should send it to the examiner within thirty days of the thirty-day letter. The written protest letter should include the following information:

- a statement that you wish to exercise your appeal rights;

- your name, address, and social security number;

- the date and symbols from the thirty-day letter;

- the tax periods or years involved;

- statement of the ajustments that you do not agree with;

- a statement of the facts supporting your position when the facts are in dispute; and

- a statement concerning the law or other authority upon which you are relying.

The statement of facts must also include a statement that they are true under penalty of perjury and must be signed by you.

The Collection of Unpaid Taxes

A tax assessment for unpaid taxes is generally based upon your tax return or an audit thereof. Assessments may include taxes shown on your tax returns, deficiencies in taxes, additional or delinquent taxes, and any applicable penalties and interest. Once an assessment has been made to your account by IRS, you will receive a bill which is a notice of tax due and a demand for payment. A jeopardy assessment may be made when the IRS has reason to believe that delay will jeopardize collection. In a jeopardy assessment you may be given notice with a demand for immediate payment. If you fail to pay your tax liability immediately in a jeopardy assessment, collection of the tax may be made without any additional notice.

If you cannot pay your tax liability in full, you should contact the local IRS office or the office from which you received your tax bill and explain your financial situation. You may be asked to complete a Collection Information Statement so that your financial situation can be evaluated. You may also be asked to borrow the funds or sell or mortgage assets to enable you to pay your tax liability. In addition, you may be allowed to pay your tax in installments with the amount of the installment determined by your overall financial picture.

In some cases, the IRS will temporarily delay collection until you are able to pay. In such a case, interest and penalties continue to accrue, since the tax debt is not forgiven. If you are entitled to a refund in subsequent tax years, it will be applied against any outstanding balance in taxes due. If you are undergoing bankruptcy proceedings, you should contact the local IRS office upon receipt of a tax bill and request a temporary stay of collection.

If you fail to pay taxes which are due, the IRS will use forced collection procedures to collect the taxes. These procedures include filing a Notice of Federal Tax Lien, serving a Notice of Levy, or seizure and sale of your property.

A tax lien is basically a claim on your property as security for the payment of taxes. Once a Notice of Federal Tax Lien is filed it becomes a public notice to all of your creditors and it also applies to any property that you acquire after filing of the notice. Total payment of the tax liability or posting of a bond will release your property from the lien.

A levy is the seizure of your property to satisfy a judgment for taxes. The tax law normally requires that the procedures below be followed before levy action can be taken:

- Assessment of tax liability;

- Submission of a tax bill to you at your last known address;

- Giving of notice of intent to levy at least ten days in advance. (The notice may be given in person, left at your residence or business, or sent by certified or registered mail to your last known address); and

- Issuance of a court order authorizing collection personnel to enter your property to take levy action.

If the IRS has reason to believe that collection may be jeopardized by delay, the ten-day waiting period and notice is waived.

Any kind of property that you own can be seized and sold to pay your tax liability, except that which is specifically exempt by the tax law. The property subject to seizure includes both personal and business property, including your personal residence. The IRS is required to give you notice of the seizure as soon as practicable. The notice must specify the sum demanded by the IRS and a description of the property to be seized. After property has been seized, the IRS will normally give you and the public notice of the proposed sale at least ten days prior to the sale of the property. The notice of sale will specify the property to be sold, the time, place, manner, and conditions of the sale. The proceeds of levy and sale will be applied against the expenses of the proceeding and against the tax liability. Any surplus remaining after application of the proceeds as mentioned above will be credited or refunded to you, unless a creditor submits a superior claim over yours. If the proceeds of the sale are less than the tax liability, you are still responsible for the unpaid balance.

The IRS will normally release seized property before it is sold if you do one of the following:

- Pay an amount equal to the IRS's interest in the property;

- Agree to a satisfactory escrow arrangement;

- Furnish acceptable bond; or

- Make acceptable agreement for payment of the tax.

You may also redeem your property prior to the sale by paying the total amount due, including interest, penalties, and any expenses of collection. Real estate may normally be redeemed within 180 days after the sale by paying the buyer of the property the amount paid for it plus interest.

Taxpayer Bill Of Rights

In 1988, Congress enacted the omnibus Taxpayer Bill of Rights Act in response to taxpayers' concerns regarding IRS procedure and practice. The Act was aimed at achieving the following objectives: codifying the relations between the IRS and taxpayers; increasing statutory protection for taxpayers; implementing new administrative procedures; and increasing notification to taxpayers regarding IRS procedures.

Some Useful IRS Publications

The following IRS publications may be useful to you and are available free from IRS by writing or calling **1-800-829-3676**:

Publication 1	-	*Your Rights as a Taxpayer*
Publication 5	-	*Appeal Rights and Preparation of Protest for Unagreed Cases*
Publication 17	-	*Your Federal Income Tax*
Publication 552	-	*Recordkeeping for Individuals and a List of Tax Publications*
Publication 556	-	*Examination of Returns, Appeal Rights, and Claims for Refund*
Publication 586A	-	*The Collection Process*
Publication 910	-	*Guide to Free Tax Services*

These publications are prepared by IRS and usually give IRS's interpretation of the tax laws. If you have questions concerning IRS's views, you should consult an accountant or tax lawyer.

NOTE: For those individuals with Internet access, a wide variety of tax-related information can be accessed at the IRS's homepage on the World Wide Web at: http://www.ustreas.gov/treasury/bureaus/irs/New_irs.html

25 *Protecting Your Privacy*

Taking Steps to Safeguard Your Privacy

The future will bring dramatic improvements in the ability to collect and disseminate personal, financial, and medical information on the general public. There is a growing concern over technology and its connection to the invasion of privacy in the workplace and at home. People are also concerned about the escalating problems of credit card, mail, and telephone fraud; unwanted mail and telemarketing calls; employer surveillance; and what they can do to keep from becoming victims.

There are many ways you can help to protect your privacy and personal records. For example, when you are filling out an application for credit, insurance, or a job you should always ask how the information you give about yourself will be used. Who has access to it? Will the information be exchanged with other companies? How long is the information kept? How often is it updated?

With credit bureaus collecting more and more information on consumers' credit habits, you need to check your credit records periodically, correct any inaccuracies, and assure that there has been no improper releases of your credit records. The major credit bureau companies will agree not to release your name and other information for marketing purposes if you request it.

Credit bureaus are required to maintain a record af all creditors or others who have requested your credit history within the past six months. Sometimes credit checks are run on you without your knowledge, usually by places that offer instant credit, check cashing, and even prospective employers. Notify the credit bureaus of any improper inquiries and request that they be removed from your report because they may have a negative impact on your credit. Also notify the Federal Trade Commission, consumer protection agencies, or other agencies which enforce credit laws.

You should always be on guard at home and elsewhere against circumstances where your privacy can be violated. Remember that conversations on cellular and cordless telephones can be easily intercepted and these devices should never be used for confidential discussions which you would not want a third party to receive.

There are several ways you can protect your privacy from unscrupulous employers and co-workers. Personal affairs should be kept separate from the work environment to the extent possible. Minimize personal telephone calls and outside activties while at work. Do not use the company's voice mail and electronic mail for personal activities; instead, use these only for work-related tasks. Be aware that many companies may monitor telephone calls, computer files, and voice and electronic mail to keep tabs on their employees. Make sure that computer documents, voice mail, and e-mail are password protected. Keep personal files which may be at the office locked in a secure place. Follow a "clean desk" policy and lock-up files when away from the office.

You can run, but it is difficult to hide from the thousands of merchants and telemarketers who are trying to get to you and your money. Telemarketers obtain information on you from many sources you may not realize, such as warranty cards, coupons, sweepstakes entries, credit card usage, video rentals, hospital visits, driver's license applications, and other sources. Even the most sensitive information such as age, income, education, and special interests may be available to telemarketers.

You should try to minimize the information that you provide on yourself in the above situations. Don't give out sensitive information about yourself in response to telephone or mail solicitations, particularly checking account and credit card numbers. If you want to buy a product based on a telephone call from an unfamiliar company, you need to ask for the name, address, and phone number where you can reach caller after considering the offer. It is best to request and read written information before deciding to buy.

Keeping Your Medical and Insurance Records Confidential

No one wants private information relating to medical treatment, hospitalization, and insurance coverage released without their permission. Every time you apply for individual life, health, or disability insurance, medical and other information about you is collected and, with your authorization, shared with a consortium of insurance companies. The Medical Information Bureau (MIB) is a databank used by over 700 insurance companies. MIB may have a brief coded report on applicants who have significant underwriting risks. The MIB uses this information to help insurers guard against fraud and high-risk coverage, such as AIDS and drug abuse.

You can obtain a free copy of our MIB files by writing or calling:

> Medical Information Bureau
> P.O. Box 105
> Essex Station
> Boston, MA 02112
> Phone: (617) 426-3660

If the insurance company originating your files believes there is sensitive medical information recorded on your file, the company may require the MIB to send your medical files only to your doctor. In any event, you need to discuss your MIB file with your doctor periodically to make sure you understand what it says. You should ask your doctor to verify the accuracy and completeness.

Doctors and other health care providers are generally under an obligation to maintain medical records in confidence unless you authorize the release thereof. Legal action can be taken against them if they violate these confidences.

How to Avoid Mail and Telemarketing Frauds

Direct mail and telemarketing is used more and more by companies to reach consumers and by charitable organizations to reach potential contributors. This is an area which is ripe for fraud and invasion of privacy. If you do not want to receive unsolicited mail advertisements and telephone solicitations, you can usually write to the companies or organizations that are contacting you and ask to be removed from their mailing and telephone lists.

The federal government has now created a National Do Not Call Registry as a free and easy way to reduce the telemarketing phone calls you get at home. Most telemarketers cannot legally call you if you have registered your phone number with the National Do Not Call Registry. However, you may still get some calls from nonprofit, charitable, and political organizations. To register, call 1-888-382-1222 or go to the Web site, *www.donotcall.gov.* The registration is good for five years or until you take your phone number off the registry. You can renew the registration after five years.

The Direct Marketing Association (DMA) operates the Mail Preference Service and Telephone Preference Service and provides telephone numbers and mailing information on consumers to subscribers. If you wish to have your name removed from the lists maintained by companies subscribing to these DMA services, you can write to:

> Mail Preference Service
> Direct Marketing Association
> P.O. Box 9008
> Farmingdale, NY 11735

> or

> Telephone Preference Service
> Direct Marketing Association
> P.O. Box 9015
> Farmingdale, NY 11735

You will still get some mail and telephone calls, but this will significantly reduce the amount.

It is important that you try to control what information is kept about you. You should refuse to give more information to telemarketers than you feel is necessary or comfortable. You should ask for follow-up explanatory materials and avoid giving any personal information unless you receive these materials. Some companies offer rebate, incentive, and warranty programs that benefit consumers. You should find out who has access to information you provide to participate in these programs. Some companies use this data to create mailing lists that are sold to marketers.

According to the U.S. Office of Consumer Affairs, more and more consumers are receiving misleading or downright fraudu-lent mail promotions. These promotions take several forms. Some examples are:

- Sweepstakes that require paying an entry fee or ordering a product
- Notices of prizes that require calling a 900 number or buying a product
- Mailings that look like they are from government agencies but are not
- Classified "employment" or "business opportunity" advertisements promising easy money for little work
- Prize awards that ask for credit card or bank account numbers

Consumers should be particularly suspicious of one of the most prevalent forms of mail fraud, notices that they have received a prize—in some cases, a very expensive prize like a car or vacation. Usually, they have to purchase a product—for example, a lifetime supply of cosmetics or large amount of vitamins—to be eligible to receive the prize. In fact, few of the prizes are awarded, and of those received, many are worthless.

The Alliance Against Fraud in Telemarketing, administered by the National Consumers League, has information about the dangers of these types of mail solicitations. You should contact your state or local consumer office or Better Business Bureau if you have any doubts about promotions you have received through the mail.

Protecting Yourself from Telephone Fraud

The Federal Trade Commission (FTC) provides these important facts for consumers on how you can protect yourself from telephone fraud. The FTC estimates that fraudulent telemarketers swindle American consumers out of more than a billion dollars each year. They promote everything from useless water purifiers to interests in nonexistent oil wells.

The heart of the telemarketing operation is usually centered in a "boiler room," a rented office space filled with desks, telephones, and experienced salespeople. These people spend their days talking to hundreds of potential victims all across the country. Fraudulent telemarketers and sellers may reach us in several ways, but the telephone always plays an important role.

You may get a telephone call from a stranger who got your number from the telephone directory or a mailing list. A telemarketer calling from a boiler room may know, through a mailing list, your age, income, hobbies, marital status, and other information—all to help personalize the call. This is the classic telemarketing scam. You may make the telephone call yourself in some cases, in response to a television, newspaper, magazine advertisement, or direct mail solicitation. However, just because you make the call does not mean the business is legitimate or that you should be any less cautious about buying or investing over the phone.

Automatic debit scams involve unauthorized debits (withdrawals) from your checking accounts. You may get a postcard or a telephone call saying you have won a free prize or can qualify for a major credit card. If you respond to the offer, the caller may ask you to read off all of the numbers at the bottom of your check. Sometimes you may not be told why this information is needed. Other times you may be told this account information will help ensure that you qualify for the offer. And, in some cases, the caller may explain this information will allow them to debit your account and ship the prize or process the fee for the credit card.

The telemarketer places your checking account information on a "demand draft," which is processed much like a check. However, unlike a check, the draft does not require your signature. Your bank then pays the telemarketer's bank. And, you may not learn of the transaction until you receive your bank statement.

Automatic debit scams involve a fraud that is hard to detect, but there are some precautions you can take. You should never give your checking account number over the phone in response to solicitations from people you do not know. If anyone asks for your checking account numbers, you should ask them why they need this information. And, you should ask to review the company's offer in writing before you agree to a purchase.

Marketers of "gold" or "platinum" cards may promise in their ads that by participating in their credit programs, which might have an initiation fee of fifty dollars or more, you will be able to get major credit cards and improve your credit rating. But generally, this is not the case. Many of these credit card marketers—who often target people in lower-income areas through direct mail, television, or newspaper ads featuring "900" numbers—do not report to credit bureaus. And rarely can they help to secure lines of credit with other creditors. In fact, some of these cards only allow you to purchase merchandise from the marketer's own catalogue—and only after you have paid an extra charge.

Be skeptical of plans promising to secure major credit cards or erase bad credit. Contact the local consumer protection agency or the local Better Business Bureau (BBB) to learn if any complaints have been lodged against a particular marketer of "gold" or "platinum" cards. And be aware that unless marketers subscribe to credit bureaus, they are unable to report any information about a person's credit experience.

Telemarketing travel scams have many variations and often involve travel packages that sound legitimate. You may get a phone call or a postcard saying that you have been selected to receive a free trip. The card will tell you to call a toll-free or "900" number for details. On the phone, skilled salespeople will tell you that, to be eligible for the free trip, you must join their travel club. Later, you may find another fee is required to make your reservations and you will have a telephone charge if you used the "900" line. In the end, you may never get your "free" trip because your reservations are never confirmed or you cannot comply with hard-to-meet or expensive conditions.

While it is sometimes difficult to tell a legitimate travel offer from a fraudulent one, there are some precautions you can take. You should always be wary of "great deals," and before you pay for the trip, you should ask detailed questions that will give you clear answers. You should ask for the travel offer in writing so you can check details. You can try to check the reliability of the travel company by calling your local consumer protection office or the local Better Business Bureau. But remember, they cannot vouch for the company, but only can tell you if they have any complaints logged under the company name.

Typical telephone investments sold by fraudulent telemarketers include coins, gemstones, interests in oil wells and gold mining operations, oil and gas leases, and the sale of precious metals such as gold and silver. Con artists direct their sales pitches to the universal desire to make money with little risk. A caller usually will say that you have been specially selected to participate in an unusual investment opportunity. The caller often requires that money, sometimes thousands of dollars, be transferred immediately because the "market is moving."

Be wary of telephone investment opportunities that are guaranteed to be risk-free and provide a high return. Before you give anyone your money, it is best to get written information about an investment, to invest in businesses you know something about, and to discuss the matter with a knowledgeable person.

If you have a complaint about a telemarketing sale, you should try to resolve complaints with the company first. If that does not work and you believe you have been defrauded, you can contact your local consumer protection agency or the Better Business Bureau to report the company.

If you believe you have been victims of a scam, you also can file a complaint with the FTC by writing to: Federal Trade Com-mission, Division of Marketing Practices, Washington, DC 20580. Although the FTC does not generally intervene in individual disputes, the information it provides may indicate a pattern of possible law violations requiring action by the Commission.

See chapter 18 for more information on how to be a smart consumer and avoid mail and telephone fraud.

Safeguarding Your Privacy with Telecommunications and the Internet
The telephone has become our primary form of communicating with each other and is likely to be surpassed by the computer in the early 21st century. The increasing use of voice mail, electronic mail, and cordless and cellular phones requires a critical look at how to protect your privacy and confidential information.

To protect your privacy on the telephone, you should keep in mind that cellular and cordless telephone conversations are easy to monitor. Never use these to conduct confidential conversations.

Some companies have taken steps to protect the privacy of voice and electronic mail. Typically a password is required to gain access to files. Several companies now make reading another person's electronic mail or listening to their voice-mail a violation of corporate ethics and may result in disciplinary action. Most of the time, however, there is a lack of adequate safeguards to protect the privacy of these messages.

Many companies may monitor voice and electronic mail to keep tabs on their employees. Therefore, it is best to consider voice and e-mail messages as non-private. You should never use these to discuss personal or other information which you would not want a third party to receive.

Most telephone companies offer a "caller ID" service. This service allows you to see the telephone number of the person calling you before you answer the telephone. If you do not recognize the incoming telephone number, or simply do not want to talk to the person, you can decide not to answer. If you are using caller ID service, you might consider using an answering machine or service so that you will not miss important calls from unfamiliar telephone numbers.

You may not want your telephone number revealed when you place a call to those who have caller ID. In such a case, you can check to see if your local telephone company offers a blocking system to prevent your telephone number from being displayed. Otherwise, you could place calls through an operator and request that our number not be revealed, or you could call from a pay phone.

Companies and organizations with 800 and 900 numbers might use a telephone number identification system to record your numbers when you call. They might also match your telephone numbers and addresses to add to customer lists for marketing purposes.

With more and more transactions taking place via the Internet, you must be careful with the use of credit card, social security numbers, and other financial information over the Internet. Ensure that you are dealing with known and reputable organizations. Make sure that they have a privacy policy which will protect your personal information. Conduct your Internet transactions over a secure network to keep hackers and other unwanted recipients from intercepting and misappropriating your information.

How to Fight Identity Theft

Because identity theft is on the rise, you must be alert to any instances and take action to protect yourself.

Remember that safeguarding your personal information is the main key to preventing you from becoming a victim of identity theft. Taking quick action to report instances of identity theft or fraud is also important in minimizing your harm.

Identity thieves have a variety of methods of gaining access to your personal information, including deception, theft, mail tampering, trash rummaging, electronic skimming devices, and impersonation of business and government officials. After identity thieves have obtained your personal information, they may use it to charge purchases to your accounts, open new accounts and loans in your name, forge checks, and engage in other fraudulent transactions.

The Federal Trade Commission (FTC) serves as the clearinghouse for consumer complaints about identity theft, and it uses the information from these complaints to monitor, investigate, and prosecute identify thieves. To file a complaint about identity theft with the FTC, contact the Consumer Response Center, 600 Pennsylvania Ave., NW, Washington, DC 20580 by mail or phone (1-877-438-4338) or the internet at *www.ftc.gov*.

If you believe that your identity has been stolen, the FTC recommends that you take these actions immediately:

1. Contact the fraud departments of each of the major credit bureaus (Equifax, Experian, and Trans Union) and tell them to flag your file with a fraud alert advising creditors to contact you for permission before opening any new accounts in your name. Also check your credit reports every year for accuracy and improper activity.

2. Contact the creditors for any accounts which have been tampered with or opened fraudulently and advise them of the situation. Follow up in writing via certified mail with return receipt to document what information the creditors received, and keep a copy for your files.

3. File a police report and keep a copy in case your creditors need proof.

4. File a complaint with the FTC.

Use the following form to track and document your actions to report identity theft:

Form 41: Chart Your Course of Action

Use this form to record the steps you've taken to report the fraudulent use of your identity. Keep this list in a safe place for future reference.

Credit Bureaus—Report Fraud

Bureau	Phone Number	Date Contacted	Contact Person	Comments
Equifax	_____	_____	_____	_____
				_____
Experian	_____	_____	_____	_____
				_____
Transunion	_____	_____	_____	_____
				_____

Bank and Credit Car Account Issuers (Contact each issuer to protect your rights under the Fair Credit Billing Act)

Issuer	Address and Phone Number	Date Contacted	Contact Person	Comments
_____	_____	_____	_____	_____
	_____			_____
_____	_____	_____	_____	_____
	_____			_____
_____	_____	_____	_____	_____
	_____			_____
_____	_____	_____	_____	_____
	_____			_____
_____	_____	_____	_____	_____
	_____			_____

Law Enforcement Authorities—Report Identity Theft

Agency	Phone Number	Date Contacted	Contact Person	Report Number	Comments
_____	_____	_____	_____	_____	_____
					_____
_____	_____	_____	_____	_____	_____
					_____
_____	_____	_____	_____	_____	_____
					_____

Appendix

Private Organizations and Foundations

American Arbitration Association
335 Madison Ave., Floor 10
New York, NY 10017
(800) 778-7879
www.adr.org

American Association for Marriage and Family Therapy
1133 15th St. NW, Suite 300
Washington, DC 20005
(202) 452-0109
www.aamft.org

American Bar Association
541 Fairbanks Ct.
Chicago, IL 60611
(312) 988-5522
www.abanet.org

American Civil Liberties Union
125 Broad St., Floor 17
New York, NY 10004
(212) 344-3005
www.aclu.org

American Marketing Association
311 S. Wacker Dr., Suite 5800
Chicago, IL 60606
(800) 262-1150
www.ama.org

Clark Office Products, Inc.
12750 Lake City Way NE
Seattle, WA 98125
(206) 362-1250

Consumer Federation of America
1424 16th St. NW, Suite 604
Washington, DC 20036
(202) 387-6121
www.consumerfed.org

Council of Better Business Bureaus
4200 Wilson Blvd., Suite 800
Arlington, VA 22203
(703) 276-0100
www.bbb.org

Experian Credit Services (TRW)
505 City Pkwy. West, Suite 200
Orange, CA 92868
(888) 397-3742
www.experian.com

HALT
1612 K St., Suite 510
Washington, DC 20006
(888) 367-4258
www.halt.org

National Association of Realtors
430 N. Michigan Ave., Suite 500
Chicago, IL 60611
(312) 329-8200
www.nar.realtor.com

National Association of State Development Agencies (NASDA)
750 First St. NE, Suite 710
Washington, DC 20002
(202) 898-1302
www.nasda.com

National Consumers League
1701 K St. NW, Suite 1201
Washington, DC 20006
(202) 835-3323
www.natlconsumersleague.org

National Foundation for Consumer Credit
8611 Second Ave.
Silver Spring, MD 20910
(800) 388-2227
www.nfcc.org

National Legal Information Services
327 13th St., Suite 2B
Philadelphia, PA 19107

Society for the Right To Die
National Council on Death and Dying
250 W. 57th St.
New York, NY 10107
(212) 246-6973

Government Departments and Offices

Administrative Office of the United States Courts
One Columbus Circle NE, Suite 4-560
Washington, DC 20544
(202) 273-1530
www.uscourts.gov

Consumer Product Safety Commission
4330 East-West Highway
Bethesda, MD 20814
(800) 638-2772
www.cpsc.gov

Copyright Office
Library of Congress
101 Independence Ave. SE
Washington, DC 20559
(202) 707-3000
www.loc.gov/copyright

Federal Mediation and Conciliation Service
2100 K St. NW
Washington, DC 20427
(202) 606-8100
www.fmcs.gov

FirstGov (U.S. Government Search Engine)
c/o GSA
1800 F St. NW, Room 5240
Washington, DC 20405
www.firstgov.gov

Internal Revenue Service
1111 Constitution Ave. NW
Washington, DC 20224
(800) 829-1040
www.irs.treas.gov

Legal Services Corp.
750 First Ave. NE, Floor 10
Washington, DC 20002
(202) 336-8800
www.lsc.gov

National Institute of Standards and Technology
Office of Energy Related Inventions
100 Bureau Dr., Stop 3460
Gaithersburg, MD 20899
(301) 975-6478
www.nist.gov

Securities and Exchange Commission
450 Fifth St. NW
Washington, DC 20549
(202) 942-7040
www.sec.gov

Small Business Administration
200 North College St., Suite A-2015
Charlotte, NC 28202
(800) 827-5722
www.sba.gov

Thomas: Legislative Information on the Internet
Library of Congress
101 Independence Ave. SE
Washington, DC 20540
http://thomas.loc.gov

United States Patent and Trademark Office
General Information Services Division
Crystal Plaza 3, Suite 2C-02
Washington, DC 20231
(800) 786-9199
www.uspto.gov

United States Department of Commerce
Herbert C. Hoover Building
1401 Constitution Ave. NW
Washington, DC 20230
(202) 482-2000
www.doc.gov

United States Government Manual, $36.00
National Archives and Records Administration
700 Pennsylvania Ave. NW
Washington, DC 20408
(800) 234-8861
www.access.gpo.gov/nara/nara001.html

United States Government Printing Office
Superintendent of Documents
PO Box 371954
(202) 512-1800
www.access.gpo.gov

United States Information Agency
301 4th St. SW
Washington, DC 20547
(202) 619-4700
www.usia.gov

Legal Resources on the Internet

The Internet can be helpful in finding information about many legal issues. A number of websites answer questions, offer legal texts, and provide referrals to attorneys. Among these sites are:

www.mycounsel.com
www.findlaw.com
www.nolo.com
www.freeadvice.com
www.lawyers.com
www.lawoffice.com
www.estateplanninglinks.com
www.law.cornell.edu
www.thelaw.com
www.uslaw.com

About the Author

Carl W. Battle is an attorney and author of several books including *Business and Legal Forms for Industrial Designers* (written with Tad Crawford and Eva Doman Bruck) and *The Patent Guide: A Friendly Guide to Protecting and Profiting from Patents* (published by Allworth Press). A founder of National Legal Information Services, Battle has been involved in a variety of seminars and legal education projects that help people understand their basic legal rights. He lives near San Francisco, California.

Index

Books from Allworth Press

Allworth Press is an imprint of Allworth Communications, Inc. Selected titles are listed below.

Estate Planning and Administration: How to Maximize Assets, Minimize Taxes, and Protect Loved Ones, Second Edition
by Edmund T. Fleming (paperback, 6 × 9, 256 pages, $14.95)

Your Living Trust and Estate Plan: How to Maximize Your Family's Assets and Protect Your Loved Ones, Third Edition
by Harvey J. Platt (paperback, 6 × 9, 336 pages, $16.95)

Your Will and Estate Plan: How to Protect Your Estate and Your Loved Ones
by Harvey J. Platt (paperback, 6 × 9, 224 pages, $16.95)

Winning the Divorce War: How to Protect Your Best Interests, Second Edition
by Ronald Sharp (paperback, 5½ × 8½, 208 pages, $16.95)

Turn You Idea or Invention into Millions
by Don Kracke (paperback, 6 × 9, 224 pages, $18.95)

Spend Your Way to Wealth
by Mike Schiano (paperback, 6 × 9, 208 pages, $16.95)

Power Speaking: The Art of the Exceptional Public Speaker
by Achim Nowak (paperback, 6 × 9, 256 pages, $19.95)

Career Solutions for Creative People: How to Balance Career Goals with Career Security
by Dr. Ronda Ormont (paperback, 6 × 9, 320 pages, $19.95)

The Entrepreneurial Age: Awakening the Spirit of Enterprise in People, Companies, and Countries
by Larry C. Farrell (hardcover, 6¼ × 9¼, 352 pages, $24.95)

Feng Shui and Money
by Eric Shaffert (paperback, 6 × 9, 256 pages, $16.95)

How to Escape Lifetime Security and Pursue Your Impossible Dream: A Guide to Transforming our Career
by Kenneth Atchity (paperback, 5½ × 8½, 208 pages, $16.95)

Fair Use, Free Use, and Use by Permission: How to Handle Copyrights in All Media
by Lee Wilson (paperback, 6 × 9, 256 pages, $24.95)

The Copyright Guide: A Friendly Guide to Protecting and Profiting from Copyrights, Third Edition
by Lee Wilson (paperback, 6 × 9, 256 pages, $19.95)

The Trademark Guide: A Friendly Guide for Protecting and Profiting from Trademarks, Second Edition
by Lee Wilson (paperback, 6 × 9, 256 pages, $18.95)